Essential Virtual SAN

Administrator's Guide to VMware® Virtual SAN

VMware Press is the official publisher of VMware books and training materials, which provide guidance on the critical topics facing today's technology professionals and students. Enterprises, as well as small- and medium-sized organizations, adopt virtualization as a more agile way of scaling IT to meet business needs. VMware Press provides proven, technically accurate information that will help them meet their goals for customizing, building, and maintaining their virtual environment.

With books, certification and study guides, video training, and learning tools produced by world-class architects and IT experts, VMware Press helps IT professionals master a diverse range of topics on virtualization and cloud computing and is the official source of reference materials for preparing for the VMware Certified Professional Examination.

VMware Press is also pleased to have localization partners that can publish its products into more than forty-two languages, including, but not limited to, Chinese (Simplified), Chinese (Traditional), French, German, Greek, Hindi, Japanese, Korean, Polish, Russian, and Spanish.

For more information about VMware Press, please visit **http://www.vmwarepress.com**.

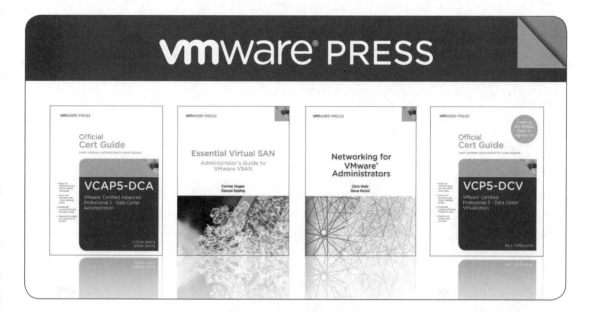

Essential
Virtual SAN

Administrator's Guide
to VMware® Virtual SAN

Cormac Hogan
Duncan Epping

vmware® PRESS

Upper Saddle River, NJ • Boston • Indianapolis • San Francisco
New York • Toronto • Montreal • London • Munich • Paris • Madrid
Capetown • Sydney • Tokyo • Singapore • Mexico City

Essential Virtual SAN

ISBN-10: 0-13-385499-X

ISBN-13: 978-0-13-385499-2

Library of Congress Control Number: 2014942087

Printed in the United States of America

First Printing: August 2014

Warning and Disclaimer

Special Sales

VMWARE PRESS PROGRAM MANAGER
David Nelson

ASSOCIATE PUBLISHER
David Dusthimer

ACQUISITIONS EDITOR
Joan Murray

TECHNICAL EDITORS
Christos Karamanolis
Paudie O'Riordan

SENIOR DEVELOPMENT EDITOR
Christopher Cleveland

MANAGING EDITOR
Sandra Schroeder

PROJECT EDITOR
Mandie Frank

COPY EDITOR
Keith Cline

PROOFREADER
Paula Lowell

INDEXER
Lisa Stumpf

EDITORIAL ASSISTANT
Vanessa Evans

DESIGNER
Chuti Prasertsith

COMPOSITOR
Bumpy Design

*We would like to dedicate this book to the VMware VSAN engineering team.
Without their help and countless hours discussing the ins and outs of
Virtual SAN, this book would not have been possible.*
—Cormac & Duncan

Contents

Foreword by Ben Fathi

When I arrived at VMware in early 2012, I was given the charter to deliver the next generation of vSphere, our flagship product. It was a humbling experience, but exhilarating at the same time. A few months into the role, I welcomed our storage group to the team, and I had the honor of working closely with a dedicated team of engineers. I saw that they were building something very unique—what I believe will be a significant turning point in the history of storage.

We set out to build a distributed fault tolerant storage system optimized for virtual environments. Our goal was to build a product that had all the qualities of shared storage (resilience, performance, scalability, and so on) but running on standard x86 servers with no specialized hardware or software to maintain. Just plug in disks and SSDs, and vSphere takes care of the rest. Add to that a policy-based management framework and you have a new operational model, one that drastically simplifies storage management.

There were problems aplenty, as is usual in all long-term software projects: long nights, low morale, competing priorities, and shifting schedules. Through it all, the team persevered. We hit a particularly painful point in June 2013. We were getting ready to ship vSphere 5.5, and I had to be the one to tell the team that they weren't ready to ship VSAN. Instead, they would have to go through a broad public beta and much more rigorous testing before we could call the product "customer-ready."

The stakes were far too high, particularly because this was VMware's first foray into software-defined storage and a key part of our software-defined data center vision.

They were disappointed, of course, not to be showcased up on stage at VMworld, but still they persevered. I think we took the right course. Six months and 12,000 beta testers later, Virtual SAN was ready: It's robust, proven, and ready for action. VSAN can scale from a modest three-node configuration in a branch office to a multi-petabyte, mega-IOPS monster capable of handling all enterprise storage needs.

The team has delivered something truly unique in the industry: a fully distributed storage architecture that's seamlessly integrated into the hypervisor.

VSAN isn't bolted on, it's built in.

Much has already been written about VSAN and how it brings something completely new to the storage world. This book, however, is different. Duncan and Cormac have worked closely with the development team all throughout the project. Not only are they intimately familiar with the VSAN architecture, but they've also deployed and managed it at scale. You're in good hands.

Ben Fathi
CTO, VMware

Foreword by Charles Fan

Earlier this year, I had the pleasure of sitting in a session by Clayton Christensen. His seminal work, *Innovator's Dilemma*, was one of my favorite business readings, and it was an awesome experience to hear Clayton in person. For the whole session, I had this surreal feeling that there were no other people in the room, just Clayton and me, and we were discussing Virtual SAN (VSAN).

The topic of the discussion? Is VSAN a disruptive innovation or a sustaining innovation?

As they were defined in Clayton's book, sustaining innovations are the technological advances that make things better, faster, more powerful to answer to the increasing demand from customers. Sustaining innovations do not require any change in the business model, business process, or target customers. This is how big companies become bigger. Given their resources and customer relationships, they almost always win against smaller companies when it comes to sustaining innovation.

However, there will be times that the technology advances outpace the growth of customer demand. At this time, the innovation comes from the bottom. Those innovations will offer a different way of getting things done, which may not deliver the same level of feature and performance initially, but they are cheaper, simpler, and often introduce the technology to more and different customers and sometimes completely change the business model. This is the disruptive innovation. It is extremely difficult for incumbent leaders to deal with disruptive innovations, and this type of innovation redefines industries. And new leaders are born.

So, is VSAN a disruptive innovation or a sustaining innovation? It might seem like a dumb question. Of course, it is a disruptive innovation. It is a radically simple, software-only, hypervisor-converged distributed storage solution fully integrated with vSphere, running on commodity hardware. It redefines both the economics and the consumption models of storage. Although it lacks (so far) a list of classic storage features and goodies, it is offering orders of magnitude more simplicity than classic enterprise storage arrays, sold to a different set of users from the storage admins, at a lower cost. Thus it is a classic disruptive innovation, similar to the point-and-shoot cameras. Compared to "real" cameras, point-and-shoot cameras had fewer features initially, but they were also radically simpler and targeted a different set of users. Guess what? Quickly there were more point-and-shoots than the real ones.

Then why the question? As a storage product, yes, VSAN is without a doubt a revolutionary product that will disrupt the entire storage industry and usher in a new era. However, if we change our perspective, and look at it as the natural extension of vSphere Server virtualization platform to the software-defined data center, it is a sustaining innovation.

VSAN is being sold to the same vSphere customers and empowers them to do more. It extends server environments into converged infrastructure. It extends the vSphere abstractions and policy-based automation from compute to storage.

So, we have a rare winner on our hands, a combination of being a sustaining innovation on top of our hypervisor platform that is natural for VMware to extend the value we offer to our customers, and at the same time a disruptive innovation that will reshape the storage industry. In other words, it is a product that will do to storage what vSphere did to servers.

The VSAN product is the result of 4 years of hard work from the entire VSAN product team. This team is more than just the core architects, developers, testers, and product managers. Duncan and Cormac are two critical members of the team who brought real-world experiences and customer empathy into the program, and they have also been two of our strongest voices back out to the world. I am really glad that they are writing this timely book, and hope you will find it as useful as I did. VSAN is a unique product that will have a lasting impact on the industry, and I welcome you to join us in this exciting journey.

Charles Fan
SVP of VMware R&D, Storage, and Availability

About the Authors

Cormac Hogan is a storage architect in the Integration Engineering team at VMware. Cormac was one of the first VMware employees at the EMEA headquarters in Cork, Ireland, back in 2005, and has previously held roles in VMware's Technical Marketing and Support organizations. Cormac has written a number of storage-related white papers and has given numerous presentations on storage best practices and new features. Cormac is the owner of CormacHogan.com, a blog site dedicated to storage and virtualization.

He can be followed on twitter **@CormacJHogan**.

Duncan Epping is a principal architect working for VMware R&D. Duncan is responsible for exploring new possibilities with existing products and features, researching new business opportunities for VMware. Duncan specializes in software-defined storage, hyper-converged platforms, and availability solutions. Duncan was among the first VMware Certified Design Experts (VCDX 007). Duncan is the owner of Yellow-Bricks.com and author of various books, including the VMware vSphere Clustering Technical Deepdive series.

He can be followed on twitter **@DuncanYB**.

About the Technical Reviewers

Christos Karamanolis is the Chief Architect and a Principal Engineer in the Storage and Availability Engineering Organization at VMware. He has more than 20 years of research and development experience in the fields of distributed systems, fault tolerance, storage, and storage management. He is the architect of Virtual SAN (VSAN), a new distributed storage system, and vSphere's policy-based storage management stack (S-PBM, VASA). Previously, he worked on the ESX storage stack (NFS client and vSCSI filters) and Disaster Recovery (vSphere Replication). Prior to joining VMware in 2005, Christos spent several years at HP Labs as a researcher working on new-generation storage products. He started his career as an Assistant Professor at Imperial College, while he also worked as an independent IT consultant. He has coauthored more than 20 research papers in peer-reviewed journals and conferences and has 24 granted patents. He holds a Ph.D. in Distributed Computing from Imperial College, University of London, U.K.

Paudie O'Riordan is a Staff Integration Liaison at VMware R&D. Formerly he worked in EMC Corporation (1996-2007) as an IT Admin, EMC Global Technical Support, Corporate Systems Engineer, and Principle Software Engineer at EMC R&D. Previously at VMware, he had a role in VMware Global Services as Senior Staff Technical Support Engineer. He holds the VCP certification (VCP4).

Acknowledgments

The authors of this book both work for VMware. The opinions expressed in the book are the authors' personal opinions and experience with the product. Statements made throughout the book do not necessarily reflect the views and opinions of VMware.

We would like to thank Christos Karamanolis and Paudie O'Riordan for keeping us honest as our technical editors. Of course, we want to thank the Virtual SAN engineering team. In particular, we want to call out two individuals of the engineering team, Christian Dickmann and once again Christos Karamanolis, whose deep knowledge and understanding of VSAN was leveraged throughout this book. We also want to acknowledge William Lam, Wade Holmes, Rawlinson Rivera, Simon Todd, Alan Renouf, and Jad El-Zein for their help and contributions to the book.

Lastly, we want to thank our VMware management team (Phil Weiss, Adam Zimman, and Mornay van der Walt) for supporting us on this and other projects.

Go VSAN!

Cormac Hogan and Duncan Epping

We Want to Hear from You!

As the reader of this book, *you* are our most important critic and commentator. We value your opinion and want to know what we're doing right, what we could do better, what areas you'd like to see us publish in, and any other words of wisdom you're willing to pass our way.

We welcome your comments. You can email or write us directly to let us know what you did or didn't like about this book—as well as what we can do to make our books better.

Please note that we cannot help you with technical problems related to the topic of this book.

When you write, please be sure to include this book's title and author as well as your name, email address, and phone number. We will carefully review your comments and share them with the author and editors who worked on the book.

Email: VMwarePress@vmware.com

Mail: VMware Press
        ATTN: Reader Feedback
        800 East 96th Street
        Indianapolis, IN 46240 USA

Reader Services

Visit our website at www.informit.com/title/9780133854992 and register this book for convenient access to any updates, downloads, or errata that might be available for this book.

Introduction

When talking about virtualization and the underlying infrastructure that it runs on, one component that always comes up in conversation is storage. The reason for this is fairly simple: In many environments, storage is a pain point. Although the storage landscape has changed with the introduction of flash technologies that mitigate many of the traditional storage issues, many organizations have not yet adopted these new architectures and are still running into the same challenges.

Storage challenges range from operational effort or complexity to performance problems or even availability constraints. The majority of these problems stem from the same fundamental problem: legacy architecture. The reason is that most storage platform architectures were developed long before virtualization existed, and virtualization changed the way these shared storage platforms were used.

In a way, you could say that virtualization forced the storage industry to look for new ways of building storage systems. Instead of having a single server connect to a single storage device (also known as a logical unit or LUN for short), virtualization typically entails having one (or many) physical server(s) running many virtual machines connecting to one or multiple storage devices. This did not only increase the load on these storage systems, it also changed the workload patterns and increased the total capacity required.

As you can imagine, for most storage administrators, this required a major shift in thinking. What should the size of my LUN be? What are my performance requirements, and how many spindles will that result in? What kind of data services are required on these LUNs, and where will virtual machines be stored? Not only did it require a major shift in thinking, but it also required working in tandem with other IT teams. Whereas in the past server admins and network and storage admins could all live in their own isolated worlds, they now needed to communicate and work together to ensure availability of the platform they were building. Whereas in the past a mistake, such as a misconfiguration or underprovisioning, would only impact a single server, it could now impact many virtual machines.

There was a fundamental shift in how we collectively thought about how to operate and architect IT infrastructures when virtualization was introduced. Now another collective shift is happening all over again. This time it is due to the introduction of software-defined networking and software-defined storage. But let's not let history repeat itself, and let's avoid the mistakes we all made when virtualization first arrived. Let's all have frank and open discussions with our fellow datacenter administrators as we all aim to revolutionize datacenter architecture and operations!

Motivation for Writing This Book

During the early stages of the product development cycle, both of us got involved with Virtual SAN. We instantly knew that this was going to be a product that everyone would be talking about and a product that people would want to know more about. During the various great water-cooler type of conversations we were having, we realized that none of the information was being captured anywhere. Considering both of us are fanatic bloggers we decided to, each independently, start writing articles. We quickly had so much material that it became impossible to release all of it as blog posts and decided to join forces and publish it in book form. After some initial research, we found VMware Press was willing to release it.

You, the Reader

This book is targeted at IT professionals who are involved in the care and feeding of a VMware vSphere environment. Ideally, you have been working with VMware vSphere for some time and perhaps you have attended an authorized course in vSphere, such as the "Install, Configure, and Manage" class. This book is not a starters guide, but there should be enough in the book for administrators and architects of all levels.

How to Use This Book

This book is split into ten chapters, as described here:

- **Chapter 1, "Introduction to VSAN":** This chapter provides a high-level introduction to software-defined storage and VSAN.

- **Chapter 2, "VSAN Prerequisites and Requirements for Deployment":** This chapter describes the requirements from a physical and virtual perspective to safely implement VSAN.

- **Chapter 3, "VSAN Installation and Configuration":** This chapter goes over the steps needed to install and configure VSAN.

- **Chapter 4, "VM Storage Policies on VSAN":** This chapter explains the concept of storage policy-based management.

- **Chapter 5, "Architectural Details":** This chapter provides in-depth architectural details of VSAN.

- **Chapter 6, "VM Storage Policies and Virtual Machine Provisioning":** This chapter describes how VM storage policies can be used to simplify VM deployment.

- **Chapter 7, "Management and Maintenance":** This chapter describes the steps for most common management and maintenance tasks.

- **Chapter 8, "Interoperability":** This chapter covers interoperability of Virtual SAN with other VMware features and products.

- **Chapter 9, "Designing a VSAN Cluster":** This chapter provides various examples around designing a VSAN cluster, including sizing exercises.

- **Chapter 10, "Troubleshooting, Monitoring, and Performance":** This chapter covers the various (command line) tools available to troubleshoot and monitor VSAN.

## Chapter 1

Introduction to VSAN

This chapter introduces you to the world of the software-defined datacenter, but with a focus on the storage aspect. The chapter covers the basic premise of the software-defined datacenter and then delves deeper to cover the concept of software-defined storage and associated solutions such as the server storage-area network (Server SAN).

Software-Defined Datacenter

VMworld, the VMware annual conferencing event, introduced VMware's vision for the software-defined datacenter (SDDC) in 2012. The SDDC is VMware's architecture for the public and private clouds where all pillars of the datacenter—compute, storage, and networking (and the associated services)—are virtualized. Virtualizing datacenter components enables the IT team to be more flexible. If you lower the operational complexity and cost while increasing availability and agility, you will ultimately lower the time to market for new services.

To achieve all of that, virtualization of components by itself is not sufficient. The platform used must be capable of being installed and configured in a fully automated fashion. More importantly, the platform should enable you to manage and monitor your infrastructure in a smart and less operationally intense manner. That is what the SDDC is all about! Raghu Raghuram (VMware senior vice president) captured it in a single sentence: The essence of the software-defined datacenter is "abstract, pool, and automate."

Abstraction, pooling, and automation are all achieved by introducing an additional layer on top of the physical resources. This layer is usually referred to as a *virtualization layer*. Everyone reading this book is probably familiar with the leading product for compute virtualization, VMware vSphere. Fewer people are probably familiar with network virtu-alization, sometimes referred to as software-defined network (SDN) solutions. VMware offers a solution named NSX that is based on the solution built by the acquired company Nicira. NSX does for networking what vSphere does for compute. These layers do not just virtualize the physical resources but also allow you to pool them and provide you with an application programming interface (API) that enables you to automate all operational aspects.

Automation is not just about scripting, however. A significant part of the automation of virtual machine (VM) provisioning (and its associated resources) is achieved through policy-based management. Predefined policies allow you to provision VMs in a quick, easy, consistent, and repeatable manner. The resource characteristics specified on a resource pool or a vApp container exemplify a compute policy. These characteristics enable you to quantify resource policies for compute in terms of reservation, limit, and pri-ority. Network policies can range from security to quality of service (QoS). Unfortunately, storage has thus far been limited to the characteristics provided by the physical storage device, which in many cases did not meet the expectations and requirements of many of our customers.

This book examines the storage component of VMware's SDDC. More specifically, the book covers how a new product called Virtual SAN (VSAN), releasing with VMware vSphere 5.5 Update 1, fits into this vision. You will learn how it has been implemented and integrated within the current platform and how you can leverage its capabilities and expand on some of the lower-level implementation details. Before going further, though, you want to have a generic understanding of where VSAN fits in to the bigger software-defined storage picture.

Software-Defined Storage

Software-defined storage is a term that has been used and abused by many vendors. Because software-defined storage is currently defined in so many different ways, consider the fol-lowing quote from VMware:

> Software Defined Storage is the automation and pooling of storage through a software control plane, and the ability to provide storage from industry standard servers. This offers a significant simplification to the way storage is provisioned and managed, and also paves the way for storage on indus-try standard servers at a fraction of the cost. (Source: http://cto.vmware.com/vmwares-strategy-for-software-defined-storage/)

A software-defined storage product is a solution that abstracts the hardware and allows you to easily pool all resources and provide them to the consumer using a user-friendly user interface (UI) or API. A software-defined storage solution allows you to both scale up and scale out, without increasing the operational effort.

Many hold that software-defined storage is about moving functionality from the traditional storage devices to the host. This is a trend that was started by virtualized versions of storage devices such as HP's StoreVirtual VSA and evolved into solutions that were built to run on many different hardware platforms. One example of such a solution is Nexenta. These solutions were the start of a new era.

Hyper-Convergence/Server SAN Solutions

In today's world, the hyper-converged/server SAN solutions come in two flavors:

- Hyper-converged appliances
- Software-only solutions

A hyper-converged solution is an appliance type of solution where a single box provides a platform for VMs. This box typically contains multiple commodity x86 servers on which a hypervisor is installed. Local storage is aggregated into a large shared pool by leveraging a virtual storage appliance or a kernel-based storage stack. Typical examples of hyper-converged appliances that are out there today include Nutanix, Scale Computing, SimpliVity, and Pivot3. Figure 1-1 shows what these appliances usually look like: a 2U form factor with four hosts.

Figure 1-1 Commonly used hardware by hyper-converged storage vendors

You might ask, "If these are generic x86 servers with hypervisors installed and a virtual storage appliance, what are the benefits over a traditional storage system?" The benefits of a hyper-converged platform are as follows:

- Time to market is short, less than 4 hours to install and deploy
- Ease of management and integration

- Able to scale out, both capacity and performance-wise

- Lower total costs of acquisition compared to traditional environments

These solutions are sold as a single stock keeping unit (SKU), and typically a single point of contact for support is provided. This can make support discussions much easier. However, a hurdle for many companies is the fact that these solutions are tied to hardware and specific configurations. The hardware used by hyper-converged vendors is often not the same as from the preferred hardware supplier you may already have. This can lead to operational challenges when it comes to updating/patching or even cabling and racking. In addition, a trust issue exists. Some people swear by server Vendor X and would never want to touch any other brand, whereas others won't come close to server Vendor X. This is where the software-based storage solutions come in to play.

Software-only storage solutions come in two flavors. The most common solution today is the virtual storage appliance (VSA). VSA solutions are deployed as a VM on top of a hypervisor installed on physical hardware. VSAs allow you to pool underlying physical resources into a shared storage device. Examples of VSAs include VMware vSphere Storage Appliance, Maxta, HP's StoreVirtual VSA, and EMC Scale IO. The big advantage of software-only solutions is that you can usually leverage existing hardware as long as it is on the hardware compatibility list (HCL). In the majority of cases, the HCL is similar to what the used hypervisor supports, except for key components like disk controllers and flash devices.

VSAN is also a software-only solution, but VSAN differs significantly from the VSAs listed. VSAN sits in a different layer and is not a VSA-based solution.

Introducing Virtual SAN

VMware's plan for software-defined storage is to focus on a set of VMware initiatives related to local storage, shared storage, and storage/data services. In essence, VMware wants to make vSphere a platform for storage services.

Historically, storage was something that was configured and deployed at the start of a project, and was not changed during its life cycle. If there was a need to change some characteristics or features of the logical unit number (LUN) or volume that were being leveraged by VMs, in many cases the original LUN or volume was deleted and a new volume with the required features or characteristics was created. This was a very intrusive, risky, and time-consuming operation due to the requirement to migrate workloads between LUNs or volumes, which may have taken weeks to coordinate.

With software-defined storage, VM storage requirements can be dynamically instantiated. There is no need to repurpose LUNs or volumes. VM workloads and requirements may change over time, and the underlying storage can be adapted to the workload at any time. VSAN aims to provide storage services and service level agreement *automation* through a software layer on the hosts that *integrates* with, *abstracts*, and *pools* the underlying hardware.

A key factor for software-defined storage is storage policy–based management (SPBM). This is also a key feature in the vSphere 5.5 release. SPBM can be thought of as the next generation of VMware's storage profile features that was introduced with vSphere 5.0. Where the initial focus of storage profiles was more about ensuring VMs were provisioned to the correct storage device, in vSphere 5.5. SPBM is a critical component to how VMware is implementing software-defined storage.

Using SPBM and vSphere APIs, the underlying storage technology surfaces an abstracted pool of storage space with various capabilities that is presented to vSphere administrators for VM provisioning. The capabilities can relate to performance, availability, or storage services such as thin provisioning, compression, replication, and more. A vSphere administrator can then create a *VM storage policy* (or profile) using a subset of the capabilities that are required by the application running in the VM. At deployment time, the vSphere administrator selects a VM storage policy. SPBM pushes the VM storage policy down to the storage layer and datastores that understand that the requirements placed in the VM storage policy will be made available for selection. This means that the VM is always instantiated on the appropriate underlying storage based on the requirements placed in the VM storage policy.

Should the VM's workload or I/O pattern change over time, it is simply a matter of applying a new VM storage policy with requirements and characteristics that reflect the new workload to that specific VM, or even virtual disk, after which the policy will be seamlessly applied without any manual intervention from the administrator (in contrast to many legacy storage systems, where a manual migration of VMs or virtual disks to a different datastore would be required). VSAN has been developed to seamlessly integrate with vSphere and the SPBM functionality it offers.

What Is Virtual SAN?

VSAN is a new storage solution from VMware, released as a beta in 2013 and made generally available to the public in March 2014. VSAN is fully integrated with vSphere. It is an object-based storage system and a platform for VM storage policies that aims to simplify VM storage placement decisions for vSphere administrators. It fully supports and is integrated with core vSphere features such as vSphere High Availability (HA), vSphere Distributed Resource Scheduler (DRS), and vMotion, as illustrated in Figure 1-2.

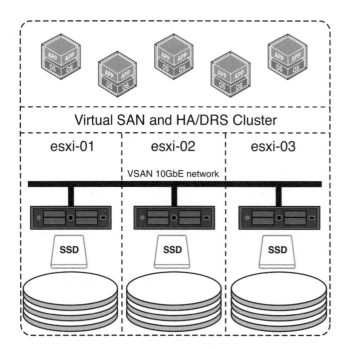

Figure 1-2 Simple overview of a VSAN cluster

VSAN's goal is to provide both resiliency and scale-out storage functionality. It can also be thought of in the context of QoS in so far as VM storage policies can be created that define the level of performance and availability required on a per-VM, or even virtual disk, basis.

VSAN is a software-based distributed storage solution that is built directly in the hypervisor. Although not a virtual appliance like many of the other solutions out there, a VSAN can best be thought of as a kernel-based solution that is included with the hypervisor. Technically, however, this is not completely accurate because components critical for performance and responsiveness such as the data path and clustering are in the kernel, while other components that collectively can be considered part of the "control plane" are implemented as native user-space agents. Nevertheless, with VSAN there is no need to install anything other than the software you are already familiar with: VMware vSphere.

VSAN is about simplicity, and when we say *simplicity*, we do mean simplicity. Want to try out VSAN? It is truly as simple as creating a VMkernel network interface card (NIC) for VSAN traffic and enabling it on a cluster level, as shown in Figure 1-3. Of course, there are certain recommendations and requirements to optimize your experience, as described in further detail in Chapter 2, "VSAN Prerequisites and Requirements for Deployment."

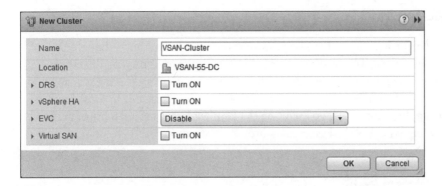

Figure 1-3 Two-click enablement

Now that you know it is easy to use and simple to configure, what are the benefits of a solution like VSAN? What are the key selling points?

- **Software defined**: Use industry standard hardware
- **Flexible**: Scale as needed and when needed, both scale up and scale out
- **Simple**: Ridiculously easy to manage and operate
- **Automated**: Per-VM and disk policy-based management
- **Converged**: Enables you to create dense/building-block-style solutions

That sounds compelling, doesn't it? Of course, there is a time and place for everything; Virtual SAN 1.0 has specific use cases. For version 1.0, these use cases are as follows:

- **Virtual desktops**: Scale-out model using predictive and repeatable infrastructure blocks lowers costs and simplifies operations
- **Test and dev**: Avoids acquisition of expensive storage (lowers total cost of ownership [TCO]), fast time to provision
- **Management or DMZ infrastructure**: Fully isolated resulting in increased security and no dependencies on the resources it is potentially managing.
- **Disaster recovery target**: Inexpensive disaster recovery solution, enabled through a feature like vSphere Replication that allows you to replicate to any storage platform

Now that you know what VSAN is, it's time to see what it looks like from an administrator's point of view.

What Does VSAN Look Like to an Administrator?

When VSAN is enabled, a single shared datastore is presented to all hosts that are part of the VSAN-enabled cluster. This is the strength of VSAN; it is presented as a datastore. Just like any other storage solution out there, this datastore can be used as a destination for VMs and all associated components, such as virtual disks, swap files, and VM configuration files. When you deploy a new VM, you will see the familiar interface and a list of available datastores, including your VSAN-based datastore, as shown in Figure 1-4.

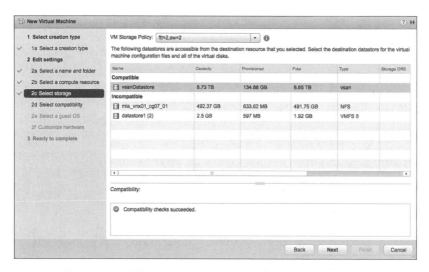

Figure 1-4   Just a normal datastore

This VSAN datastore is formed out of host local storage resources. Typically, all hosts within a VSAN-enabled cluster will contribute performance (flash) and capacity (magnetic disks) to this shared datastore. This means that when your cluster grows, your datastore will grow with it. VSAN is what is called a scale-out storage system (adding hosts to a cluster), but also allows scaling up (adding resources to a host).

Each host that wants to contribute storage capacity to the VSAN cluster will require at least one flash device and one magnetic disk. At a minimum, VSAN requires three hosts in your cluster to contribute storage; other hosts in your cluster could leverage these storage resources without contributing storage resources to the cluster itself. Figure 1-5 shows a cluster that has four hosts, of which three (esxi-01, esxi-02, and esxi-03) contribute storage and a fourth does not contribute but only consumes storage resources. Although it is technically possible to have a nonuniform cluster and have a host not contributing storage, we do highly recommend creating a uniform cluster and having all hosts contributing storage for overall better utilization, performance, and availability.

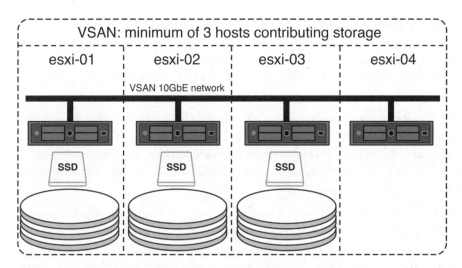

Figure 1-5 Nonuniform VSAN cluster example

Today's boundary for VSAN in terms of both size and connectivity is a vSphere cluster. This means that at most 32 hosts can be connected to a VSAN datastore. Each host can run a supported maximum of 100 VMs, allowing for a total combined of 3,200 VMs within a 32-host VSAN cluster, of which 2,048 VMs can be protected by vSphere HA.

As you can imagine, with just regular magnetic disks it would be difficult to provide a good user experience when it comes to performance. To provide optimal user experience, VSAN relies on flash. Flash resources are used for read caching and write buffering. Every write I/O will go to flash first, and eventually will be destaged to magnetic disks. For read I/O it will depend, although in a perfect world all read I/O will come from flash. Chapter 5, "Architectural Details," describes the caching and buffering mechanisms in much greater detail.

To ensure VMs can be deployed with certain characteristics, VSAN enables you to set policies on a per-virtual disk or a per-VM basis. These policies help you meet the defined service level objectives (SLOs) for your workload. These can be performance-related characteristics such as read caching or disk striping, but can also be availability-related characteristics that ensure strategic replica placement of your VM's disks (and other important files).

If you have worked with VM storage policies in the past, you might now wonder whether all VMs stored on the same VSAN datastore will need to have the same VM storage policy assigned. The answer is no. VSAN allows you to have different policies for VMs provisioned to the same datastore and even different policies for disks from the same VM.

As stated earlier, by leveraging policies, the level of resiliency can be configured on a per-virtual disk granular level. How many hosts and disks a mirror copy will reside on depends on the selected policy. Because VSAN uses mirror copies defined by policy to provide resiliency, it does not require a local RAID set. In other words, hosts contributing to VSAN storage capacity should simply provide a set of disks to VSAN.

Whether you have defined a policy to tolerate a single host failure or, for instance, a policy that will tolerate up to three hosts failing, VSAN will ensure that enough replicas of your objects are created. The following example illustrates how this is an important aspect of VSAN and one of the major differentiators between VSAN and most other virtual storage solutions out there.

EXAMPLE: We have configured a policy that can tolerate one failure and created a new virtual disk. This means that VSAN will create two identical storage objects and a witness. The witness is a component tied to the VM that allows VSAN to determine who should win ownership in the case of a failure. If you are familiar with clustering technologies, think of the witness as a quorum object that will arbitrate ownership in the event of a failure. Figure 1-6 may help clarify these sometimes-difficult-to-understand concepts. This figure illustrates what it would look like on a high level for a VM with a virtual disk that can tolerate one failure. This can be the failure of a host, NICs, disk, or flash device, for instance.

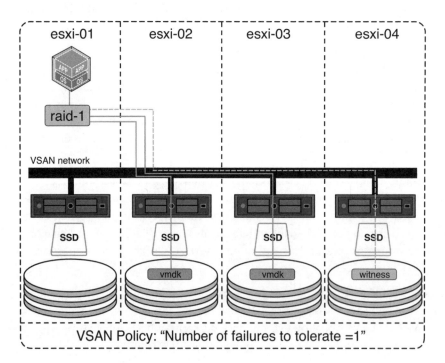

Figure 1-6 VSAN failures to tolerate

In Figure 1-6, the VM's compute resides on the first host (esxi-01) and its virtual disks reside on the other hosts (esxi-02 and esxi-03) in the cluster. In this scenario, the VSAN network is used for storage I/O, allowing for the VM to freely move around the cluster without the need for storage components to be migrated with the compute. This does, however, result in the first requirement to implement VSAN. VSAN requires at a minimum one dedicated 1Gbps NIC port, but VMware recommends a 10GbE for the VSAN network.

Yes, this might still sound complex, but in all fairness, VSAN masks away all the complexity, as you will learn as you progress through the various chapters in this book.

Summary

To conclude, vSphere Virtual SAN (VSAN) is a brand-new, hypervisor-based distributed storage platform that enables convergence of compute and storage resources. It enables you to define VM-level granular SLOs through policy-based management. It allows you to control availability and performance in a way never seen before, simply and efficiently.

This chapter just scratched the surface. Now it's time to take it to the next level. Chapter 2 describes the requirements for installing and configuring VSAN.

## Chapter 2

VSAN Prerequisites and Requirements for Deployment

Before delving into the installation and configuration of VSAN, it's necessary to discuss the requirements and the prerequisites. VMware vSphere 5.5 Update 1 (U1) is the foundation of every VSAN-based virtual infrastructure.

VMware vSphere 5.5

VMware vSphere 5.5 U1 consists of two major components: the vCenter Server management platform and the ESXi hypervisor. To install and configure VSAN, both vCenter Server and ESXi are required.

VMware vCenter Server provides a centralized management platform for VMware vSphere environments. It is the solution used to provision new virtual machines (VMs), configure hosts, and perform many other operational tasks associated with managing a virtualized infrastructure.

To run a fully supported VSAN environment, the vCenter Server 5.5 U1 platform is the minimum requirement. VSAN can be managed by both the Windows version of vCenter Server and the vCenter Server Appliance (VCSA). VSAN is configured and monitored via the vSphere Web Client, and this also needs to be the 5.5 U1 version. VSAN can also be fully configured and managed through the command-line interface (CLI) and vSphere application programming interface (API) for those wanting to automate some (or all) of the aspects of VSAN configuration, monitoring, or management. Although a single cluster can contain only one VSAN datastore, a vCenter Server instance can manage multiple VSAN and compute clusters.

ESXi 5.5 U1

VMware ESXi is an enterprise-grade virtualization product that allows you to run multiple instances of an operating system in a fully isolated fashion on a single server. It is a bare-metal solution, meaning that it does not require a guest OS and has an extremely thin footprint. ESXi is the foundation for the large majority of virtualized environments worldwide.

VSAN requires a minimum of three ESXi hosts (where each host has local storage and is contributing this storage to the VSAN datastore) to form a *supported* VSAN cluster. This is to allow the cluster to meet the minimum availability requirements of tolerating at least one host failure. The VSAN cluster supports a maximum of 32 ESXi hosts in the cluster, an increase from the 8 hosts that were originally supported during the VSAN beta release. The ESXi hosts must be running version 5.5 U1 at a minimum.

At a minimum, it is recommended that a host has at least 6GB of memory. If you configure a host to contain the maximum number of disk groups, we recommend that the host is configured with a minimum of 32GB of memory. The host memory requirement is directly related to the number of physical disks in the host and the number of disk groups configured on the host. You will learn more about this in Chapter 9, "Designing a VSAN Cluster."

ESXi Boot Considerations

When it comes to installing an ESXi for VSAN-based infrastructure, you have various options to consider regarding where to place the ESXi image. ESXi can be installed on a local magnetic disk, USB flash drive, or SD card. With the current version of VSAN, stateless booting of ESXi (auto-deploy) is not supported. By deploying ESXi to a USB flash drive or SD card, you have the added advantage of not consuming a magnetic disk for the image. This disk can then be consumed by VSAN to create the distributed, shared VSAN datastore used for deploying VMs.

For hosts with less than 512GB of memory, USB/SD is supported. For hosts with a memory configuration larger than 512GB, ESXi needs to be installed on a local disk. The reason for this is that VSAN will use the core dump partition to store VSAN traces that can be used by VMware Global Support Services and the VMware Engineering team for root cause analysis. VSAN traces are discussed in more detail in Chapter 10, "Troubleshooting, Monitoring, and Performance." When installing ESXi on USB or SD, note that you should use a device that has a minimum capacity of 8GB.

If the host does not have USB/SD and a local disk is used to install ESXi, this disk cannot be part a disk group and therefore cannot be used to contribute storage to the VSAN datastore. So, in an environment where the number of disk slots is a constraint, it is recommended to use USB/SD.

VSAN Requirements

Before enabling VSAN, it is highly recommended that the vSphere administrator validate that the environment meets all the prerequisites and requirements. To enhance resilience, this list also includes recommendations from an infrastructure perspective:

- Minimum of three ESXi hosts
- Minimum of 6GB memory per host to install ESXi
- VMware vCenter Server
- One hard disk for hosts contributing storage to VSAN datastore
- One flash device for hosts contributing storage to VSAN datastore
- One boot device to install ESXi on
- Pass-through/JBOD mode capable disk controller preferred
- Dedicated 1GbE network port for VSAN VMkernel interface

VMware Hardware Compatibility Guide

Before installing and configuring ESXi, validate that your configuration is on the official VMware compatibility guide for VSAN, which you can find at the following website:

http://vmwa.re/vsanhcl

VSAN has strict requirements when it comes to disks, flash devices, and disk controllers. With all the various options, configuring the perfect VSAN host can be a complex exercise. Before reading about all the components, you will want to learn about an alternative: VSAN Ready Nodes.

VSAN Ready Nodes

VSAN Ready Nodes are a great alternative to manually selecting components. Various vendors have gone through the exercise for you and created configurations that are called *VSAN Ready Nodes*. These VSAN Ready Nodes consist of tested and certified hardware only and, in our opinion, provide an additional guarantee. VSAN Ready Nodes are also listed in the compatibility guide, as shown in Figure 2-1.

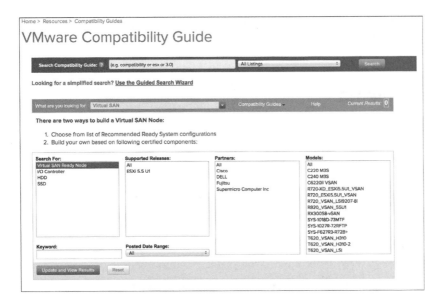

Figure 2-1   Virtual SAN Ready Nodes configurations

For the more adventurous types, or those who prefer a particular server model or vendor that is not currently listed in the VSAN Ready Nodes compatibility guide, some specifics for the various components, such as storage controllers and disk drives, must be called out. The sections that follow highlight these considerations in more detail.

Storage Controllers

Each ESXi host participating in the VSAN cluster requires a disk controller. It is recommended that this disk controller is capable of running in what is commonly referred to as *pass-through mode*, *HBA mode*, or *JBOD mode*. In other words, the disk controller should provide the capability to pass up the underlying magnetic disks and solid-state disks (SSDs) as individual disk drives without a layer of RAID sitting on top. The result of this is that ESXi can perform operations directly on the disk without those operations being intercepted and interpreted by the controller. VSAN will take care of any RAID configuration when policy attributes such as availability and performance for VMs are defined. The VSAN compatibility guide will call out the disk controllers that have successfully passed testing.

Every server vendor has many different disk controllers that can be selected when configuring a new server. We have listed a couple of controllers for the most commonly used server brands, and a couple of generic LSI disk controllers that are often used with brands like SuperMicro:

- Dell PERC H200

- HP H220i

- IBM ServeRAID M1015 SAS/SATA

- LSI 2008, LSI 9207-8i, LSI 9211-8i, LSI 9240-8i

These disk controllers were in the compatibility guide at the time of writing this book, but you should validate your respective controller against the VMware compatibility guide before purchasing it. In some cases, the compatibility guide has changed because of firmware changes, for instance.

During the VSAN beta, there were challenges with the AHCI onboard controllers that are installed on many low-end motherboards. These disk controllers are typically used in home labs, and the driver, which came with ESXi, unfortunately contained an issue that resulted in disks randomly being reported with a "Permanent Device Loss" state. These AHCI controllers also result in a lower performance because they were not designed for the VSAN use case. These controllers are not usually in the VMware compatibility guide, however, and it is not recommended to use these controllers for production or serious lab environments.

In some scenarios, hardware may have already been acquired and the disk controllers that are available do not support pass-through mode. In those scenarios, you can use RAID-0.

Disk Controller RAID-0

For disk controller adapters that do not support pass-through/HBA/JBOD mode, VSAN supports disk drives presented via a RAID-0 configuration. Volumes can be used by VSAN if they are created using a RAID-0 configuration that contains only a single drive. This needs to be done for both the magnetic disks and the SSDs. This can be done using the disk controller software/firmware. Administrators need to understand, however, that when SSDs are exposed to a VSAN leveraging a RAID-0 configuration, in many cases the drive is not recognized as a flash device because these characteristics are masked by the RAID-0 configuration. If this occurs, you will need to mark the drive as a flash device using esxcli. The following example shows how this can be done. There is also an example that shows how to address another common device presentation issue: how to mark a device as local. In some environments, devices can be recognized as shared volumes even though they are local to the ESXi host. This is because some SAS controllers allow devices to be accessed from more than one host. In this case, the devices, although local, are shown as shared (not local). These devices are not considered for use by VSAN because VSAN does not currently support the use of SAN or other shared volumes. In this scenario, we create a rule that configures the device mpx.vmhba2:C0:T0:L0 as being a local device and a flash device:

```
esxcli storage nmp satp rule add –satp VMW_SATP_LOCAL –device
mpx.vmhba2:C0:T0:L0 –option "enable_local enable_ssd"
```

When using RAID-0 instead of pass-through, you must take into consideration certain operational impacts. When pass-through is used, drives are (in most scenarios) instantly recognized, and there is no need to configure the drives as local/SSD. On top of that, when a RAID-0 set is used, the drive is bound to that RAID-0 configuration. This means that the RAID-0 set has a 1:1 relationship with a given drive. If this drive fails and needs to be replaced with a new drive, this relationship is broken and a new RAID-0 set with a new drive must be manually created. The effort involved will differ per RAID controller used, whereas with a drive in pass-through mode, replacing the drive is a matter of removing and inserting.

Performance and RAID Caching

VMware has carried out many performance tests using various types of disk controllers and RAID controllers. In most cases, the performance difference between pass-through and RAID-0 configurations was negligible.

When utilizing RAID-0 configurations, you should disable the storage controllers write cache so as to provide VSAN full control. When the storage controller cache cannot be completely disabled in a RAID-0 configuration, you should configure the storage controller cache for 100% read cache, effectively disabling the write cache.

Magnetic Disks

Each ESXi host must have at least one magnetic disk when contributing capacity to the VSAN cluster. Additional magnetic disks will obviously increase capacity, and may also increase performance as VM storage objects can be striped across multiple spindles. Also for consideration, a higher number of magnetic disks lead to a larger number of capacity balancing options when required. Each disk will be part of a disk group. At most, a VSAN host can have 5 disk groups, each containing 7 magnetic disks, resulting in a maximum of 35 magnetic disks, as depicted in Figure 2-2.

VSAN supports the various types of disks ranging from high-capacity 7200 RPM SATA drives to lower-capacity but better performing 15K RPM SAS drives. A large portion of VM storage I/O performance will be met by flash devices, but note that any I/O that needs to come from disk will be bound by the performance characteristics of those spindles. Chapter 9 provides various examples that demonstrate the impact of choosing SATA over SAS and vice versa. For now, we would like to provide the following list that gives an indication of the number of input/output operations per second (IOPS) that a disk type can provide:

- **7,200 RPM SATA:** 80 IOPS

- **10,000 RPM SAS:** 130 IOPS

- **15,000 RPM SAS:** 175 IOPS

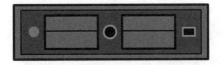

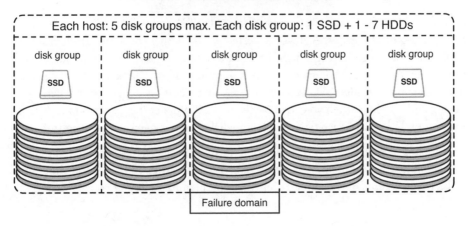

Figure 2-2 Maximum disks and disk group configuration

Flash Devices

Each ESXi host must have at least one flash device when contributing capacity to a VSAN cluster. This flash device is utilized by VSAN as both a write buffer and a read cache and fronts a group of magnetic disks. Each disk group requires one flash device. Because VSAN can have a maximum of five disk groups per host, the maximum number of flash devices per host is also five. The more flash capacity in a host, the greater the performance will be because more I/O can be cached/buffered.

For the best VSAN performance, VMware is recommending customers to use flash devices with at least 20,000 IOPS, with a lifespan of 5 years with 10 writes per cell per day. VMware supports various types of flash, ranging from SSDs to PCIe flash devices. VMware has published a list of supported PCIe flash devices and SSDs in the VMware compatibility guide. Before procuring new equipment, review the VMware compatibility guide to ensure that your configuration is a supported configuration.

The designated flash device classes specified within the VMware compatibility guide are as follows:

- **Class A**: 2,500–5,000 writes per second

- **Class B**: 5,000–10,000 writes per second

- **Class C**: 10,000–20,000 writes per second

- **Class D**: 20,000–30,000 writes per second

- **Class E**: 30,000+ writes per second

This question often arises: "Can I use a consumer grade SSD and will VSAN work?" From a technical point of view, VSAN works perfectly fine with a consumer grade SSD; however, in most cases, consumer-grade SSDs have much lower endurance guarantees and different (lower) performance characteristics. Although it might be attractive from a price point to use a consumer-grade SSD, we like to stress that VSAN is dependent on flash for both buffering and caching; when your drive fails, this will impact the disk group to which this SSD is bound. When the flash device fails, the disk group is marked as unhealthy.

After having looked at the various SSDs and PCIe flash devices, we have concluded that it is almost impossible to recommend a brand or type of flash to use. This decision should be driven by the requirements of the applications that you plan to deploy in your VMs running on VSAN.

Network Requirements

This section covers the requirements and prerequisites from a networking perspective for VSAN. VSAN is a distributed storage solution and therefore heavily leans on the network for intra-host communication. Consistency and reliability are the keys.

Network Interface Cards

Each ESXi host must have at least one 1GbE network interface card (NIC) dedicated to VSAN. However, as a best practice, VMware and the authors of this book are recommending 10GbE NICs. For redundancy, you can configure a team of NICs on a per-host basis. We consider this a best practice, but it is not necessary to build a fully functional VSAN cluster.

Supported Virtual Switch Types

VSAN is supported on both VMware vSphere Distributed Switches (VDS) and VMware standard switches (VSS). There are some advantages to using a Distributed Switch that will be covered in Chapter 3, "VSAN Installation and Configuration." No other virtual switch types are supported in the initial release of VSAN.

VMkernel Network

On each ESXi host that wants to participate in a VSAN cluster, a VMkernel port for VSAN communication must be created. The VMkernel port is labeled Virtual SAN Traffic and is new in vSphere 5.5. This port is used for inter-cluster node communication. It is also used for reads and writes when one of the ESXi hosts in the cluster owns a particular VM but the actual data blocks making up the VM files are located on a different ESXi host in the cluster. In this case, I/O will need to traverse the network configured between the hosts in the cluster, as depicted in Figure 2-3, where VMkernel interface vmk2 is used for VSAN traffic by all the hosts in the VSAN cluster. The VM residing on esxi-01 does all of its reads and writes leveraging the VSAN network.

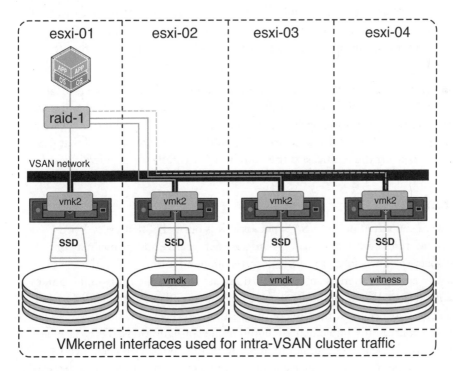

Figure 2-3 VSAN traffic

VSAN Network Traffic

The protocol used by VSAN is a proprietary protocol. VMware has not published a specification of the protocol. This is similar to the approach taken for other VMware products and features such as vMotion, Fault Tolerance, vSphere Replication, and other VMware proprietary protocols, where VMware deems the information proprietary. The VSAN network is used for three different traffic types. It is important to know these because they introduce a requirement for your physical network switch configuration:

- **Multicast heartbeats**: These are used to discover all participating VSAN hosts in the cluster, as well as to determine the state of a host. Compared to other traffic types, multicast heartbeats generate very few packets.

- **Multicast and unicast packets from the clustering service (CMMDS)**: This traffic does metadata updates like object placement and statistics. These generate more network traffic than the heartbeats, but it's still a very small percentage.

- **Storage traffic (for example, reads, writes)**: This is the majority of network traffic. Any host within the cluster can talk to any other host over unicast.

To ensure that VSAN hosts can communicate properly, it is required that multicast traffic is enabled on the physical switch on Layer 2. If multicast communication is not possible between the ESXi hosts in the VSAN cluster over the VSAN traffic network, the VSAN cluster will not form correctly.

Although multicast is just a small percentage of the total network traffic, it is a critical part. The majority of traffic in a VSAN cluster will be storage traffic as storage read and write I/O go over the network. Ensuring optimal network bandwidth is important. VMware recommends that physical switches that support real multicast traffic are used and that lower-end switches that convert the multicast traffic into broadcast traffic be avoided if possible.

Jumbo Frames

Jumbo frames are supported on the VSAN network. It is our belief that every VSAN deployment is different, both from a server hardware perspective and from a network hardware perspective. Therefore, it is difficult to recommend for or against the use of jumbo frames. In addition, there is an operational impact in implementing jumbo frames on non-greenfield sites. When jumbo frames are not consistently configured end to end, network problems may occur. At the time of this writing, however, no known issues exist on VSAN with inconsistently implemented jumbo frame configurations. Tests have been conducted to prove the benefits of jumbo frames, but results so far have been inconclusive. In some scenarios, a performance improvement of 15 percent is measured and a decrease of CPU utilization is observed. In other scenarios, no performance increase or CPU utilization decrease has been measured.

In an operationally mature environment where a consistent implementation can be guaranteed, the use of jumbo frames is left to the administrator's discretion.

NIC Teaming

Another potential way of optimizing network performance is teaming of NICs. NIC teaming in ESXi is transparent to VSAN. You can team NICs in various ways. To allow VSAN to use multiple physical NIC ports, it is possible to implement either physical teaming (EtherChannels) or create multiple VSAN VMkernel interfaces. Chapter 3 covers the configuration details and parameters in more detail. Note, however, that there is no guarantee that VSAN network traffic will be able to utilize the full bandwidth of multiple physical NICs at the same time; various factors play a part, including the size of the cluster, the number of NICs, and the number of different IP addresses used.

Network I/O Control

Although it is recommended to use 10GbE NICs, there is no requirement to solely dedicate these cards to the VSAN network. NICs can be shared with other traffic types; however, you might consider using network I/O control (NIOC) to ensure that the VSAN traffic is guaranteed a certain amount of bandwidth over the network in the case where congestion of the network arises. This is especially true if a 10GbE NIC shared with (for instance) vMotion traffic, which is infamous for utilizing all available bandwidth when possible. NIOC requires the creation of a VDS because NIOC is not available with VSS. Luckily, the distributed switch is included with the VSAN license.

Chapter 3 provides various examples of how NIOC can be configured for the various types of network configurations.

Firewall Ports

When you are enabling VSAN, a number of ESXi firewall ports are automatically opened (both ingoing and outgoing) on each ESXi host that participates in the VSAN cluster. The ports are used for inter-cluster host communication and for communication with the storage provider on the ESXi hosts. Table 2-1 provides a list of VSAN-specific network ports.

Table 2-1 ESXi Ports and Protocols Opened by VSAN

Name	Port	Protocol
Cmmds	12345, 23451	UDP
RDT	2233	TCP
Vsanvp	8080	TCP

Summary

Although configuring VSAN literally takes a couple of clicks, it is important to take the time to ensure that all requirements are met and to ensure that all prerequisites are in place. A stable storage platform starts at the foundation, the infrastructure on which it is enabled. Before moving on to Chapter 3, you should run through this checklist to confirm that all requirements have been met:

- vSphere 5.5 U1.

- Three hosts minimum.

- 6GB memory per host minimum.

- When exceeding 512GB of host memory, it is required to install ESXi on magnetic disk. USB flash drives or SD cards are not supported.

- Certified disk controller.

- At least one certified flash device per host contributing capacity.

- At least one certified magnetic drive per host contributing capacity.

- Dedicated 1GbE NIC port or shared 10GbE NIC port for VSAN.

- Multicast enabled on VSAN network (Layer 2).

The following list identifies additional recommendations, which are not requirements for a fully functional VSAN but which might be desirable from a production standpoint:

- Network switch redundancy for VSAN

- Jumbo frames consistently implemented end to end

VSAN Installation and Configuration

This chapter describes in detail the installation and configuration process, as well as all initial preparation steps that you might need to consider before proceeding with a VSAN cluster deployment. You will find information on how to correctly set up network and storage devices, as well as some helpful tips and tricks on how to deploy the most optimal VSAN configuration.

VSAN Networking

Network connectivity is the heart of any VSAN cluster. VSAN cluster hosts use the network for virtual machine (VM) I/O but also to communicate their state between one another. Consistent and correct network configuration is key to a successful VSAN deployment. Because the majority of disk I/O will either come from a remote host, or will need to go to a remote host, VMware recommends leveraging a 10GbE infrastructure. Note that although 1GbE is fully supported, it could become a bottleneck in large-scale deployments.

VMware vSphere provides two different types of virtual switch, both of which are fully supported with VSAN:

- The VMware standard virtual switch (VSS) provides connectivity from VMs and VMkernel ports to external networks but is local to an ESXi host.

- A vSphere Distributed Switch (VDS) gives central control of virtual switch administration across multiple ESXi hosts. A VDS can also provide additional networking features over and above what a VSS can offer, such as network I/O control (NIOC), that can provide quality of service (QoS) on your network. Although a VDS normally requires a particular vSphere edition, VSAN includes a VDS independent of the vSphere edition you are running.

VMkernel Network for VSAN

All ESXi hosts participating in a VSAN network need to communicate with one another. A new VMkernel type called Virtual SAN Traffic, introduced in vSphere 5.5, is now available for VSAN traffic. A VSAN cluster will not successfully form until a VSAN VMkernel port is available on each ESXi host participating in the VSAN cluster. The vSphere administrator must create a VSAN VMkernel port on each ESXi host in the cluster before the VSAN cluster forms (see Figure 3-1).

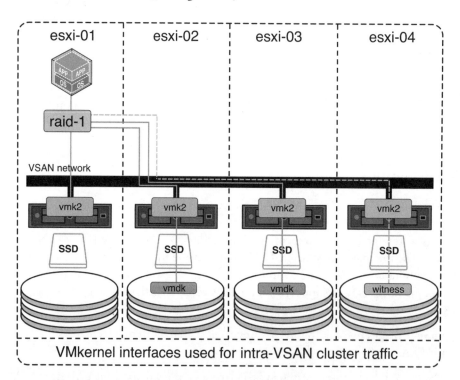

Figure 3-1   VMkernel interfaces used for intra-VSAN cluster traffic

Without a VMkernel network for VSAN, the cluster will not form successfully. If communication is not possible between the ESXi hosts in the VSAN cluster, only one ESXi host will join the VSAN cluster. Other ESXi hosts will not be able to join. A warning message will display when there are communication difficulties between ESXi hosts in the cluster. If the cluster is created before the VMkernel ports are created, a warning message is also displayed regarding communication difficulties between the ESXi hosts. Once the VMkernel ports are created and communication is established, the cluster will form successfully.

VSAN Network Configuration: VMware Standard Switch

With a VSS, creating a port group for VSAN network traffic is relatively straightforward. By virtue of installing an ESXi host, a VSS is automatically created to carry ESXi network management traffic and VM traffic. You can use an already-existing standard switch and its associated uplinks to external networks to create a new VMkernel port for VSAN traffic. Alternatively, you may choose to create a new standard switch for the VSAN network traffic VMkernel port (see Figure 3-2), selecting some new uplinks for the new standard switch.

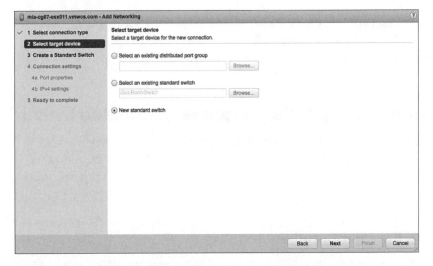

Figure 3-2   Add Networking Wizard: Virtual switch selection/creation

In this example, we have decided to create a new standard switch or vSwitch. As you progress through the Add Networking Wizard, after selecting the appropriate uplinks for this new standard switch, you will get to the port properties shown in Figure 3-3. This is where the appropriate network service for the VMkernel port is selected. For VSAN, a new traffic type called **Virtual SAN traffic** is available for selection.

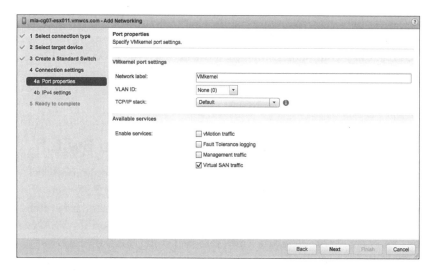

Figure 3-3   Enabling the Virtual SAN traffic service on a port

Complete the wizard, and you will have a standard switch configured with a VMkernel port group to carry the VSAN traffic. Of course, this step will have to be repeated for every ESXi host in the VSAN cluster.

VSAN Network Configuration: vSphere Distributed Switch

In the case of a VDS, a distributed port group needs to be configured to carry the VSAN traffic. Once the distributed port group is created, VMkernel interfaces on the individual ESXi hosts can then be created to use that distributed port group. The sections that follow describe this process in greater detail.

Step 1: Create the Distributed Switch

Although the official VMware documentation makes no distinction regarding which versions of Distributed Switch you should be using, the authors recommend using the latest version (5.5) of the Distributed Switch with VSAN. This is the version that the authors used in their VSAN tests. Note that if Distributed Switch version 5.5 is used, all ESXi hosts attaching to this distributed switch must be running ESXi version 5.5. Earlier versions of ESXi will not be able to utilize this distributed switch.

One of the steps when creating a distributed switch is to select whether NIOC is enabled or disabled. We recommend leaving this at the default option of enabled. Later on, we discuss the value of NIOC in a VSAN environment.

Step 2: Create a Distributed Port Group

The steps to create a distributed port group are relatively straightforward:

1. Using the vSphere Web Client, navigate to the VDS object in the vCenter Server inventory.

2. Select the option to create a new distributed port group.

3. Provide a name for the distributed port group.

4. Set the characteristics of the port group, such as the type of binding, allocation, and the number of ports that can be attached to the port group, as shown in Figure 3-4.

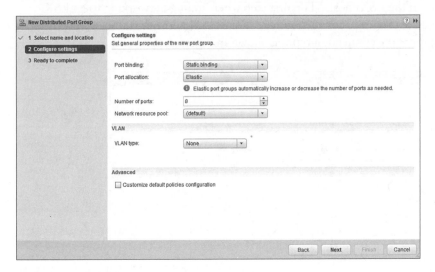

Figure 3-4   Distributed port group settings

One important consideration with the creation of the port group is the port allocation settings and the number of ports associated with the port group. Note that the default number of ports is eight and that the allocation setting is elastic by default. This means that when all ports are assigned, a new set of eight ports is created. A port group with an allocation type of elastic can automatically increase the number of ports as more devices are allocated. With the port binding set to static, a port is assigned to the VMkernel port when it connects to the distributed port group. If you plan to have a 16-host or a 32-host VSAN cluster, you could consider configuring a greater number of ports for the port group instead of the default of 8. This means that in times of maintenance and outages, the ports always stay available for the host until such time as it is ready to rejoin the cluster, and it means that the switch doesn't incur any overhead by having to delete and re-add the ports.

When creating a Distributed Switch and distributed port groups, there are a lot of additional options to choose from, such as port binding type. These options are well documented in the official VMware vSphere documentation, and although we discussed port allocation in a little detail here, most of the settings are beyond the scope of this book. Readers who are unfamiliar with these options can find explanations in the official VMware vSphere documentation. However, you can simply leave these Distributed Switch and port groups at the default settings and VSAN will deploy just fine with those settings.

Step 3: Build VMkernel Ports

Once the distributed port group has been created, you can now proceed with building the VMkernel ports on the ESXi hosts. The first step when adding networking to an ESXi host is to select an appropriate connection type. For VSAN network traffic, **VMkernel Network Adapter** is the connection type, as shown in Figure 3-5.

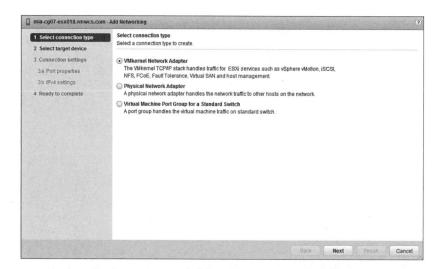

Figure 3-5   VMkernel connection type

The next step is to select the correct port group or distributed port group with which to associate this VMkernel network adapter. We have previously created a distributed port group, so we select that distributed port group, as shown in Figure 3-6.

Once the distributed port group has been selected, it is now time to select the appropriate connection settings for this VMkernel port. In the first part of the connection settings, the port properties are populated. This is where the services associated with the VMkernel port are selected. In this case, we are creating a VMkernel port for VSAN traffic, so that would be the service that should be selected, as shown in Figure 3-7. By default, there will be only one TCP/IP stack to choose. Options for configuring different network stacks may be found in official VMware documentation and are beyond the scope of this book, but suffice it to say that different network stacks can be configured on the ESXi host and have different properties such as default gateways associated with each network stack.

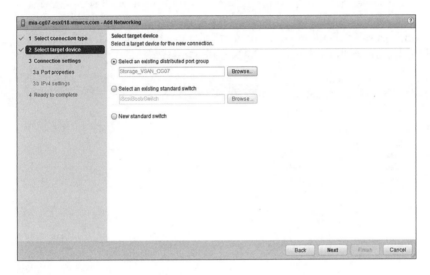

Figure 3-6   VMkernel target device

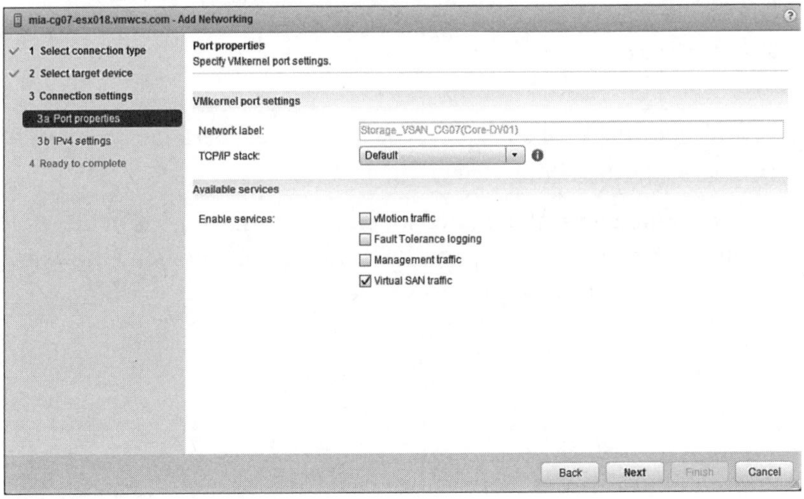

Figure 3-7   VMkernel port properties

Once the correct service (**Virtual SAN traffic**) has been chosen, the next step is to popu-
late the IPv4 settings of the VMkernel adapter, as shown in Figure 3-8. IPv6 is not supported in VSAN 1.0. You have two options available for IPv4 settings: DHCP or static.
The Dynamic Host Configuration Protocol is a standardized network protocol that is used
to provide network configuration details to other devices over the network. If DHCP is
chosen, a valid DHCP server needs to exist on the network to provide valid IPv4 information to the ESXi host for this VMkernel port. In this example, we have chosen to go with a
static configuration, so a valid IP address and subnet mask must be provided. Both DHCP
and static IP addresses are supported for the VSAN traffic interface.

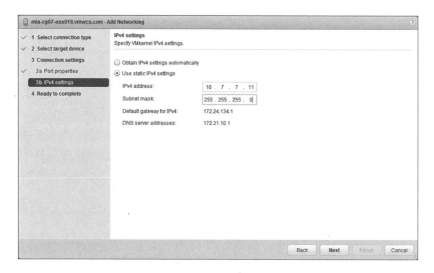

Figure 3-8   VMkernel IPv4 settings

With all the details provided for the VMkernel port, you can double-check the configuration before finally creating the port, as illustrated in Figure 3-9.

This VMkernel port configuration must be repeated for each of the ESXi hosts in the
VSAN cluster. When this configuration is complete, the network configuration is now in
place to allow for the successful formation of the VSAN cluster.

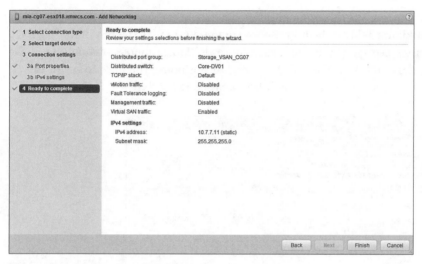

Figure 3-9   VMkernel ready to complete

Possible Network Configuration Issues

If the VSAN VMkernel is not properly configured, a configuration warning will be displayed in the Virtual SAN > General section on the Manage tab of your VSAN cluster object. If you click the information icon next to the "Misconfiguration detected" message, further details related to the network status will display, as shown in Figure 3-10.

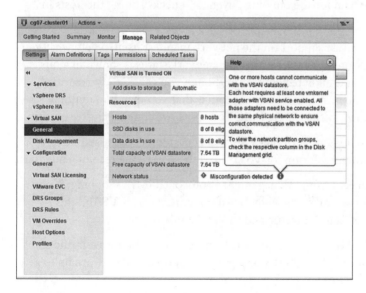

Figure 3-10   Network configuration warning

Another place to observe VSAN communication issues is in the summary view of the ESXi host as shown in Figure 3-11. If the host cannot communicate with the rest of the VSAN cluster, the message displayed in the Summary tab reads "Host cannot communicate with all other nodes in the VSAN enabled cluster." At this point, you need to revisit the VMkernel port properties and ensure that it has been set up correctly.

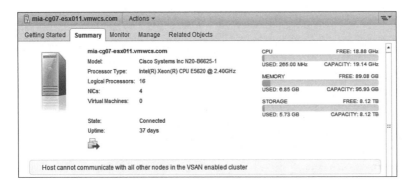

Figure 3-11   Host cannot communicate

Another issue that has surprised a number of customers is the reliance on multicast traffic. One of the requirements for VSAN is to allow multicast traffic on the VSAN network between the ESXi hosts participating in the VSAN cluster; however, multicast is used only for relatively infrequent operations. For example, multicast is used for the initial discovery of hosts in the VSAN cluster and for the ongoing "liveness" checks among the hosts in the cluster.

So, how does this lack of multicast support on the network manifest itself? Well, what you will see after enabling VSAN on the cluster is that the network status is shown in a mis-configured state ("Misconfiguration detected"), even though you can ping/vmkping all the VSAN interfaces on all the hosts. Another symptom is that you may find multiple single host VSAN clusters formed, with a single ESXi host in its own unique cluster partition.

How do you resolve it? Well, a number of our VSAN beta customers discussed some options on the VMware community forum for VSAN, and these were the recommendations:

- **Option 1**: Disable Internet Group Management Protocol (IGMP) snooping. Now this will allow *all* multicast traffic through; but if the only traffic is VSAN, this should be a negligible amount of traffic and should be safe to use.

- **Option 2**: Configure IGMP snooping querier. If there is other multicast traffic and you are concerned that disabling IGMP snooping might open the network up to a flood of multicast traffic, this is a preferred option.

Customers who ran into this situation stated that both methods worked for them; however, we recommend that you refer to your switch provider documentation on how to handle multicast configurations. Some switches convert multicasts to broadcasts, and the packets will be sent to all ports. VMware recommends that customers should avoid using these switches with VSAN if at all possible. The smarter switches that use IGMP snooping have the capability to send the multicast packets on ports where the multicast has been requested, and these switches are more desirable in VSAN deployments. The reason for this recommendation is that simple switches that turn multicast traffic into broadcast traffic can flood a network and affect other non-VSAN hosts attached to the switch.

One final point is to explain how you can figure out which host or hosts are partitioned from the cluster. The easiest way is to use the Disk Management view under the VSAN Manage tab and then the Disk Groups view. This contains a column called Network Partition Groups. This column will show a group number to highlight which partition a particular host resides in. In the example in Figure 3-12, one of the hosts is unable to communicate with the other hosts in the cluster and so is placed in a different network partition group.

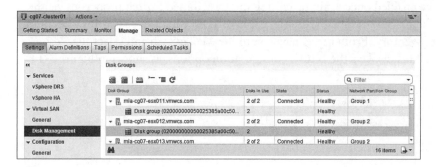

Figure 3-12   Network partition group

If the cluster is successfully formed and all hosts are communicating, all hosts in this view will have the same network partition number.

Network I/O Control Configuration Example

As previously mentioned, network I/O control (NIOC) can be used to guarantee bandwidth for VSAN cluster communication and I/O. NIOC is available only on VDS, not on VSS. Indeed, VDS are only available with some of the higher vSphere editions; however, VSAN includes VDS irrespective of the vSphere edition used.

If you are using an earlier version of a distributed switch prior to 5.5, although not explicitly called out in the vSphere documentation, we recommend upgrading to version 5.5 of the Distributed Switch if you plan to use it with VSAN. This is simply a cautionary recommendation as we did all of our VSAN testing with this version of Distributed Switch.

A new traffic type is now available in the vSphere 5.5 version of NIOC. It is called *Virtual SAN Traffic* and provides QoS on VSAN traffic. Although this QoS configuration might not be necessary in some VSAN cluster environments, it is a good feature to have available if VSAN traffic appears to be impacted by other traffic types sharing the same 10GbE network interface card. An example of a traffic type that could impact VSAN is *vMotion*. By its very nature, vMotion traffic is "bursty" and might claim the full available bandwidth on a network interface card (NIC) port, impacting other traffic types sharing the NIC, including VSAN traffic. Leveraging NIOC in those situations will avoid a self-imposed denial-of-service (DoS) attack.

Setting up NIOC is quite straightforward, and once configured it will guarantee a certain bandwidth for the VSAN traffic between all hosts. NIOC is enabled by default when a VDS is created. If the feature was disabled during the initial creation of the Distributed Switch, it may be enabled once again by editing the Distributed Switch properties via the vSphere Web Client. To begin with, use the vSphere Web Client to select the VDS in the vCenter Server inventory. From there, navigate to the Manage tab and select the Resource Allocation view. This displays the NIOC configuration options, as shown in Figure 3-13.

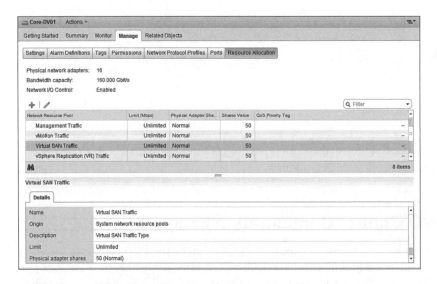

Figure 3-13   NIOC resource allocation

To change the resource allocation for the VSAN traffic in NIOC, simply edit the properties of the VSAN traffic network resource pool. Figure 3-14 shows the modifiable configuration options.

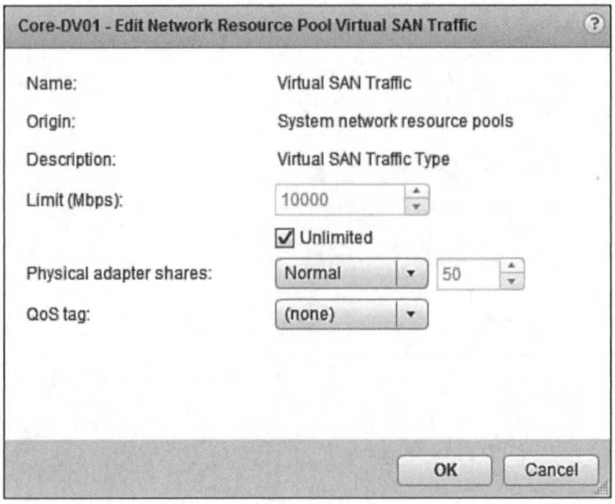

Figure 3-14 NIOC configuration

By default, the limit is set to Unlimited, physical adapter shares are set to 50, and there is no QoS tag. The Unlimited value means that VSAN network traffic is allowed to consume all the network bandwidth when there is no congestion. If congestion arises, the physical adapter shares come into place. These shares are compared with the share values assigned to other traffic types to determine which traffic type gets priority.

The QoS tag requires some further explanation. It simply isn't good enough to define a priority for network traffic at the host; you need to inform the whole infrastructure that a particular traffic type is prioritized once it leaves the ESXi host. This is where the QoS tag comes in. The QoS tag is actually an IEEE 802.1p tag. The IEEE 802.1p tag provides a 3-bit field called the Priority Control Point (PCP) to specify a level of prioritization. This is within the Ethernet frame header. This allows network packets to be grouped into one of seven different traffic classes. The higher the tag number, the higher the priority of the traffic. This allows external devices such as switches and routers to identify which traffic is prioritized. The example in Figure 3-15 sets the VSAN traffic QoS tag to 5 and the shares value to High, which is equivalent to 100.

With VSAN deployments, VMware is recommending a 10GbE network infrastructure. In these deployments, two 10GbE network ports are usually used, and are connected to two physical 10GbE capable switches to provide availability. The various types of traffic will need to share this network capacity, and this is where NIOC can prove invaluable.

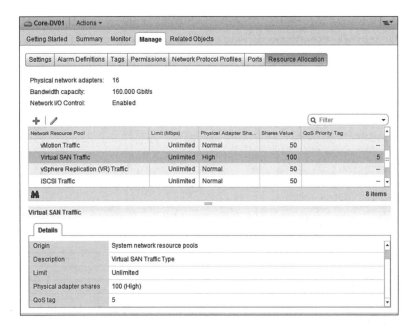

Figure 3-15   VSAN traffic network resource pool

We do not recommend setting a limit on the VSAN traffic. The reason for this is because a limit is a "hard" setting. In other words, if a 2Gbps limit is configured on the VSAN traffic, the traffic will be limited even when additional bandwidth is available on the network. Therefore, you should not use limits because of this behavior. Instead, you should use shares and "artificially limit" your traffic types based on resource usage and demand.

Design Considerations: Distributed Switch and Network I/O Control

To provide QoS and performance predictability, VSAN and NIOC should go hand in hand. Before discussing the configuration options, the following types of networks are being considered:

- Management network

- vMotion network

- Virtual SAN network

- VM network

This design consideration assumes 10GbE redundant networking links and a redundant switch pair for availability. Two scenarios will be described. These scenarios are based on the type of network switch used:

1. Redundant 10GbE Switch setup *without* "link aggregation" capability
2. Redundant 10GbE Switch setup *with* "link aggregation" capability

NOTE

Link aggregation (IEEE 802.3ad) allows users to use more than one connection between network devices. It basically combines multiple physical connections into one logical connection, and provides a level of redundancy and bandwidth improvement.

In both configurations, recommended practice dictates that you create the following port groups and VMkernel interfaces:

- 1 × management network VMkernel interface
- 1 × vMotion VMkernel interface (with all interfaces in the same subnet)
- 1 × VSAN VMkernel interface
- 1 × VM port group

To simplify the configuration, you should have a single VSAN and vMotion VMkernel interface. It is, however, possible to create multiple VSAN and multiple vMotion VMkernel interfaces. When these configurations are being created, you *must* place the VSAN VMkernel interfaces on different subnets.

To ensure traffic types are separated on different physical ports, we will leverage standard Distributed Switch capabilities. We will also show how to use shares to avoid noisy neighbor scenarios.

Scenario 1: Redundant 10GbE Switch Without "Link Aggregation" Capability

In this configuration, two individual 10GbE uplinks are available. It is recommended to separate traffic and designate a single 10GbE uplink to VSAN for simplicity reasons. The recommended minimum amount of bandwidth per traffic type is as follows:

- **Management network**: 1GbE
- **vMotion VMkernel interface**: 5GbE

- **VM network**: 2GbE

- **VSAN VMkernel interface**: 10GbE

Various traffic types will share the same uplink. The management network, VM network, and vMotion network traffic are configured to share uplink 1, and VSAN traffic is configured to use uplink 2. With the network configuration done this way, sufficient bandwidth exists for all the various types of traffic when the VSAN cluster is in a normal or standard operating state.

To make sure that no single traffic type can impact other traffic types during times of contention, NIOC is configured, and the shares mechanism is deployed.

When defining traffic type network shares, this scenario works under the assumption that there is only one physical port available and that all traffic types share that same physical port for this exercise.

This scenario also takes a worst-case scenario approach into consideration. This will guarantee performance even when a failure has occurred. By taking this approach, we can ensure that VSAN always has 50 percent of the bandwidth at its disposal while leaving the remaining traffic types with sufficient bandwidth to avoid a potential self-inflicted DoS.

Table 3-1 outlines the recommendations for configuring shares for the traffic types.

Table 3-1 Recommended Share Configuration by Traffic Type (Scenario 1)

Traffic Type	Shares	Limit
Management Network	20	N/A
vMotion VMkernel Interface	50	N/A
VM Port Group	30	N/A
Virtual SAN VMkernel Interface	100	N/A

When selecting the uplinks used for the various types of traffic, you should separate traffic types to provide predictability and avoid noisy neighbor scenarios. The following configuration is recommended:

- Management network VMkernel interface = Explicit failover order =
  Uplink 1 active / Uplink 2 standby

- vMotion VMkernel interface = Explicit failover order =
  Uplink 1 active / Uplink 2 standby

- VM port group = Explicit failover order = Uplink 1 active / Uplink 2 standby

- Virtual SAN VMkernel interface = Explicit failover order =
  Uplink 2 active / Uplink 1 standby

Setting an explicit failover order in the Teaming and Failover section of the port groups is recommended for predictability (see Figure 3-16). The explicit failover order always uses the highest-order uplink from the list of active adapters that passes failover detection criteria.

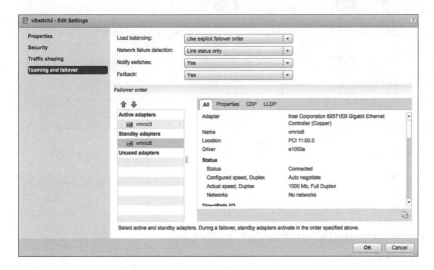

Figure 3-16   Using explicit failover order

Separating traffic types allows for optimal storage performance while also providing sufficient bandwidth for the vMotion and VM traffic (see Figure 3-17). Although this could also be achieved by using the Load Based Teaming (LBT) mechanism, note that that the LBT load balancing period is 30 seconds, potentially causing a short period of contention when "bursty" traffic share the same uplinks. Also note that when troubleshooting network issues, it might be difficult to keep track of the relationship between the physical NIC port and VMkernel interface. Therefore, this approach also provides a level of simplicity to the network configuration.

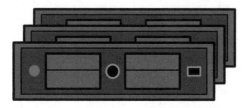

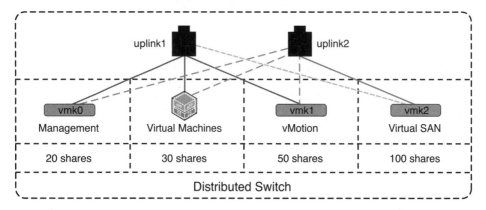

Figure 3-17   Distributed Switch, failover order, and NIOC configuration

Scenario 2: Redundant 10GbE Switch with Link Aggregation Capability

In this next scenario, there are two 10GbE uplinks set up in a teamed configuration (often referred to as EtherChannel or link aggregation). Because of the physical switch capabilities, the configuration of the virtual layer will be extremely simple. We will take the previous recommended minimum bandwidth requirements into consideration for the design:

- **Management network**: 1GbE
- **vMotion VMkernel**: 5GbE
- **VM port group**: 2GbE
- **VSAN VMkernel interface**: 10GbE

When the physical uplinks are teamed (link aggregation), the Distributed Switch load-balancing mechanism is required to be configured with one of the following configuration options:

- IP-Hash
- Link Aggregation Control Protocol (LACP)

IP-Hash is a load-balancing option available to VMkernel interfaces that are connected to multiple uplinks on an ESXi host. An uplink is chosen based on a hash of the source and destination IP addresses of each packet. For non-IP packets, whatever is located at those IP address offsets in the packet is used to compute the hash.

LACP is supported on vSphere 5.5 Distributed Switches. This feature allows you to connect ESXi hosts to physical switches by means of dynamic link aggregation. LAGs (link aggregation groups) are created on the distributed switch to aggregate the bandwidth of the physical NICs on the ESXi hosts that are in turn connected to LACP port channels.

LACP support was introduced in vSphere Distributed Switch version 5.1, but enhanced support was introduced in the 5.5 versions. If you are running an earlier version of the Distributed Switch, you should upgrade to the 5.5 versions.

The official vSphere networking guide has much more detail on IP-hash and LACP support and should be referenced for additional details.

It is recommended to configure all port groups and VMkernel interfaces to use either LACP or IP-Hash depending on the type of physical switch being used:

- Management network VMkernel interface = LACP / IP-Hash

- vMotion VMkernel interface = LACP / IP-Hash

- VM port group = LACP / IP-Hash

- VSAN VMkernel interface = LACP / IP-Hash

Because various traffic types will share the same uplinks, you also want to make sure that no traffic type can affect other types of traffic during times of contention. For that, the NIOC shares mechanism is once again used.

Working under the same assumptions as before that there is only one physical port available and that all traffic types share the same physical port, we once again take a worst-case scenario approach into consideration. This approach will guarantee performance even in a failure scenario. By taking this approach, we can ensure that VSAN always has 50 percent of the bandwidth at its disposal while giving the other traffic types sufficient bandwidth to avoid a potential self-inflicted DoS situation arising.

When both uplinks are available, this will equate to 10GbE for VSAN traffic. When only one uplink is available (due to NIC failure or maintenance reasons), the bandwidth is also cut in half, giving a 5GbE bandwidth.

Table 3-2 outlines the recommendations for configuring shares for the traffic types.

Table 3-2   Recommended Share Configuration by Traffic Type (Scenario 2)

Traffic Type	Shares	Limit
Management Network	20	N/A
vMotion VMkernel Interface	50	N/A
VM Port Group	30	N/A
VSAN VMkernel Interface	100	N/A

Figure 3-18 depicts this configuration scenario.

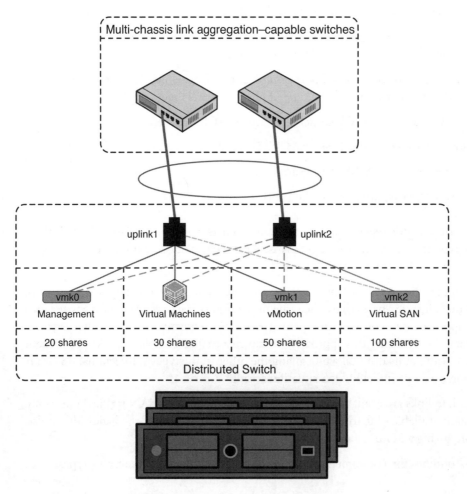

Figure 3-18   Distributed Switch configuration for link aggregation

Either of the scenarios discussed here should provide an optimal network configuration for your VSAN cluster.

Creating a VSAN Cluster

The creation of a VSAN cluster is identical in many respects to how a vSphere administrator might set up a vSphere Distributed Resource Scheduler (DRS) or vSphere High Availability (HA) cluster. A cluster object is created in the vCenter Server inventory, and one can either choose to enable the VSAN cluster functionality and then add in the hosts to the cluster, or add the hosts first, and then enable VSAN on the cluster. The net result from enabling VSAN on a cluster is to have all of the ESXi hosts in the VSAN cluster access a shared, distributed VSAN datastore. In VSAN 1.0, only a single VSAN datastore can be created. Therefore, all local storage is consumed by this single VSAN datastore.

The VSAN datastore is made up from the local storage of each of the ESXi hosts in the cluster. The size of the VSAN datastore is entirely dependent on the number of hosts in the VSAN cluster and the number of magnetic disks in the ESXi hosts participating in the VSAN cluster.

When you enable the VSAN functionality, a single option is displayed asking the administrator to choose a manual or automatic cluster. This simply refers to whether the vSphere administrator would like VSAN to discover all the local disks on the hosts and automatically add them to the VSAN datastore or if the vSphere administrator would like to manually select which disks to add to the cluster. Note that when configuring VSAN on an existing cluster, vSphere HA needs to be disabled before enabling VSAN. Chapter 8, "Interoperability," discusses the changes relevant to vSphere HA.

The Role of Disk Groups

VSAN uses the concept of a disk group as a container for magnetic disks and solid-state drives (SSD) or PCIe flash devices. VMs that have their storage deployed on a disk drive in a particular disk group will leverage the caching capabilities of the SSD or flash device in the same disk group only. The disk group can be thought of as an aggregate hybrid device that uses flash for performance and magnetic disk drives for capacity. You must take into account a number of considerations for disk groups, which we will look at in detail now. In the future, when we refer to SSDs in the context of VSAN disk groups, we also infer PCIe flash devices.

Disk Group Maximums

In VSAN 1.0, there are a maximum number of five disk groups per host. Each of these disk groups can contain a maximum of one SSD and seven magnetic disks. This means that the VSAN datastore maximum size is seven magnetic disks × five disk groups × number of ESXi hosts in the cluster × size of the magnetic disk. As you see, this is quite scalable and can produce a very large distributed datastore.

Why Configure Multiple Disk Groups in VSAN?

Disk groups can contain at most one SSD. In the event that a vSphere administrator finds that there are multiple SSDs in an ESXi host that want to participate in a VSAN cluster, multiple disk groups would have to be created. The vSphere administrator can then decide the ratio of SSD to magnetic disks if performance was a requirement. If the SSD to magnetic disk ratio is high, the greater the size of the cache that will be available for I/O acceleration. Alternatively, a vSphere administrator may decide to keep a constant SSD to magnetic ratio across all disk groups for consistent VM performance. Chapter 5, "Architectural Details," discusses in detail the role of the SSDs. For the moment, it is sufficient to understand that SSDs do not contribute toward VSAN datastore capacity but instead act as an I/O accelerator for VMs as it is leveraged as read cache (70 percent) and a write buffer (30 percent).

Another reason for multiple disk groups is that it allows a vSphere administrator to define their failure domain. With multiple disk groups with a single SSD and a few magnetic disks, should the SSD in that disk group fail, the failure domain is limited to only those magnetic disks in that disk group. With one very large disk group containing lots of magnetic disks, an SSD failure can impact a greater number of VMs. The failure domain should also be a consideration when designing disk group configurations.

Figure 3-19 shows a VSAN cluster that contains five hosts, and each host contains one SSD and seven magnetic disk drives. Should the SSD in any of the hosts fail, only the magnetic disks in the same disk group are affected. The SSD failure does not impact any other hosts or disk groups in the cluster. Indeed, if there were another disk group containing its own SSD and magnetic disks on the same host, it would not be impacted by the SSD failure either. This is what we mean when we say that a disk group can be used to define a failure domain.

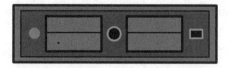

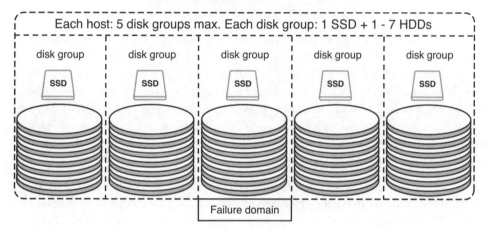

Figure 3-19   Disk groups define failure domains.

SSD to Magnetic Disk Ratio

When designing your VSAN environment from a hardware perspective, realize that VSAN heavily relies on SSD for performance. As a rule of thumb, VMware recommends 10 percent flash capacity of the expected consumed total virtual disk capacity before "failures to tolerate" has been taken into account. VMware also supports lower ratios. Larger ratios will, in fact, improve the performance of VMs by virtue of the fact that more I/O can be cached. SSDs will function as read cache and write buffer capacity for VMs in VSAN.

The 10 percent value is based on the assumption that the majority of working data sets are about 10 percent. Using this rule of thumb (and it is just a rule of thumb) to cover the majority of workloads means that live data from the application running in your VM should be in flash.

For example, assume that we have 100 VMs. Each VM has a 100GB virtual disk, of which anticipated usage is 50GB on average. In this scenario, this would result in the following:

10% of (100 * 50GB) = 500GB

This total amount of flash capacity should be divided by the number of ESXi hosts in the VSAN cluster. If you have five hosts, in this example that would lead to 100GB of flash capacity recommended per host.

Automatically Add Disks to VSAN Disk Groups

In some cases, it might be useful to take control and configure VSAN in manual mode, but in most scenarios it makes more sense to let VSAN deal with this. If automatic mode is chosen during the VSAN cluster creation workflow, VSAN will automatically discover local magnetic disks and local SSDs on each host and build disk groups on each host in the cluster. Note that these SSDs and magnetic disks will be claimed by VSAN only if they are empty and contain no partition information. VSAN will not claim disks that are already being used or have been used in the past and contain residual data. For VSAN to claim these disks, they will first have to be wiped clean.

Each host with valid storage will have a disk group containing their local magnetic disks and SSDs. Suffice it to say that a disk group can be thought of as a container of magnetic disks and SSDs. As stated previously, each disk group can only contain a single SSD and a maximum of seven magnetic disks, but there may be multiple disk groups defined per ESXi host. Finally, after all of this is completed, the VSAN datastore is created, and its size reflects the capacity of all the magnetic disks across all the hosts in the cluster, less some metadata overhead.

ESXi hosts that are part of the VSAN cluster but do not contribute storage to the VSAN datastore can still access the VSAN datastore. This is a very advantageous feature of VSAN, because a VSAN cluster can now be scaled not just on storage requirements, but also on compute requirements. Note, however, that VMware recommends uniformly configured clusters for better load balancing, availability, and overall performance.

Handling Is_local or Is_SSD Issues

Note that although automatic mode will claim "local" disks, most ESXi hosts with SAS controllers will have their disks show up as "remote," and VSAN will not auto-claim these disks. In this case, the vSphere administrator must manually create the disk groups, even though the cluster is set up in automatic mode.

Although previously discussed in Chapter 2, "VSAN Prerequisites and Requirements for Deployment," it is worth reiterating that some SAS controllers can have devices shared by more than one host. When ESXi detects one of these controller types, it marks the devices as shared even though it is more than likely that these devices are only in use by a single ESXi host. Nevertheless, when VSAN sees this shared flag (the flag and its actual setting are Is_Local: False), it will not claim the disk just in case more than one ESXi host is sharing it. VSAN expects and needs devices to be marked as local before it will claim them. This is why user intervention is needed to mark these devices as local so that VSAN can claim them. You might think that this is an overcautious approach, but the last thing VSAN wants to do is claim a disk it shouldn't claim.

Depending on the type of flash used, it can also occur that your flash device is not recognized as such. In both scenarios, it is also possible to manually mark the devices as either "local" or as "ssd" by using the esxcli command. The following example shows how to do that. Although we already touched on this command for RAID-0 configurations in Chapter 2, it is worth revisiting it here once again in some more detail.

The first step is to create a new SATP rule. The rule contains the disk device to mark as SSD and the —option parameter set to enable_ssd. In this case, my device is identified by mpx.vmhba0:C0:T0:L0:

```
# esxcli storage nmp satp rule add --satp VMW_SATP_LOCAL --device
mpx.vmhba0:C0:T0:L0 --option=enable_ssd
```

The next step is to reclaim the device so that the new rule is applied:

```
# esxcli storage core claiming reclaim -d mpx.vmhba0:C0:T0:L0
```

Finally, verify that the device is being seen as an SSD device:

```
# esxcli storage core device list --device=mpx.vmhba0:C0:T0:L0
mpx.vmhba0:C0:T0:L0
   Display Name: Local VMware Disk (mpx.vmhba0:C0:T0:L0)
   .

   .

   .

   Model: Virtual disk
   Revision: 1.0
   SCSI Level: 2
   Is Pseudo: false
   Status: on
   Is RDM Capable: false
   Is Local: true
   Is Removable: false
   Is SSD: true
   Is Offline: false
   Is Perennially Reserved: false
   Thin Provisioning Status: unknown
   .

   .

   .
```

A similar process may be followed to address the Is_Local property when devices behind a SAS controller show up as Is_Local: false. This command must be run against all the disks that you want VSAN to claim, be they magnetic disks or SSDs. It will also have to be run on all hosts that want to participate in a VSAN cluster and contribute storage to the VSAN datastore but have disks marked as remote.

Manually Adding Disks to a VSAN Disk Group

As mentioned earlier, as you create the VSAN cluster, you have the option to manually add disks. If this option is selected, the VSAN cluster is still formed; however, the VSAN datastore is 0 bytes in size initially. The administrator will have to manually create disk groups on a per-host basis and add between one and seven magnetic disks per disk group and at most one SSD disk to each of the disk groups. After each disk group is created on a per-host basis, the size of the VSAN datastore will grow according to the amount of magnetic disk capacity that is added. Note that the SSDs function as read caches and write buffers and are not included in the capacity of the VSAN datastore.

You might wonder when this option would be used. One possible reason could be that when VSAN constructs disk groups it will always try to do this in a consistent manner; however, due to many different server configurations, especially those using SAS for disk connectivity, the manual method may be an important approach over the automatic method. SAS reports devices with unique identifiers instead of on a port-by-port basis. Therefore, a disk in disk slot 1 of one host may be part of disk group 1 in ESXi host 1, while disk in disk slot 1 may become part of disk group 2 in ESXi host 2. When disks need to be replaced for whatever reason, it is of the utmost importance that the correct disk is removed and replaced with a new one. Therefore, a vSphere administrator may want to manually configure the disk groups so that the disks are easily identifiable.

Disk Group Creation Example

Disk group creation is necessary only if the cluster is created in manual mode. If the cluster is created in automatic mode, the disk groups are automatically created for you, using all available disks on the host. The mechanism to create a disk group is quite straightforward. You need to remember some restrictions, however, as mentioned previously:

- At most, there can be one SSD per disk group.
- At most, there can be seven magnetic disks per disk group.

Multiple disk groups may be created if a host has more than seven magnetic disks or more than one SSD. To create a disk group, the cluster must first of all be configured in manual mode, as shown in Figure 3-20.

Figure 3-20   Turning on VSAN

Once the cluster is created, there will be no storage devices claimed by VSAN. The next
step is to manually create disk groups. Navigate to the Disk Management section under
VSAN management in the vSphere Web Client. From here, you select a host in the cluster and click the icon to create a new disk group. This will display all available disks (SSD
and magnetic disks) in the host, as shown in Figure 3-21.

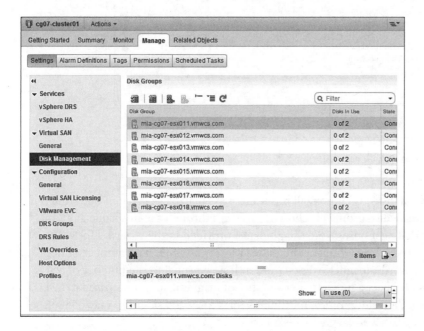

Figure 3-21   VSAN Disk Management

At this point, vSphere administrators have a number of options available. They can decide
to claim all disk from all hosts if they want, or they can individually build disk groups one

host at a time. The first option is useful if disks show up as not local, such as disks that may be behind a SAS controller. For more granular control, however, administrators may like to set up disk groups one host at a time for more control.

When you decide to configure disk groups manually, the vSphere Web Client provides a very intuitive user interface (UI) to do this. From the UI, you can select the magnetic disks and SSDs that form the disk group on a per-host basis, as shown in Figure 3-22.

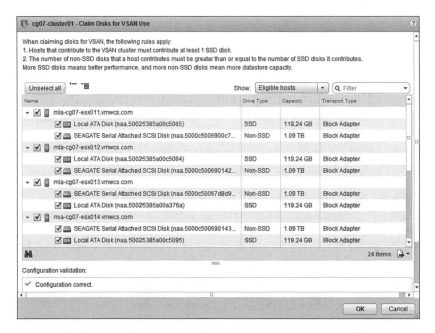

Figure 3-22 Claiming disks for VSAN

If the first icon (claim disks) is chosen, all hosts and disks may be selected in one step. If the second icon (create disk groups) is chosen, this steps through the hosts one at a time, claiming disks for that host only. Note the guidance provided in the wizard. Hosts that contribute storage to the VSAN must contribute at least one SSD. The number of non-SSD disks (in other words, magnetic disks) must at least be equal to the number of SSDs. In reality, you would expect a much higher number of magnetic disks compared to SSDs. And just to reiterate the configuration maximums for VSAN, a disk group may contain only one SSD but up to seven magnetic disks.

After the disk groups have been created, the VSAN datastore is created. This VSAN datastore can now be used for the deployment of VM.

VSAN Datastore Properties

The size of a VSAN datastore is governed by the number of magnetic disks per ESXi host and the number of ESXi hosts in the cluster. There is some metadata overhead to also consider. For example, if a host has seven × 2TB magnetic disks in the cluster, and there are eight hosts in the cluster, the raw capacity is as follows:

7 × 2TB × 8 = 112TB raw capacity

At this point, your VSAN is configured.

Once the VSAN datastore is formed, a number of datastore capabilities are surfaced up into vCenter Server. These capabilities will be used to create the appropriate VM storage policies for VMs and their associated virtual machine disk (VMDK) storage objects deployed on the VSAN datastore. These include stripe width, component failures to tolerate, force provisioning, and provisioned capacity. Before deploying VMs, however, you first need to understand how to create appropriate VM storage policies that meet the requirements of the application running in the VM.

VM storage policies and VSAN capabilities will be discussed in greater detail later in Chapter 4, "VM Storage Policies on VSAN," but suffice it to know for now that these capabilities form the VM policy requirements. These allow a vSphere administrator to specify requirements based on performance, availability, and data services when it comes to VM provisioning. The next chapter discusses VM storage policies in the context of VSAN and how to correctly deploy a VM using VSAN capabilities.

Summary

If everything is configured and working as designed, VSAN can be configured in just a few clicks. However, it is vitally important that the infrastructure is ready in advance. Identifying appropriate magnetic disk drives for capacity, sizing your flash resources for performance, and verifying that your networking is configured to provide the best availability and performance are all tasks that must be configured and designed up front.

Now the VSAN cluster is up and running, let's make use of it. We touched on the topic of VM storage policies. These should be created to reflect the requirements of the application running in your VM. We look at how to do this in the next chapter.

## Chapter 4

VM Storage Policies on VSAN

In vSphere 5.0, VMware introduced a feature called Profile-Driven Storage. Profile-Driven Storage is a feature that allows vSphere administrators to easily select the correct datastore on which to deploy virtual machines (VMs). The selection of the datastore is based on the capabilities of that datastore. Throughout the life cycle of that VM, Profile-Driven Storage allows the administrator to check whether its underlying storage is still *compatible*. In other words, does the datastore on which the VM resides still have the correct capabilities for this VM? The reason why this is useful is because if the VM is migrated to a different datastore for whatever reason, the administrator can ensure that it has moved to a datastore that continues to meet its requirements. If the VM is migrated to a datastore without paying attention to the capabilities of the destination storage, the administrator can still check the compliance of the VM storage from the vSphere client at any time, and take corrective actions if it no longer resides on a datastore that meets its storage requirements (that is, move it back to a compliant datastore).

However, VM storage policies and storage policy-driven management have taken this a step further. In the previous paragraph, we described a sort of storage quality of service driven by the storage. All VMs residing on the same datastore would inherit the capabilities of the datastore. With VSAN, the storage quality of service no longer resides with the datastore; instead, it is enforced by the VM storage policy associated with the VM and the VM disks (VMDKs).

Introducing Storage Policy-Based Management in a VSAN Environment

VSAN leverages this approach to VM deployment, using an updated method called storage policy-based management (SPBM). All VMs deployed to a VSAN datastore must use a VM storage policy, although if one is not specifically created, a default one is assigned to the VM. The VM storage policy contains one or more VSAN capabilities. This chapter will describe the VSAN capabilities. After the VSAN cluster has been configured and the VSAN datastore has been created, VSAN surfaces up a set of capabilities to the vCenter Server. These capabilities, which are surfaced by the vSphere APIs for Storage Awareness (VASA) storage provider (more on this shortly) when the cluster is configured successfully, are used to set the availability, capacity, and performance policies on a per-VM (and VMDK) basis when that VM is deployed on the VSAN datastore.

As previously mentioned, this differs significantly from the previous VM storage profile mechanism that we had in vSphere in the past. With this VM Storage profile feature, the capabilities were associated with datastores, and these were used for VM placement.

What we have now is a mechanism whereby we can specify the requirements of the VM, and the VMDKs, and use these to create a policy. This policy is then sent to the storage layer, asking it to build a storage object for this VM that meets these policy requirements. In fact, a VM can have multiple policies associated with it, different policies for different VMDKs.

By way of explaining capabilities, policies, and profiles, capabilities are what the underlying storage is capable of providing by way of availability, performance, and reliability. These capabilities are visible in vCenter. The capabilities are then used to create a VM storage policy (or just policy for short). A policy may contain one or more capabilities, and these capabilities reflect the requirements of your VM or application running in a VM. Previous versions of vSphere used the term *profiles*, but these are now known as *policies*.

Deploying VMs on a VSAN datastore is very different from previous approaches in vSphere. In the past, an administrator would present a logical unit number (LUN) or volume to a group of ESXi hosts and—in the case of block storage—partition, format, and build a VMFS file system to create a datastore for storing VM files. In the case of network-attached storage (NAS), a Network File System (NFS) volume is mounted to the ESXi host, and once again a VM is created on the datastore. There is no way to specify a RAID-0 stripe width for these VMDKs, nor is there any way to specify a RAID-1 replica for the VMDK.

In the case of VSAN, the approach to deploying VMs is quite different. Consideration must be given to the availability, performance, and reliability factors of the application running in the VM. Based on these requirements, an appropriate VM storage policy must be created and associated with the VM during deployment.

There are five capabilities in the initial release of VSAN, as illustrated in Figure 4-1.

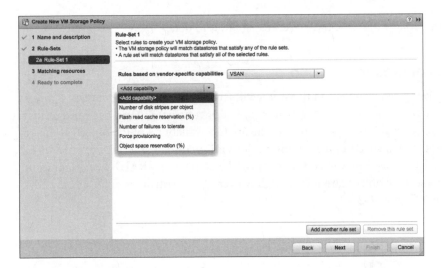

Figure 4-1   VSAN capabilities that can be used for VM storage policies

You can select the capabilities when a VM storage policy is created. VM storage policies are essential in VSAN deployments because they define how a VM is deployed on a VSAN datastore. Using VM storage policies, you can define the capabilities that can provide the number of VMDK RAID-0 stripe components or the number of RAID-1 mirror copies of a VMDK.

The sections that follow highlight where you should use these capabilities when creating a VM storage policy and when to tune these values to something other than the default. Remember that a VM storage policy will contain one or more capabilities.

In the initial release of VSAN, five capabilities are available for selection to be part of the VM storage policy. As an administrator, you can decide which of these capabilities can be added to the policy, but this is, of course, dependent on the requirements of your VM. For example, what performance and availability requirements does the VM have? The capabilities are as follows:

- Number of failures to tolerate
- Number of disk stripes per object

- Flash read cache reservation
- Object space reservation
- Force provisioning

The sections that follow describe the VSAN capabilities in detail.

Number of Failures to Tolerate

This capability sets a requirement on the storage object to tolerate at least *number of failures to tolerate failures in the cluster*. This is the number of concurrent host, network, or disk failures that may occur in the cluster and still ensure the availability of the object. If this property is populated, it specifies that configurations must contain at least *number of failures to tolerate* + 1 replicas. You can consider this in the context of a RAID-1 configuration, where the VM's storage objects are mirrored; however, the mirroring is done across ESXi hosts, as shown in Figure 4-2.

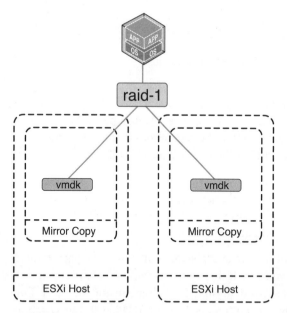

Figure 4-2 Number of failures to tolerate results in a RAID-1 configuration.

Note that this requirement will create a configuration for the VM that may also contain an additional number of witness objects being instantiated to ensure that the VM is available (maintain quorum) even in the presence of up to *number of failures to tolerate* concurrent host failures (see Table 4-1). Witness objects provide a quorum when failures occur in the cluster or a decision has to be made when a split-brain situation arises. These witness objects will be discussed in much greater detail later in the book, but suffice it to say that witness objects play an integral part in maintaining VM availability during failures and maintenance tasks.

One aspect worth noting is that any disk failure on a single host is treated as a "failure" for this metric. Therefore, the VM may not persist if there is a disk failure on host A and a host failure of host B when number of failures to tolerate is set to 1.

Table 4-1   Witness and Hosts Required to Meet Number of Failures to Tolerate Requirement

Number of Failures to Tolerate	Mirror Copies/ Replicas	Witness Objects	Minimum Number of ESXi Hosts
0	1	0	1
1	2	1	3
2	3	2	5
3	4	3	7

If no policy is chosen when a VM is deployed, the default policy will set the number of failures to tolerate to 1. When a new policy is created, the default value of number of failures to tolerate is also 1. This means that even if this capability is not specified in the policy, it is implied.

Number of Disk Stripes Per Object

This capability defines the number of physical disks across which each replica of a storage object (for example, VMDK) is striped. This can be considered in the context of a RAID-0 configuration where I/O traverses a number of physical disk spindles. Typically, when the number of disk stripes per object is defined, the number of failures to tolerate is also defined, because what is "performance" without "availability"? Figure 4-3 shows what a combination of these two capabilities could result in.

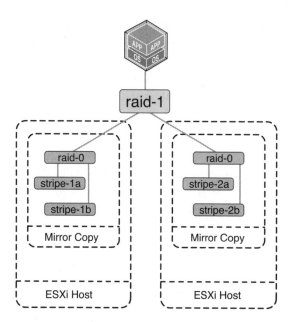

Figure 4-3   Storage object configuration when stripe width set is to 2 and failures to tolerate is set to 1

To understand the impact of stripe width, let's examine it first in the context of write operations and then in the context of read operations.

Because all writes go to the solid-state disk (SSD) write buffer, the value of an increased stripe width may or may not improve performance. This is because there is no guarantee that the new stripe will use a different SSD; the new stripe may be placed on a magnetic disk in the same disk group and thus the new stripe will use the same SSD. If the new stripe is placed in a different disk group, either on the same host or on a different host, and thus leverages a different SSD, performance might improve. However, you as the vSphere administrator have no control over this behavior. The only occasion where an increased stripe width could definitely add value is when there are many, many writes to destage from SSD to magnetic disk. In this case, having a stripe could improve destage performance.

From a read perspective, an increased stripe width will help when you are experiencing many read cache misses. Consider the example of a VM consuming 2,000 read operations per second and experiencing a hit rate of 90 percent, and there are 200 read operations that need to be serviced from magnetic disk. In this case, a single magnetic disk that can provide 150 input/output operations per second (IOPS) is not able to service all of those read operations, so an increase in stripe width would help on this occasion to meet the VM I/O requirements.

In general, the default stripe width of 1 should meet most, if not all VM workloads. Stripe width is a capability that should change only when write destaging or read cache misses are identified as a performance constraint.

Flash Read Cache Reservation

This capability is the amount of flash capacity reserved on the SSD or a flash device as read cache for the storage object. It is specified as a percentage of the logical size of the storage object (that is, VMDK). This is specified as a percentage value (%), with up to four decimal places. This fine granular unit size is needed so that administrators can express sub 1% units. Take the example of a 1TB VMDK. If you limited the read cache reservation to 1% increments, this would mean cache reservations in increments of 10GB, which in most cases is far too much for a single VM.

Note that you do not have to set a reservation to get cache. All VMs equally share the read cache of an SSD. The reservation should be left unset (default) unless you are trying to solve a real performance problem and you believe dedicating read cache is the solution. If you add this capability to the VM storage policy and set it to a value 0 (zero), however, you will not have any read cache assigned to the VM that uses this policy. In the initial version of VSAN, there is no proportional share mechanism for this resource when multiple VMs are consuming read cache, so every VM consuming read cache will share it equally.

Object Space Reservation

All objects deployed on VSAN are thinly provisioned. This means that no space is reserved at VM deployment time but rather space is consumed as the size of the VM storage grows. The object space reservation capability defines the percentage of the logical size of the VM storage object that may be reserved during initialization. The object space reservation is the amount of space to reserve specified as a percentage of the total object address space. This is a property used for specifying a thick provisioned storage object. If object space reservation is set to 100 percent, all of the storage capacity requirements of the VM storage are reserved up front (thick). This will be lazy zeroed thick (LZT) format and not eager zeroed thick (EZT). The difference between LZT and EZT is that EZT virtual disks are zeroed out at creation time; LZT virtual disks are zeroed out at first write time.

Force Provisioning

If the force provisioning parameter is set to a nonzero value, the object will be provisioned even if the policy specified in the VM storage policy is not satisfied by the datastore. The VM will be shown as noncompliant in the VM Summary tab in and relevant VM storage policy views in the UI. If there is not enough space in the cluster to satisfy the reservation requirements of at least one replica, however, the provisioning will fail even if force provisioning is turned on. When additional resources become available in the cluster, VSAN will bring this object to a compliant state. Remember that this parameter should be used only when *absolutely* needed and as an exception. When used by default, this could easily lead to scenarios where VMs, and all data associated with it, are at risk. Use with caution!

VASA Vendor Provider

As part of the VSAN cluster creation step, each ESXi host has a VSAN storage provider registered with vCenter. This uses the vSphere APIs for Storage Awareness (VASA) to surface up the VSAN capabilities to the vCenter Server. The capabilities can then be used to create VM storage policies for the VMs deployed on the VSAN datastore. If you are familiar with VASA and have used it with traditional storage environments, you'll find this functionality familiar; however, with traditional storage environments that leverage VASA, some configuration work needs to be done to add the storage provider for that particular storage. In the context of VSAN, a vSphere administrator does not need to worry about registering these; these are automatically registered when a VSAN cluster is created.

An Introduction to VASA

VASA allows storage vendors to publish the capabilities of their storage to vCenter Server, which in turn can display these capabilities in the vSphere Web Client. VASA may also provide information about storage health status, configuration info, capacity and thin provisioning info, and so on. VASA enables VMware to have an end-to-end story regarding storage. Traditionally, this enabled storage arrays to inform the VASA storage provider of capabilities, and then the storage provider informed vCenter Server, so now users can see storage array capabilities from vSphere Web Client. Through VM storage policies, these storage capabilities are used in the vSphere Web Client to assist administrators in choosing the right storage in terms of space, performance, and service level agreement (SLA) requirements. This was true for both traditional storage arrays, and now it is true for VSAN also; however, there is a notable difference in workflow when using VASA and VM storage policies when comparing traditional storage to VSAN. With traditional storage, VASA historically surfaced information about the datastore capabilities and a vSphere administrator had to choose the appropriate storage on which to place the VM. With VSAN, you define the capabilities you want to have for your VM storage in a VM storage policy. This policy information is then pushed down to VSAN, basically informing it that these are the requirements you have for storage. VASA will then tell you whether VSAN can meet these requirements, effectively communicating compliance information on a per-storage object basis. The major difference is that this functionality is now working in a bidirectional mode. Previously, VASA would just surface up capabilities. Now it not only surfaces up capabilities, but it also verifies whether VM requirements are being met based on the contents of the policy.

Storage Providers

Figure 4-4 illustrates an example of what the storage provider looks like. When a VSAN cluster is created, the VASA storage provider from every ESXi host in the cluster is registered to the vCenter Server. In a four-node VSAN cluster, the VASA VSAN storage provider configuration would look similar to this.

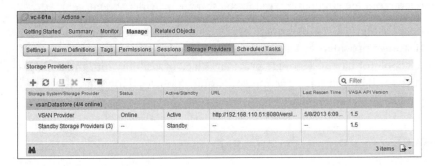

Figure 4-4   A VSAN storage provider, added when the VSAN cluster is created

You can always check the status of the storage providers by navigating in the Web Client to the vCenter Server inventory item, selecting the **Manage** tab and then the **Storage Providers** view. One VSAN provider should always be online. The other storage providers should be in standby mode.

In VSAN clusters that have more than eight ESXi hosts, and thus more than eight VASA storage providers, the list of storage providers is shortened to eight in the user interface (UI) for display purposes. The number of standby storage providers is still displayed correctly; you simply won't be able to interrogate them.

VSAN Storage Providers: Highly Available

You might ask why every ESXi host registers this storage provider. The reason for this is high availability. Should one ESXi host fail, another ESXi host in the cluster can take over the presentation of these VSAN capabilities. If you examine the storage providers shown in Figure 4-4, you will see that only one of the VSAN providers is online. The other storage providers from the other three ESXi hosts in this four-node cluster are in a standby state. Should the storage provider that is currently active go offline or fail for whatever reason (most likely because of a host failure), one of the standby providers will be promoted to active.

There is very little work that a vSphere administrator needs to do with storage providers to create a VSAN cluster. This is simply for your own reference. However, if you do run into a situation where the VSAN capabilities are not surfacing up in the VM storage policies section, it is worth visiting this part of the configuration and verifying that at least one of the storage providers is active. If you have no active storage providers, you will not discover any VSAN capabilities when trying to build a VM storage policy. At this point, as a troubleshooting step, you could consider doing a refresh of the storage providers by clicking on the refresh icon (orange circular arrows) in the storage provider screen.

What should be noted is that the VASA storage providers do not play any role in the data path for VSAN. If storage providers fail, this has no impact on VMs running on the VSAN datastore. The impact of not having a storage provider is lack of visibility into the underlying capabilities, so you will not be able to create new storage policies. However, already running VMs and policies are unaffected.

Changing VM Storage Policy On-the-Fly

Being able to change a VM storage policy on-the-fly is quite a unique aspect of VSAN. We will use an example to explain the concept of how you can change a VM storage policy on-the-fly, and how it changes the layout of a VM without impacting the application or the guest operating system running in the VM.

Consider the following scenario, briefly mentioned earlier in the context of stripe width. A vSphere administrator has deployed a VM with the default VM storage policy, which is that the VM storage objects should have no disk striping and should tolerate one failure. The layout of the VM disk file would look something like Figure 4-5.

The VM and its associated applications initially appeared to perform satisfactorily with a 100 percent cache hit rate; however, over time, an increasing number of VMs were added to the VSAN cluster. The vSphere administrator starts to notice that the VM deployed on the VSAN is getting a 90 percent read cache hit rate. This implies that 10 percent of reads need to be serviced from magnetic disk. At peak time, this VM is doing 2,000 read operations per second. Therefore, there are 200 reads that need to be serviced from magnetic disk (the 10 percent of reads that are cache misses). The specifications on the magnetic disks imply that each disk can do 150 IOPS, meaning that a single disk cannot service these additional 200 IOPS. To meet the I/O requirements of the VM, the vSphere administrator correctly decides to create a RAID-0 stripe across two disks.

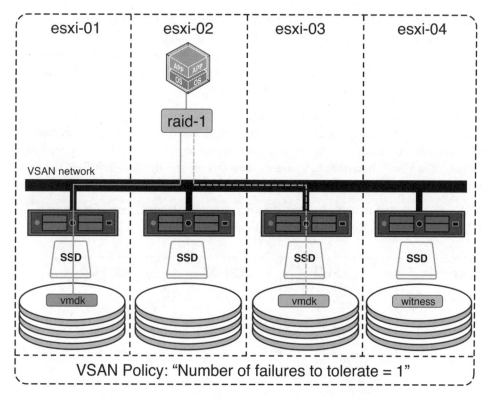

Figure 4-5   VSAN policy with the capability number of failures to tolerate = 1

On VSAN, the vSphere administrator has two options to address this.

The first option is to simply modify the VM storage policy currently associated with the VM and add a stripe width requirement to the policy; however, this would change the storage layout of all the other VMs using this policy.

Another approach is to create a brand-new policy that is identical to the previous policy but has an additional capability for stripe width. This new policy can then be attached to the VM suffering from cache misses. Once the new policy is associated with the VM, the administrator can synchronize the new/updated policy with the VM. VSAN takes care of changing the underlying VM storage layout required to meet the new policy, *while the VM is still running*. It does this by mirroring the new storage objects with the additional components (in this case RAID-0) to the original storage objects.

The workflow to change the VM storage policy can be done in two ways; either the original current VM storage policy can be edited to include the new capability of a stripe width = 2, or a new VM storage policy can be created that contains the failures to tolerate = 1 and stripe width = 2. The latter is probably more desirable because you may have other VMs using the original policy, and editing that policy will affect all VMs using it. When the new policy is created, this can be associated with the VM and the storage objects in a number of places in the Web Client. In fact, policies can be changed at the granularity of individual VM storage objects if necessary.

After making the change the new components reflecting the new configuration (for example, a RAID-0 stripe) will enter a state of reconfiguring. This will temporarily build out additional objects, in addition to keeping the original objects, so additional space will be needed on the VSAN datastore to accommodate this on-the-fly change. When the new objects are ready and the configuration is completed, the original objects are discarded.

Your VM storage objects may now reflect the changes in the Web Client—for example, a RAID-0 stripe as well as a RAID-1 replica configuration, as shown in Figure 4-6.

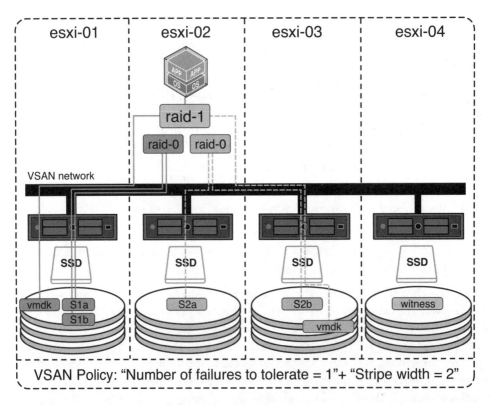

Figure 4-6   VSAN RAID-0 and RAID-1 configuration

Compare this to the tasks you would have to perform on many traditional storage arrays to achieve this. It would involve, at the very least, the following:

- The migration of VMs from the original datastore

- The decommissioning of said LUN/volume

- The creation of a new LUN with the new storage requirements (different RAID level)

- Possibly the reformatting of the LUN with VMFS in the case of block storage

Finally, you have to migrate your VMs back to the new datastore. After the new storage objects have been created and synchronized, the older storage objects will be automatically removed. Note that VSAN is capable of striping across disks, disk groups, and hosts when required, as depicted in Figure 4-6, where stripe S1a and S1b are located on the same host but stripe S2a and S2b are located on different hosts.

We have not shown that there are, of course, additional witness components that could be created with such a change to the configuration. For a VM to continue to access all its components, greater than 50 percent of the components of that object must still be available in the cluster. Therefore, changes to the VM storage policy could result in additional witness components being created.

You can actually see the configuration changes taking place in the vSphere UI during this process. Select the VM that is being changed, click its **Manage** tab, and then choose the **VM Storage Policies** view, as shown in Figure 4-7. Although this view does not show all the VM storage objects, it does display the VM Home namespace, and the VMDKs are visible.

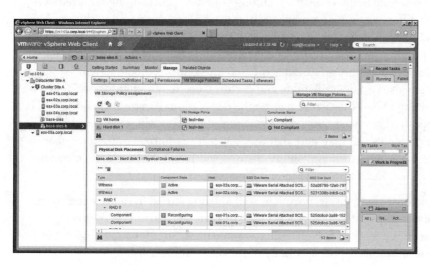

Figure 4-7   VM Storage Policy view in the vSphere client showing component reconfiguration

Objects, Components, and Witnesses

A number of new concepts have been introduced in this chapter so far, including some new terminology. Chapter 5, "Architectural Details," covers in greater detail objects, components, and indeed witness disks, as well as which VM storage objects are impacted by a particular capability in the VM storage policy. For the moment, it is enough to understand that on VSAN, a VM is no longer represented by a set of files but rather a set of storage objects. There are four types of storage objects:

- VM Home namespace
- VMDKs
- VM Swap
- Delta disks

Although the vSphere Web Client displays only the VM Home namespace and the VMDKs (hard disks), we will show ways of looking at the other storage objects, namely delta and VM Swap, in Chapter 10, "Troubleshooting, Monitoring, and Performance," when we look at various monitoring tools available to VSAN.

VM Storage Policies

VM storage policies work in an identical fashion to storage profiles introduced in vSphere 5.0, insofar as you simply build a policy containing your VM provisioning requirements. There is a major difference in how storage policies work when compared to the original storage profiles feature. With storage profiles, you simply used the requirements in the policy to select an appropriate datastore when provisioning the VM. In storage policies, not only does it select the appropriate datastore, but also informs the underlying storage layer that there are also certain availability and performance requirements associated with this VM. So while the VSAN datastore may be the destination datastore when the VM is provisioned with a VM storage policy, settings within the policy will stipulate additional requirements. For example, it may state that this VM has a requirement for a number of replica copies of the VM files for availability, a stripe width and read cache requirement for high performance, and a thin provisioning requirement.

VM storage policies are held inside VSAN, as well as being stored in the vCenter inventory database. Every object stores its policy inside its own metadata. This means that vCenter is not required for VM storage policy enforcement. So if for some reason the vCenter Server is unavailable, policies can continue to be enforced.

Enabling VM Storage Policies

VM storage policies will be automatically enabled on a cluster when VSAN is enabled on the cluster. Although VM storage policies are normally only available with certain vSphere editions, a VSAN license will also provide this feature. To enable or disable VM storage policies manually, you must navigate to the vSphere client Home location and select **Rules and Profiles**. Once in Rules and Profiles, you will find the VM Storage Policies section. Click **VM Storage Policies**, and from there you will see a number of icons, one of which enables the VM Storage Policy functionality, as shown in Figure 4-8. This may be enabled on a per-host or a per-cluster basis. Enabling VSAN automatically enables VM Storage Policies.

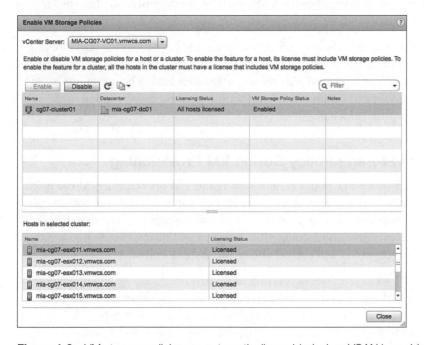

Figure 4-8 VM storage policies are automatically enabled when VSAN is enabled.

NOTE

Disabling VM storage policies on a cluster is not automatic based on disabling VSAN. Users still need to manually disable VM storage policies if they so want.

Creating VM Storage Policies

Once VM storage policies are enabled, another icon in this window allows a vSphere administrator to create individual policies. As already mentioned, a number of VSAN capabilities are surfaced up by VASA related to availability and performance, and it is at this point that the administrator must decide what the requirements are for the applications running inside of the VMs from a performance and availability perspective. For example, how many component failures (hosts, network, and disk drives) does the administrator require this VM to tolerate and continue to function? Also, is the application running in this VM demanding from an IOPS perspective? If so, an adequate read cache should be provided as a possible requirement so that the performance requirement is met. Other considerations includes whether the VM should be thinly provisioned or thickly provisioned.

One other point to note is that vSphere 5.5 also supports the use of tags for provisioning. Therefore, instead of using VSAN datastore capabilities for the creation of requirements within a VM storage policy, tag-based policies may also be created. The use of tag-based policies is outside the scope of this book, but further information may be found in the generic vSphere storage documentation.

Assigning a VM Storage Policy During VM Provisioning

The assignment of a VM storage policy is done during the VM provisioning. At the point where the vSphere administrator must select a destination datastore, the appropriate policy is selected from the drop-down menu of available VM storage policies. The datastores are then separated into compatible and incompatible datastores, allowing the vSphere administrator to make the appropriate and correct choice for VM placement.

This matching of datastores does not necessarily mean that the datastore will meet the requirements in the VM storage policy. What it means is that the datastore understands the set of requirements placed in the policy. It may still fail to provision this VM if there are not enough resources available to meet the requirements placed in the policy.

This four-node cluster example creates a policy that contains a number of failures to tolerate = 2. A four-node cluster cannot meet this policy, but when the policy is created, the VSAN datastore shows up as a matching resource, Also, when provisioning VMs using this policy, the VSAN datastore shows up as compliant, as Figure 4-9 demonstrates.

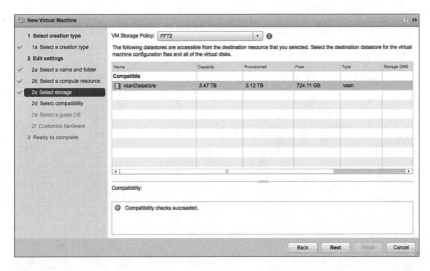

Figure 4-9 The VSAN datastore is compliant even though policy cannot be met.

If you continue with the deployment of the VM, however, the create VM operation will fail. This is an important point to keep in mind: Just because VSAN tells you it is compliant with a particular policy, this in no way implies that it can deploy a VM that uses the policy.

Summary

You may have used VM storage *profiles* in the past. VM storage *policies* differ significantly. Although we continue to use VASA, the vSphere APIs for Storage Awareness, VM storage policies have allowed us to switch the storage QoS away from datastores and to the VMs. VMs, or more specifically the applications running in VMs, can now specify their own requirements using a policy that contains underlying storage capabilities around performance, reliability, and availability.

## Chapter 5

Architectural Details

This chapter examines some of the underlying architectural details of Virtual SAN. We have already touched on a number of these aspects of VSAN, including the use of flash for caching I/O, the role of VASA in surfacing up VSAN capabilities, VM storage policies, witness disks, the need for pass-through RAID controllers, and so on.

This chapter covers these features in detail, in addition to the new architectural concepts and terminology that is introduced by VSAN. Although most vSphere administrators will never see these low-level constructs, it will be useful to have a generic understanding of the services that make up VSAN when troubleshooting or when analyzing log files. Before examining some of the lower-level details, here is one concept that we need to discuss first as it is the core of VSAN: distributed RAID.

Distributed RAID

VSAN is able to provide highly available and excellent performing VMs through the use of distributed RAID. From an availability perspective, distributed RAID simply implies that the VSAN environment can withstand the failure of one or more ESXi hosts (or components in that host, such as a disk drive) and continue to provide complete functionality for all your VMs. To ensure that VMs perform optimally, VSAN distributed RAID provides the ability to divide virtual disks across multiple physical disks and hosts.

A point to note, however, is that VM availability and performance is now defined on a per-VM basis through the use of storage policies, or even better on a per-virtual disk basis. Using a storage policy, administrators can now define how many host or disk failures a VM can tolerate in a VSAN cluster and across how many hosts and disks a virtual disk is laid out. If you choose not to set an availability requirement in the storage policy, a host or disk failure can certainly impact your VM's availability.

VSAN uses RAID-1 (synchronous mirroring) across hosts to meet the availability and reliability requirement of storage objects deployed on the system. The number of mirrored copies of the VM storage objects depends on the VM's storage policy. Depending on the VM storage policy, you could have up to three mirrors of a VM disk (VMDK) across a 32-node VSAN cluster for availability. By default, VSAN deploys VMs with an availability factor; there is a single mirror copy of the VM storage objects for every VM deployed on VSAN. This can be changed based on the policy selected during VM provisioning, however.

Depending on the number of disk stripes per object policy setting, a VM disk object may be "striped" across a number of disk spindles to achieve a desired performance. Performance of VM storage objects can be improved via a RAID-0 configuration; however, a stripe configuration does not always necessitate an improvement in performance. The section "Stripe Width Policy Setting," later in this chapter, explains the reasons for this as well as when it is useful to increase the stripe width of a VMDK in the VM storage policy.

You might wonder why VMware didn't use a more space-efficient approach such as RAID-5 or RAID-6 rather than this RAID-1 approach. The reason behind using RAID-1 is that RAID-5 and RAID-6 require read-modify-write if the write operation is less than a full stripe width. Therefore, many writes would require additional disk read operations, which would require more (and possibly smaller) drives to maintain a consistent performance for the storage. This would increase the overall cost of the system.

Objects and Components

It is important to understand the concept that the VSAN datastore is an *object storage system* and that VMs are now made up of a number of different storage objects (as opposed to the traditionally being made up of a set of files).

We have not spoken in great detail about object and components so far, so before we go into detail about the various types of objects, let's start with the definition and concepts of an object and component on VSAN.

An *object* is an individual storage block device, compatible with SCSI semantics. It may be created on demand and at any size, although VMDKs are limited to 2TB – 512 bytes in the initial release of VSAN. Objects now replace logical unit numbers (LUNs) as the main unit of storage on VSAN. In VSAN, the typical use cases for a storage block device are individual VMDKs, VM Home namespace, VM Swap, and of course, delta disks if a snapshot is taken of the VMDK. Each "object" in VSAN has its own RAID tree that turns the requirements into an actual layout on physical devices. When a VM storage policy is selected during VM deployment, the requirements around availability and performance in the policy applies to the VM objects.

Components are leaves of the object's RAID trees—that is, a "piece" of a component that is stored on a particular "flash device + magnetic disk" combination (in a physical disk group). A component gets transparent caching/buffering from flash, with its data "at rest" on magnetic disk.

A VM can have four different types of objects on a VSAN datastore as follows, but each VM can have multiples of some of these objects associated with it:

- The VM Home or "namespace directory"
- A swap object (if the VM is powered on)
- Virtual disks/VMDKs
- Delta disks (each an object) created for snapshots

There is another component called the witness. The witness component is very important and special. Although it does not directly contribute toward VM storage, it is nonetheless an important component required to determine a quorum for a VM's storage objects in the event of a failure in the cluster. We will return to the witness component shortly, but for the moment let's concentrate on VM storage objects.

Of the four objects, the VM namespace may need a little further explanation. All VMs files, excluding VMDKs, deltas (snapshots), and swap, reside in an area called the *VM namespace* on VSAN. The typical files found in the VM Home namespace are the .vmx, the .log files, .vmdk descriptor files, and snapshot deltas, descriptors files and everything else one would expect to find in a VM Home directory.

So what about components? Each storage object is deployed on VSAN as a RAID tree, and each leaf of the tree is said to be a component. For instance, if I choose to deploy a VMDK with a stripe width of 2, a RAID-0 stripe would be configured across at a minimum two disks for this VMDK. The VMDK would be the object, and each of the stripes would be a component of that object.

Similarly, if I specified that my VMDK should be able to tolerate at least one failure in the cluster (host, disk, or network), a RAID-1 mirror of the VMDK object would be created, with one replica component on one host and another replica component on another host in my VSAN cluster. Finally, if I asked for both striping and availability, my striped components would be mirrored across hosts, giving me a RAID 0+1 configuration.

Note that delta disks are created when a snapshot is taken of a VM. A delta disk inherits the same policy as the parent disk (stripe width, replicas, and so on).

The swap object is created only when the VM is powered on.

Component Limits

Two limits apply in relation to components in VSAN. It is important to understand these because they are hard limits and essentially will limit the number of VMs you can run on a single host and in your cluster. The limitations of VSAN 1.0 are as follows:

- **Maximum number of components per host limit**: 3,000

- **Maximum number of components per object**: 64 (including stripe width and replica copies)

Components per host include components from powered-off VMs. VSAN distributes components across the various hosts in the cluster and will always try to achieve an even distribution of components for balance. However, some hosts may have more components than others, which is why VMware recommends, as a best practice, that hosts participating in a VSAN cluster be similarly or identically configured. Components are a significant sizing consideration when designing and deploying a VSAN cluster, as discussed in further detail in Chapter 9, "Designing a VSAN Cluster."

The vSphere Web Client enables administrators to interrogate objects and components of the VM Home namespace and the VMDKs of a VM. Figure 5-1 provides an example of one such layout. The VM has one hard disk, which is mirrored across two different hosts, as you can see in the "hosts" column, where it shows the location of the components.

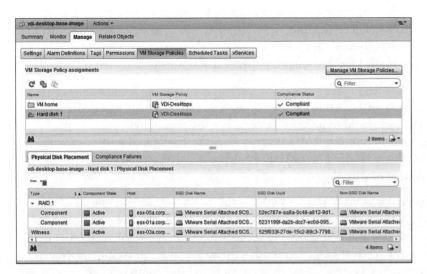

Figure 5-1   Physical disk placement

Virtual Machine Storage Objects

As stated earlier, the four storage objects are VM Home namespace, VM Swap, VMDK, and delta disks, as illustrated in Figure 5-2.

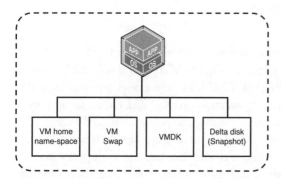

Figure 5-2   VM storage objects

We will now look at how characteristics defined in the VM storage policy impact these storage objects. Note that not all the VM storage objects implement these policies.

Virtual Machine Home Namespace

The namespace contains everything that's not a dedicated object. So, for example, this includes, but is not limited to, the following:

- The .vmx, .vmdk (the descriptor portion), .log files that the VMX uses
- Digest files for CBRC (Content-Based Read Cache) for VMware Horizon View
- The memory snapshots when you take VM snapshots
- vSphere Replication and Site Recovery Manager files
- Guest customization files
- Files created by other solutions

VSAN leverages VMFS as the file system within the VM namespace object per VM in order to store all the files of the VM. This is a fully fleshed, vanilla VMFS. That is, it includes the cluster capabilities, so that we can support all the solutions that use locks on VMFS (for example, vMotion, vSphere High Availability [HA]). This appears as an automounted subdirectory when you examine the ESXi hosts' file systems. However, although it is a vanilla VMFS being used, it does not have the same limitations as VMFS has in other environments because the number of hosts connected to these VM Home namespace VMFS volumes is at most two (for example, during a vMotion), whereas in traditional environments the same VMFS volume is shared between dozens of hosts. In other words, VSAN leverages these vanilla VMFS volumes in a completely different way, allowing for greater scale and better performance.

For the VM Home, a special VM storage policy is used. For the most part, the VM Home storage object does not inherit the same requirements as the VMDKs. If you think about it, why would you want to give something like the VM Home namespace a percentage of flash read cache or a stripe width? You wouldn't, which is why the VM Home namespace does not have these settings applied even when they are in the policy. The VM Home namespace does, however, inherit the number of failures to tolerate setting. This allows the VM to survive multiple hardware failures in the cluster. So, because high performance is not a major requirement for the VM Home namespace storage object, VSAN overwrites the inherited policy settings so that stripe width is always set to 1 and read cache reservation is always set to 0 percent. It also has object space reservation set to 0 percent so that it is always thinly provisioned. This avoids the VM Home namespace object consuming unnecessary resources, and makes these resources available to objects that might need them, such as VMDKs.

One other important note is that if force provisioning is set in the policy, the VM Home namespace object also inherits that, meaning that the VM will be deployed even if the full complement of resources is not available.

Virtual Machine Swap

For the VM Swap object, the default policy is to set number of failures to tolerate to 1. Swap objects are also provisioned 100 percent up front, without the need to set object space reservation to 100 percent in the policy. This means, in terms of admission control, VSAN will not deploy the VM unless there is enough disk space for the VM Swap object.

VMDKs and Deltas

As you have seen, VM Home namespace and VM Swap have their own default policies when a VM is deployed. Therefore, it is only the VMDKs and snapshot files (delta disks) of these disk files that obey all the characteristics that are set in the VM storage policies.

Because VSAN objects may be made up of multiple components, each VMDK and delta has its own RAID tree configuration when deployed on VSAN.

Witnesses and Replicas

As part of the RAID tree, each object usually has multiple replicas, also often referred to as components. We mentioned that alongside VM storage objects, one or more witness components *may* also get created. Witnesses are part of each and every object in the RAID tree. They are components that make up a leaf of the RAID tree, but they do not contain data, only metadata. They are there to be tiebreakers and are used for quorum determination in the event of failures in the VSAN cluster.

Let's take the easiest case to explain their purpose: Suppose, for example, that we have deployed a VM that has a stripe width setting of 1 and it also has number of failures to tolerate setting of 1. In this case, two replica copies of the VM need to be created. Effectively, this is a RAID-1 with two replicas; however, with two replicas, there is no way to differentiate between a network partition and a host failure. Therefore, a third entity called the witness is added to the configuration. For an object on VSAN to be available, two conditions have to be met:

- The RAID tree must allow for data access. (RAID-1 needs at least one intact replica, RAID-0 needs all stripes intact.)

- There must be more than 50 percent of all components available.

In the preceding example, only when there is access to one replica copy and a witness, or two replica copies, would you be able to access the object. That way, at most one part of the cluster can ever access an object in the event of a network partition.

A common question is whether the witness consumes any space on the VSAN datastore. A witness consumes about 2MB of space for metadata on the VSAN datastore. Although insignificant to most, when running many VMs with many disks, it could be something to consider when running through your sizing and scaling exercises.

Object Layout

The next question people usually ask is how objects are laid out in a VSAN environment. As mentioned, the VM Home namespace for storing the VM configuration files is formatted with VMFS. All other VM disk objects (whether VMDKs or snapshots) are instantiated as distributed storage objects in their own right.

Although we believe that you should not care where objects reside, we understand that with a new solution you may have the desire to have a better understanding of physical placement. VMware expected that administrators would have this desire; therefore, the vSphere user interface allows vSphere administrators to interrogate the layout of a VM object and see where each component (stripes, replicas, witnesses) that make up a storage object reside, as shown in Figure 5-3.

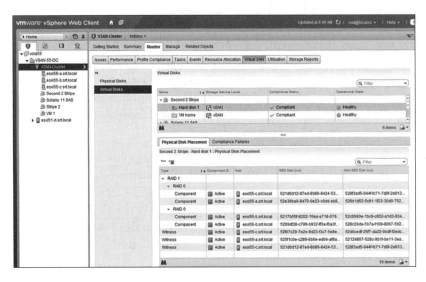

Figure 5-3   RAID-1, RAID-0, and witnesses

VSAN will never let components of different replicas (mirrors) share the same host for availability purposes.

Note that we do not see the VM Swap file objects. The swap file UUID is currently not available through the VIM application programming interface (API), so neither the Ruby vSphere Console (also known as RVC, covered later in Chapter 10) nor the vSphere Web Client can show this information. However, there is a method to retrieve swap file information, as demonstrated shortly. Snapshot/delta disk objects are not visible in the vSphere user interface (UI) either, but these objects implicitly inherit the same policy settings as the VMDK base disk against which the snapshot is taken.

We have been talking about the concept of VM storage policies for a while now; let's now consider this further.

Default VM Storage Policy

VMware encourages administrators to create their own policies with VSAN and not rely on the default policy settings. However, if you decide to deploy a VM on a VSAN datastore without selecting a policy, a default policy is applied. The default policy has been created with very specific characteristics to prevent administrators from unintentionally putting VMs and the associated data at risk when, for whatever reason, a policy is not selected. We have seen this happening fairly often when administrators create VMs in a hurry and simply forget to select a policy. However, we do need to stress that VMware strongly encourages administrators to create their own VM storage policies, even when the requirements are the same as those in the default policy. For one thing, it enables the administrator to do meaningful compliance reporting. VMware also strongly discourages administrators from editing or changing the default policy, but there may occasions where this is necessary, as discussed shortly.

The default policy can be observed from the `esxcli` command, let's inspect it:

```
~ # esxcli vsan policy getdefault
Policy Class   Policy Value
-----------    ------------------------------------------------------------
cluster        (("hostFailuresToTolerate" i1))
vdisk          (("hostFailuresToTolerate" i1))
vmnamespace    (("hostFailuresToTolerate" i1))
vmswap         (("hostFailuresToTolerate" i1) ("forceProvisioning" i1))
~ #
```

From this, we can deduce that the storage objects will always be deployed with a `hostFailuresToTolerate` set to 1. In other words, this storage object will be deployed in a RAID-1 mirror. (Note that although this command-line interface [CLI] states that this is `hostFailuresToTolerate`, the vSphere Web Client refers to it as number of failures to tolerate, and it actually covers network and disk failures, too.)

Notice that vdisk (which refers to VMDK) is also there. This implies that if a VM is deployed without a policy, the VMDK and any subsequent snapshot delta will also be replicated.

The cluster policy reference is a default setting for any objects that do not correspond to a VM storage object. At this point in time, there are no non-VM storage objects, but there may be going forward.

A final point is related to force provisioning. Currently, force provisioning is only explicitly enabled for VM Swap. If we would like to, for instance, bootstrap vCenter Server on a single-host VSAN cluster, this would not be possible with the current setting. The reason for this that the creation of the VM will fail as the default policy is `hostFailuresToTolerate` is 1, and only a single host is available, and so VSAN cannot adhere to these requirements. To allow for this to work, a change in default profile is needed, and `forceProvisioning` will need to be set to 1 for all object types. You can do this using the following command:

```
~ # esxcli vsan policy setdefault -c vdisk
-p "((\"hostFailuresToTolerate\" i1) (\"forceProvisioning\" i1))"
~ # esxcli vsan policy setdefault -c vmnamespace -p
"((\"hostFailuresToTolerate\" i1) (\"forceProvisioning\" i1))"
```

This will then result in the following change for the default VSAN policy:

```
~ # esxcli vsan policy getdefault
Policy Class  Policy Value
------------  -----------------------------------------------------
cluster       (("hostFailuresToTolerate" i1))
vdisk         (("hostFailuresToTolerate" i1) ("forceProvisioning" i1))
vmnamespace   (("hostFailuresToTolerate" i1) ("forceProvisioning" i1))
vmswap        (("hostFailuresToTolerate" i1) ("forceProvisioning" i1))
```

Now that we have looked at the default policy, we will shortly take a look at what an administrator can define.

VSAN Software Components

This section briefly outlines some of the software components that make up the distributed software layer.

Much of this information will not be of particular use to vSphere administrators on a day-to-day basis. All of this complexity is hidden away in how VMware has implemented the installation and configuration of VSAN to a few simple mouse clicks. However, we did want to highlight some of the major components behind the scenes for you because, as mentioned in the introduction, you may see messages from time to time related to these components appearing in the vSphere UI and the VMkernel logs, and we want to provide you with some background on what the function is of these components. Also, when you begin to use the RVC in Chapter 10, a number of the outputs will refer to these software components, which is another reason why we are including this brief outline.

The VSAN architecture consists of four major components, as illustrated in Figure 5-4 and described in more depth in the sections that follow.

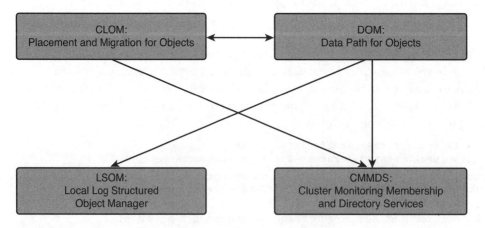

Figure 5-4   VSAN software components

Component Management

The VSAN Local Log Structured Object Manager (LSOM) works at the physical disk level. It is the LSOM that provides for the storage of VM storage object components on the local disks of the ESXi hosts, and it includes both the read caching and write buffering for these objects. When we talk in terms of components, we are talking about one of the striped components that make up a RAID-0 configuration, or one of the replicas that makes up a RAID-1 configuration. Therefore, LSOM works with the magnetic disks and solid-state disks (SSDs) on the ESXi hosts. To recap, the SSDs are used as a cache and a nonvolatile write buffer in front of the magnetic disks.

Another way of describing the LSOM is to state that it is responsible for providing persistence of storage for the VSAN cluster. By this, we mean that it stores the components that make up VM storage objects as well as any configuration information and the VM storage policy.

LSOM reports events for these devices, for example, if a device has become unhealthy. The LSOM is also responsible for retrying I/O if transient device errors occur.

LSOM also aids in the recovery of objects. On every ESXi host boot, LSOM performs an SSD log recovery. This entails a read of the entire log that ensures that the in-memory state is up to date and correct. This means that a reboot of an ESXi host that is participating in a VSAN cluster can take longer than an ESXi host that is not participating in a VSAN cluster.

Data Paths for Objects

The Distributed Object Manager (DOM) provides distributed data access paths to objects built from local (LSOM) components. The DOM is responsible for the creation of reliable, fault-tolerant VM storage objects from local components across multiple ESXi hosts in the VSAN cluster. It does this by implementing distributed RAID types for objects.

DOM is also responsible for handling different types of failures such as I/O failing from a device and unable to contact a host. In the event of an unexpected host failure, during recovery DOM must resynchronize all the components that make up every object. Components publish a bytesToSync value periodically to show the progress of a synchronize operation.

Object Ownership

We discuss object owners from time to time in this chapter. Let's elaborate a little more about what object ownership is. For every storage object in the cluster, VSAN elects an owner for the object. The owner can be considered the storage head responsible for coordinating who (internally within VSAN) can do I/O to the object. The owner basically is the entity that ensures consistent data on the distributed object by performing a transaction for every operation that modifies the data/metadata of the object.

As an analogy, in NFS configurations, consider the concept of NFS server and NFS client. Only certain clients can communicate successfully with the server. In this case, the VSAN storage object owner can be considered along the same lines as an NFS server, determining which clients can do I/O and which clients cannot. The final part of object ownership is the concept of a component manager. The component manager can be thought of as the network front end of LSOM (in other words, how a storage object in VSAN can be accessed).

An object owner communicates to the component manager to find the leaves on the RAID tree that contain the components of the storage object. Typically, there is only one client accessing the object. However, in the case of a vMotion operation, multiple clients may be accessing the same object. In the vast majority of cases, the owner entity and client co-reside on the same node in the VSAN cluster.

Placement and Migration for Objects

The Cluster Level Object Manager (CLOM) is responsible for ensuring that an object has a configuration that matches its policy (that is, that the requested stripe width is implemented or that there are a sufficient number of replicas in place to meet the availability requirement of the VM). Effectively, CLOM takes the policy assigned to an object and applies a variety of heuristics to find a configuration in the current cluster that will meet that policy. It does this while also load balancing the resource utilization across all the nodes in the VSAN cluster.

DOM then applies a configuration as dictated by CLOM. CLOM distributes components across the various ESXi hosts in the cluster. CLOM tries to create some sort of balance, but it is not unusual for some hosts to have more components, capacity used/reserved, or flash read cache used/reserved than others.

Each node in a VSAN cluster runs an instance of *CLOM*. Each instance of CLOM is responsible for the configurations and policy compliance of the objects owned by the DOM on the ESXi host where it runs so it needs to communicate with Cluster Monitoring, Membership and Directory Service (CMMDS) to be aware of ownership transitions. CLOM only communicates with entities on the node where it runs. It does not use the network.

Cluster Monitoring, Membership, and Directory Services

The purpose of Cluster Monitoring, Membership, and Directory Services (CMMDS) is to discover, establish, and maintain a cluster of networked node members. It manages the physical cluster resources inventory of items such as hosts, devices, and networks and stores object metadata information such as policies, distributed RAID configuration, and so on in an in-memory database. The object metadata is always also persisted on disk. It is also responsible for the detection of failures in nodes and network paths.

Other software components browse the directory and subscribe to updates to learn of changes in cluster topology and object configuration. For instance, DOM can use the content of the directory to determine the nodes storing the components of an object and the paths by which those nodes are reachable.

Note that CMMDS forms a cluster (and elects a master) only if there is multicast network connectivity between the hosts.

CMMDS is used to elect "owners" for objects. The owner of an object will perform all the RAID tasks for a particular object, as discussed earlier.

Host Roles (Master, Slave, Agent)

When a VSAN cluster is formed, you may notice through esxcli commands that each ESXi host in a VSAN cluster has a particular role. These roles are for the VSAN clustering service *only*. The clustering service (CMMDS) is responsible for maintaining an updated directory of disks, disk groups, and objects that resides on each ESXi host in the VSAN cluster. This has nothing to do with managing objects in the cluster or doing I/O to an object by the way; this is simply to allow nodes in the cluster to keep track of one another. The **clustering service** is based on a master (with a backup) and agents, where all nodes send updates to the master and the master then redistributes them to the agents, using a reliable ordered multicast protocol that is specific to VSAN. This is the reason why the VSAN network must be able to handle multicast traffic, as discussed in the earlier chapters of this book. Roles are applied during a cluster discover, at which time the ESXi hosts participating in the VSAN cluster elect the master. A vSphere administrator has no control over which role a cluster member takes.

A common question is why a backup role is needed. The reason for this is because if the ESXi host that is currently in the master role suffers a catastrophic failure and there is no backup, all ESXi hosts must reconcile their entire view of the directory with the newly elected master. This would mean that all the nodes in the cluster might be sending all their directory contents from their respective view of the cluster to the new master. By having a backup, this negates the requirement to send all of this information over the network, and thus speeds up the process of electing a new master node.

An important point to make is that, to a user or even a vSphere administrator, the ESXi node that is elected the role of master has no special features or other visible differences. Because the master is automatically elected, even on failures, and given that the node has no user visible difference in abilities, doing operations on a master node versus any other node doesn't matter at all.

Reliable Datagram Transport

The Reliable Datagram Transport (RDT) is the communication mechanism within VSAN. By default, it uses TCP at the transport layer. It creates and tears down TCP connections (sockets) on demand.

RDT is built on top of the VSAN clustering service. The clustering service uses heartbeats to determine link state. If a link failure is detected, RDT will drop connections on the path and choose a different healthy path.

When an operation needs to be performed on a VSAN object, DOM uses RDT to talk to the owner of the VSAN object. Because the RDT promises reliable delivery, users of the RDT can rely on it to retry requests after path or node failures, which may result in a change of object ownership and hence a new path to the owner of the object. The CMMDS (via its heart beating and monitoring functions) and the RDT are responsible for handling timeouts and path failures.

On-Disk Formats

Before looking at the various I/O-related flows, let's briefly discuss the on-disk formats used by VSAN.

Flash Devices

VMware uses its own proprietary on-disk format for the flash devices used by VSAN. The read cache portion of the flash device has its own on-disk format, and there is also a log-structured format for the write buffer portion of the flash device. Both the formats are new and are specially designed to boost the endurance of the flash device beyond the basic functionality provided by the flash device firmware.

Magnetic Disks

It may come as a surprise to some, but VMware continues to use Virtual Machine File System (VMFS) for VSAN, but not the traditional VMFS. Instead, there is a new format unique to VSAN called VMFS Local (VMFS-L). VMFS-L is the on-disk file system format of the local storage on each ESXi host in VSAN. The standard VMFS file system is specifically designed to work in clustered environments where many hosts are sharing a datastore. It was not designed with single-host/local disk environments in mind, and certainly not distributed datastores. VMFS-L was introduced for use cases like distributed storage. Primarily, the clustered on-disk locking and associated heartbeats on VMFS have been removed. These are necessary only when many hosts share the file system. They are unnecessary when only a single host is using it. Now instead of placing a SCSI reservation on the volume to place a lock on the metadata, a new lock manager is implemented that avoids using SCSI reservation completely. VMFS-L does not require on-disk heartbeating either. Now it simply updates an in-memory copy of the heartbeat (because no other host needs to know about the lock). Tests have shown that VMFS-L can provision disks in about half the time of standard VMFS with these changes incorporated.

VSAN I/O Flow

In the next couple of paragraphs, we will trace the I/O flow on both a read and a write operation from an application within a guest OS when the VM is deployed on a VSAN datastore. We will look at a read operation when the stripe width value is set to 2, and we will look at a write operation when the component failures to tolerate is set to 1. This will give you an understanding of the underlying I/O flow, and this can be leveraged to get an understanding of the I/O flows when other capability values are specified. Before we do, let's first look at the role of flash in the I/O path.

The Role of the SSD

As mentioned in the previous section, SSDs (and by that we also mean flash devices) have two purposes in VSAN: They behave as both a read cache and a write buffer. This dramatically improves the performance of VMs. In some respect, VSAN can be compared to a number of "hybrid" storage solutions in the market, which also use a combination of SSD and magnetic disks to increase the performance of the I/O, but which have the ability to scale out capacity based on low-cost SATA or SAS magnetic disk drives.

Purpose of Read Cache

The purpose of the read cache is to maintain a list of commonly accessed disk blocks by VMs. This reduces the I/O read latency in the event of a cache hit; that is, the disk block is in cache and does not have to be retrieved from magnetic disk. The actual block that is being read by the application running in the VM may not be on the same ESXi host where the VM is running. In this case, the VSAN directory service is referenced to find whether the block may be in the cache of another ESXi host in the cluster. If it transpires that there is a cache miss, the data is retrieved directly from magnetic disk, but of course this will incur a latency penalty and could also impact the number of input/output operations per second (IOPS) achievable by VSAN. We discussed the directory service already, but suffice it to say that this service maintains a list of objects that reside in the VSAN cluster, and is referenced to determine information like object owner and location.

VSAN always tries to make sure that it sends a given read request to the same mirror so that the block only gets cached once in the cluster; in other words, it is cached only on one SSD, and that SSD is on the ESXi host that contains the mirror where the read requests are sent. Because cache space is relatively expensive, this mechanism optimizes how much cache you require for VSAN. Correctly sizing VSAN cache and SSD has a very significant impact on performance in steady state.

Purpose of Write Cache

The write cache behaves as a write-back buffer. The writes are acknowledged when they enter the prepare stage on SSD. The fact that we can use SSD for writes also reduces the latency for write operations.

Because the writes go to SSD, we must, of course, ensure that there is a copy of the data block elsewhere in the VSAN cluster. All VMs deployed to VSAN have an availability policy setting that ensures at least one additional copy of VM data is available. This includes the write cache contents. Once a write is initiated by the application running inside of the guest OS, the write is forked to both the local write cache on the owning host, and to the write cache on the remote host or hosts. Writes are buffered in the SSD or flash device associated with the disk group where the components of the VMDK storage object resides.

This means that in the event of a host failure, we also have a copy of the in-cache data and so no corruption will happen to the data; the VM will simply reuse the replicated copy of the cache as well as the replicated disk data.

Anatomy of a VSAN Read

For an object within a VSAN datastore, it is possible that there are multiple replicas (RAID-1) when the failures to tolerate value is set to a value greater than 0 in the VM storage policy. In other words, reads may be spread across replicas. Different reads may be sent to different replicas according to their logical block address (LBA) on disk. This is to ensure that VSAN does not necessarily consume more read cache than necessary.

Taking the example of an application in the VM issuing a read request, the cluster service (CMMDS) is first consulted to determine owner of the data. If the block is present in read cache on owner, the read is serviced from the SSD read cache. If a read miss occurs, and the block is not in cache, the next step is to read the data from the magnetic disk.

As mentioned, the owner of the object splits the reads across the components that go to make up that object, so that a given block is cached on at most one node, maximizing the effectiveness of the SSD cache. In many cases, the cluster service may return a different host as the owner of the data, and the data may have to be transferred over the network if the data is on an SSD or magnetic disk of a different ESXi host. Once the data is retrieved, it is returned to the requesting ESXi host and the read is served up to the application.

Figure 5-5 gives an idea of the steps involved in a read operation on VSAN. In this particular example, the stripe width setting is 2, and the VM's storage object is striped across disks that reside on different hosts. (Each stripe is therefore a component, to use the correct VSAN terminology.) Note that Stripe-1a and Stripe-1b reside on the same host, while Stripe-2a and Stripe-2b reside on different hosts. In this scenario, our read needs to come from Stripe-2b. When the clustering service is referenced, the owner does not have the block that the application within the VM wants to read. Therefore, the read will go over the 10GbE network to retrieve the data block.

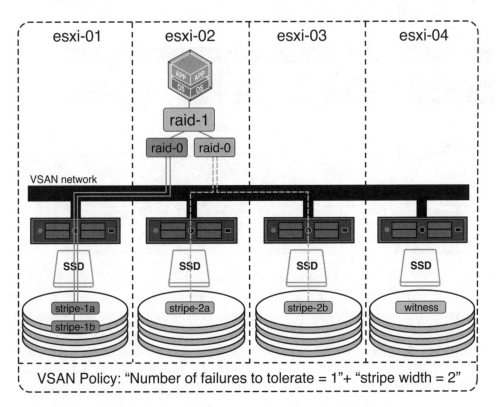

Figure 5-5   VSAN I/O flow: Failures to tolerate = 1 + stripe width = 2

Anatomy of a VSAN Write

Now that we know how a read works, let's take a look at a write operation. When a new VM is deployed, its components are stored on multiple hosts. VSAN does not have the notion of data locality and as such it could be possible that your VM runs on esxi-01 from a CPU and memory perspective, while the components of the VM are stored on both esxi-02 and esxi-03, as shown in Figure 5-6.

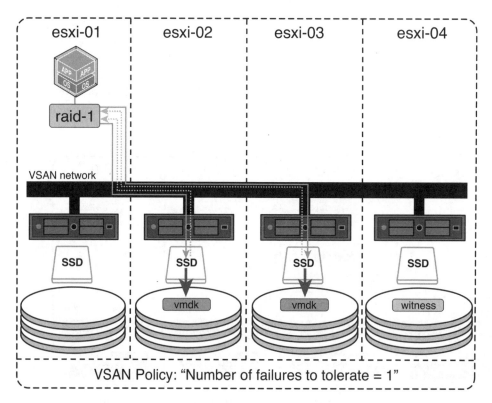

Figure 5-6   VSAN I/O flow: Write acknowledgment

When an application within a VM issues a write operation, the owner of the object clones the write operation. The write is sent to the SSD on esxi-02 and is also sent across the 10Gb network to the SSD on esxi-03 in *parallel*. The write is acknowledged when the write reaches the SSD, and the prepare operation is initiated. The owner waits for ACK from both hosts and completes I/O. Later, the write will be destaged as part of a batch commit to magnetic disk. This happens independent from each other. In other words, esx-02 may destage writes at a different time than esxi-03. This is not coordinated because it depends on various things such as how fast the buffer is filling up—how much capacity is left and where data is stored on magnetic disks.

Retiring Writes to Magnetic Disks

Writes across virtual disks from applications and guest OSs running inside a VM deployed on VSAN accumulate on flash over time. VSAN has an elevator algorithm implemented that periodically flushes the writes in buffer to magnetic disk in address order.

VSAN enables write buffering on the magnetic disks to maximize performance. The magnetic disk write buffers are flushed before discarding writes from SSD, however. As mentioned earlier, when destaging writes, VSAN considers the location of the I/O. This is done via a proximal algorithm. The algorithm determines what the most optimal batch of writes is for destaging based on proximity. In other words, LBAs in close proximity to one another on the magnetic disk are grouped for improved performance.

The heuristics used for this are sophisticated and take into account many parameters such as rate of incoming I/O, queues, disk utilization, and optimal batching. This is a self-tuning algorithm that decides how often writes on the SSD destage to magnetic disk.

Data Locality

A question that usually comes now is this: What about data locality? Is cache (for instance) kept local to the VM? Does the VM cache and the VMDK storage object need to travel with the VM each time vSphere Distributed Resource Scheduler (DRS) migrates a VM due to a compute imbalance? The answer is no; VSAN does not have the concept of data locality.

The reason for this is straightforward: Considering that read I/O is at most one network hop away and that the latency incurred on 10GbE is minimal compared to, for instance, kernel latency and even flash latency, the cost of moving data around simply does not weigh up against the benefits (especially when you consider the fact that by default vSphere DRS runs once every 5 minutes at a minimum, which can result in VMs being migrated to a different host every 5 minutes). VSAN instead focused on load balancing of storage resources across the cluster in the most efficient and optimal way, because this is more beneficial and cost-effective to VSAN.

This is a fundamental difference between VSAN and other so-called server SAN solutions. Note that we explicitly stated *read I/O*, because with write I/O with any solution there will be a network hop as data always needs to be stored on multiple hosts for resiliency purposes. If there is a specific requirement to provide a form of data locality, however, it is good to know that VSAN integrates with CBRC (in memory read cache for VMware View), and this can be enabled without the need to make any changes to your VSAN configuration.

Storage Policy-Based Management

In the introduction of the book, you learned that storage policy-based management (SPBM) now plays a major role in the policies and automation for VMware's software-defined storage vision. Chapter 4, "VM Storage Policies on VSAN," covered some of the basics of SPBM in combination with VSAN and showed that by using SPBM administrators could specify a set of requirements for a VM. More specifically, it defines a set of requirements for the application running in the VM. This set of requirements is pushed down to the storage layer, and the storage layer now checks if the storage objects for this VM can be instantiated with this set of requirements. For instance, is there an available number of stripe widths if this is a requirement? Or are there enough hosts in the cluster to provide the number of failures to tolerate? If the requirements are understood, the VSAN datastore is said to be a matching resource, and is highlighted as such in the provisioning wizard. Later, when the VM is deployed, it is said to be compliant from a storage perspective in its own summary window. If the VSAN datastore is overcommitted, or cannot meet the striping performance requirement, it is not shown as a matching resource in the deployment wizard. If the VM is still deployed to the VSAN datastore even though it shows up as not matching, the VM will be displayed as noncompliant in its summary window.

To summarize, SPBM provides an automated policy-driven mechanism for selecting an appropriate datastore for VMs in a traditional environment based on the requirements placed in the VM's storage policy. Within a VSAN-enabled environment, SPBM determines how VMs are provisioned and laid out.

Let's now take a closer look at the concept of SPBM for VSAN-based infrastructures.

VSAN Capabilities

This section examines the VSAN capabilities that can be placed in a VM storage policy. These capabilities, which are surfaced by the VASA provider for the VSAN datastore when the cluster is configured successfully, highlight the availability and performance policies that can be set on a per-object basis. We explicitly did not say *VM* as an object can even be a virtual disk.

If you overcommit on the capabilities (that is, put a capability in the policy that can no longer be met by the VSAN datastore), the VSAN datastore will no longer appear as a matching resource during provisioning, and the VM will also show noncompliant in its Summary tab.

While on the subject of VSAN capabilities, let's revisit them and discuss them in more detail.

Number of Failures to Tolerate Policy Setting

In Chapter 4, we looked at which of the VM storage policy settings affect VM storage objects. With that in mind, let's look at number of failures to tolerate (FTT for short) in greater detail; this is probably the most used capability VSAN has to offer.

This capability sets a requirement on the storage object to tolerate at least n failures. In this case, n refers to the number of concurrent host, network, or disk failures that may occur in the cluster while still ensuring the availability of the VM's storage objects, and thus allowing the VM to continue to run or be restarted by vSphere HA depending on the type of failure that occurred. If this property is populated in the VM storage policy, it specifies that storage objects must contain at least $n + 1$ replicas.

Note that a VM will remain accessible on a VSAN datastore only as long as its storage objects remains available. To recap what has been discussed before, a VM deployed on the VSAN datastore will have a number of storage objects such as VM Home namespace, VM Swap, VMDK, and snapshot deltas. For the VM to remain accessible, more than 50 percent of the components that make up the VM's storage objects must be available.

Let's take a simple policy example to clarify. If you deploy a VM that has number of failures to tolerate = 1 as the only policy setting, you may see the VMDK storage object deployed, as shown in Figure 5-7.

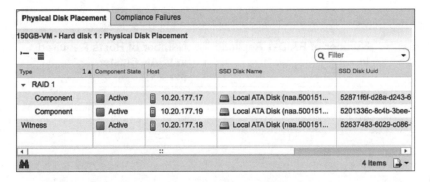

Figure 5-7   Simple physical disk placement example with failures to tolerate = 1

It is important to understand that storage objects are made up of components. There are two components making up the RAID-1 mirrored storage object—one on host 17 and the other on host 19. These are the mirror replicas of the data that make failure tolerance possible. But what is this witness object on host 18? Well, remember that 50 percent of the components must remain available. In this example, if you didn't have a witness and host 17 failed, you would lose 1 component (50 percent). Even though you still had a valid replica available, more than 50 percent of the components would not be available. This is the reason for the witness disk. The witness is also used to determine who is still in the cluster in the case of split-brain scenarios.

The witness itself is essentially a piece of metadata; it is only about 2MB in size, and so it doesn't consume a lot of space. As you create storage objects with more and more components, additional witnesses may get created, as shown in Figure 5-8. This is entirely dependent on the RAID configuration and how VSAN decides to place components.

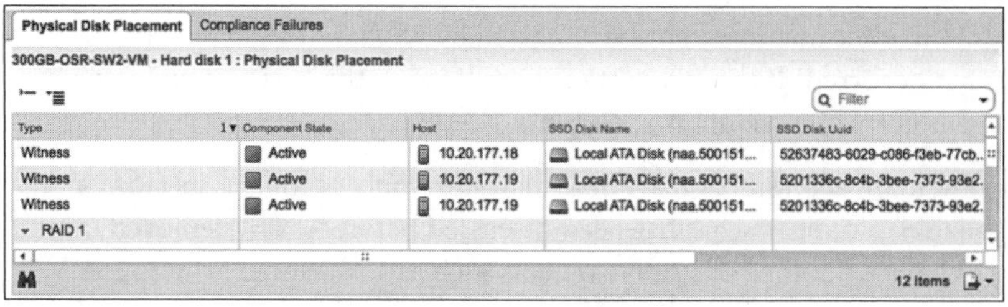

Physical Disk Placement
Compliance Failures
300GB-OSR-SW2-VM - Hard disk 1 : Physical Disk Placement
Filter
Type
Component State
Host
SSD Disk Name
SSD Disk Uuid
Witness
Active
10.20.177.18
Local ATA Disk (naa.500151...
52637483-6029-c086-f3eb-77cb...
Witness
Active
10.20.177.19
Local ATA Disk (naa.500151...
5201336c-8c4b-3bee-7373-93e2.
Witness
Active
10.20.177.19
Local ATA Disk (naa.500151...
5201336c-8c4b-3bee-7373-93e2.
RAID 1
12 items

Figure 5-8 Additional witnesses may get created.

Now that you understand the concept of the witness, the next question is this: How many hosts do you need in the VSAN cluster to accommodate *n* number of failures to tolerate? Table 5-1 outlines this solution.

Table 5-1 Relationship Between Failures to Tolerate, Replicas, and Hosts Required

Number of Failures to Tolerate (*n*)	Number of RAID-1 Replicas (*n* + 1)	Number of Hosts Required in VSAN Cluster (2*n* + 1)
1	2	3
2	3	5
3	4	7

If you try to specify a number of failures to tolerate value that is greater than that which can be accommodated by the VSAN cluster, you will not be allowed to do so. Figure 5-9 depicts an example of trying to set number of failures to tolerate to 2 in a three-node cluster.

New Virtual Machine
Cannot complete file creation operation.
The policy requires 5 hosts contributing storage, only found 3 in the cluster.
Failed to create object.

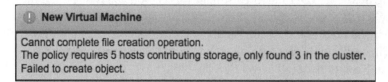

Figure 5-9 Failures to tolerate requires a specific number of hosts.

Best Practice for Number of Failures to Tolerate

The recommended practice for number of failures to tolerate is 1, unless you have a pressing concern to provide additional availability to allow VMs to tolerate more than one failure. Note that increasing number of failures to tolerate would require additional disk capacity to be available for the creation of the extra replicas.

VSAN has multiple management workflows to warn/protect against accidental decommissioning of hosts that could result in VSAN's being unable to meet the number of failures to tolerate policy of given VMs.

Then the question arises: What is the minimal number of hosts for a VSAN cluster? From a support point of view, the number is three; however, what about scenarios where you need to do maintenance and want to maintain the same level of availability during maintenance hours?

To comply with a number of failures to tolerate = 1 policy, you need three hosts at a minimum at all times. Even if one host fails, you can still access your data, because with three hosts and two mirror copies and a witness, you will still have more than 50 percent of your copies available. But what happens when you place one of those hosts in maintenance mode, as shown in Figure 5-10?

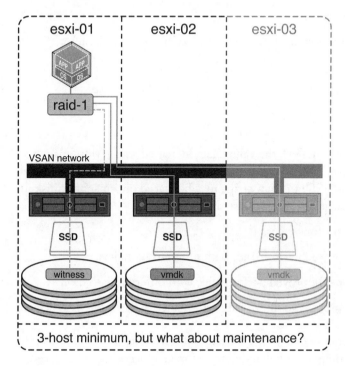

Figure 5-10 VSAN: Minimum number of hosts

When both remaining hosts keep functioning as expected, all VMs will continue to run. If another host fails, you have a challenge as at this point the remaining host will have less than 50 percent of the components of your VM. As a result, VMs cannot be restarted (nor do any I/O) because the component will not have an owner.

Stripe Width Policy Setting

The second most popular capability is definitely number of disk stripes per object. We will refer to this as stripe width for the purposes of keeping things simple. The first thing to discuss is when striping can be beneficial to VMs in a VSAN environment. The reason we are bringing this up is that you need to be aware that all I/O in VSAN goes to flash. To be more correct, all writes go to the write buffer on flash, and we try to service all reads from the read cache on flash, too. Some reads may have to be serviced by magnetic disk if the data is not in cache (read cache miss), however.

So, where can a stripe width increase help?

- It may be possible to improve write performance of a VM's storage objects if they are striped across different disk groups or indeed striped to a disk located on another host.

- When there are read cache misses.

- Possible performance improvements during destaging of blocks from flash to magnetic disk.

Let's elaborate on these a bit more.

Performance: Writes

Because all writes go to SSD (write buffer), the value of an increased stripe width may or may not improve performance for your VM I/O. This is because there is no guarantee that the new stripe will use a different SSD; the new stripe may be placed on a magnetic disk in the same disk group, and thus the new stripe will use the same SSD.

There are three different scenarios for stripes:

- **Striping across hosts**: Improved performance with different flash devices

- **Striping across disk groups**: Improved performance with different flash devices

- **Striping in the same disk group**: No improved performance (using same flash device)

At the moment, VSAN does not have data gravity/locality of reference, so it is not possible to stipulate where a particular component belonging to a storage object should be placed;

this is left up to the VSAN component placement algorithms, which try to place storage components down on disk in a balanced fashion across all nodes in the cluster.

Therefore, in conclusion, adding a stripe width may not result in any improved write performance for VM I/O, but allows for the potential of improved performance.

Performance: Read Cache Misses

Let's look at the next reason for increasing the stripe width policy setting; this is probably the primary reason for doing so. In situations where the data set of a VM is too big or the workload is so random that the read cache miss rates can overwhelm the throughput of a single spindle, it can be beneficial to ensure that multiple spindles are used when reading.

From a read perspective, an increased stripe width helps when you are experiencing many read cache misses. If you consider the earlier example of a VM consuming 2,000 read operations per second and experiencing a hit rate of 90 percent, there are 200 read operations that need to be serviced from magnetic disk. In this case, a single magnetic disk that can provide 150 IOPS cannot service all of those read operations, so an increase in stripe width would help on this occasion to meet the VM I/O requirements.

How can you tell whether you have read cache misses? Unfortunately, today this information is not available within vSphere web client. However the RVC VSAN Observer Tool provides a lot of detailed information, including read cache hit rate, as shown in Figure 5-11. In this case, the read cache hit rate is 100 percent, meaning that there is no point in increasing the stripe width, because all I/O is being served by flash.

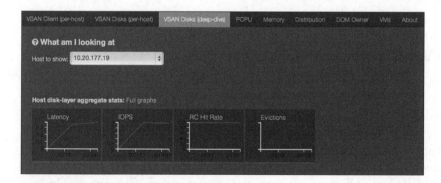

Figure 5-11   100 percent, no evictions

So in this case, if read cache misses were occurring in your VSAN, increasing the stripe width will improve the performance for I/Os that need to be serviced from magnetic disk, if a single spindle was not enough to handle the requests.

Performance: SSD Destaging

The final reason for increasing the stripe width relates to destaging blocks from SSD to magnetic disk. There is an important consideration regarding SSD destaging: What sorts of workloads are running on VSAN? By way of an example, if you are doing virtual desktop infrastructure (VDI) deployment and you have hundreds of VMs, then it is likely that VSAN needs to destage to all of the magnetic disk anyway. Changing the stripe width on the VMs won't help (because all spindles are already in use). If you have 99 VMs doing almost no writes and thus little destaging, however, and one VM doing tons of writes and thus a lot of destaging, then we expect a performance improvement in destage if that one VM is configured with a higher stripe width.

How can you tell whether your SSD has lots of blocks to be destaged? You may use the VSAN Observer Tool available with vCenter Server 5.5 U1 and later. The VSAN Observer Tool is part of the RVC, and the view shown in Figure 5-12 is taken from the VSAN Disks (deep-dive): Device-level stats option. Chapter 10 covers both RVC and the VSAN Observer in greater detail.

Figure 5-12   VSAN Observer SSD info

Striping on VSAN Outside of Policy Setting

Those who have been looking at the Web Client regularly, where you can see the placement of components, may have noticed that VSAN created a stripe width for your VMDK even when you did not explicitly ask it to. Or you've placed a stripe width of 2 in your policy and you observe a stripe width of 3 being created. VSAN will split VMDKs as it sees fit when there are space constraints. VSAN will use disk striping when a virtual disk (VMDK) is larger than any single chunk of free space. Essentially, VSAN hides the fact that even when there are small physical disks on the hosts, administrators can still create very large VMDKs. Therefore, it is common to see large VMDKs split across multiple spindles, even when no stripe width is specified in the VM storage policy. VSAN will use disk striping when a virtual disk (VMDK) is larger than any single spindle.

By default, an object will also be split at 256GB, and can have multiple 256GB chunks striped across multiple spindles even though striping may not have been a policy requirement. It can be split even before it reaches 256GB when free disk space makes VSAN think that there is a benefit in doing so. Note that just because there is a standard split at 256GB, it doesn't mean all new chunks will go onto different magnetic disks. It may, or may not, depending on overall balance and free capacity.

Let's look at what some of our tests have shown as that may make things a bit clearer for you.

Test 1

We created a 150GB VM on a VSAN datastore consisting of 136GB magnetic disks, with a policy of number of failures to tolerate (FTT) = 1. We got a simple RAID-1 for our VMDK with two components, each replica having just one component (so no striping). Now this is because the VM is deployed on the VSAN datastore as thin by default, so even though we created a 150GB VM, because it is thin it can sit on a single 136GB magnetic disk, as demonstrated in Figure 5-13.

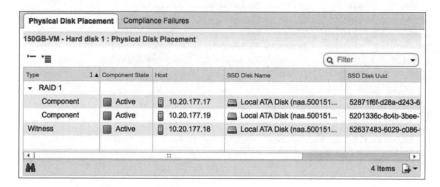

Figure 5-13   Simple physical disk placement: Single witness component

Test 2

We created a 150GB VM, with a policy of FTT = 1 and object space reservation (OSR) = 100 percent. Now we get another RAID-1 of my VMDK, but each replica is made up of a RAID-0 with two components. OSR is essentially specifying a thickness for the VM. Because we are guaranteeing space, our VM needs to span at least two magnetic disks, and therefore a stripe is being used.

Test 3

We created a 300GB VM, with a policy of FTT = 1, OSR = 100 percent, and stripe width (SW) = 2. We got another RAID-1 of our VMDK as before, but now each replica is made up of a RAID-0 with *three* components. Here, even with a SW = 2 setting, my VMDK requirement is still too large to span two magnetic disks. A third magnetic disk is required in this case, as shown in Figure 5-14.

We can conclude that striping is used for VMDKs that are larger than a single magnetic disk, even if a stripe width is not specified in the policy.

Type	1▲	Component State	Host	SSD Disk Name	SSD Disk Uuid
▾ RAID 1					
▾ RAID 0					
Component		▪ Active	▯ 10.20.177.18	▱ Local ATA Disk (naa.500151...	52637483-6029-c086-
Component		▪ Active	▯ 10.20.177.19	▱ Local ATA Disk (naa.500151...	5201336c-8c4b-3bee-
Component		▪ Active	▯ 10.20.177.18	▱ Local ATA Disk (naa.500151...	52637483-6029-c086-
▾ RAID 0					
Component		▪ Active	▯ 10.20.177.17	▱ Local ATA Disk (naa.500151...	52871f6f-d28a-d243-6
Component		▪ Active	▯ 10.20.177.17	▱ Local ATA Disk (naa.500151...	52871f6f-d28a-d243-6
Component		▪ Active	▯ 10.20.177.17	▱ Local ATA Disk (naa.500151...	52871f6f-d28a-d243-6
Witness		▪ Active	▯ 10.20.177.19	▱ Local ATA Disk (naa.500151...	5201336c-8c4b-3bee-
Witness		▪ Active	▯ 10.20.177.19	▱ Local ATA Disk (naa.500151...	5201336c-8c4b-3bee-
Witness		▪ Active	▯ 10.20.177.18	▱ Local ATA Disk (naa.500151...	52637483-6029-c086-

Figure 5-14   More complex deployment: Multiple witness components needed

Stripe Width Maximum

In this initial release of VSAN, the maximum stripe width that can be defined is 12. This can be striping across magnetic disks in the same host, or across hosts. Remember that when you specify a stripe width and an FTT value, there has to be at least stripe width (SW) × FTT number of spindles before VSAN is able to satisfy the policy requirement. This means that the larger the number of FTT and SW, the more complex the placement of object and associated components will become. The number of disk stripes per object setting in the VM storage policy means stripe across "at least" this number of magnetic disks per mirror." VSAN may, when it sees fit, use additional stripes.

Figure 5-15 shows a screenshot taken for a VM storage policy screen, with the information icon selected for further details. The reference to HDD in the help screen actually stands for hard disk drive, what we have been calling magnetic disks in this book.

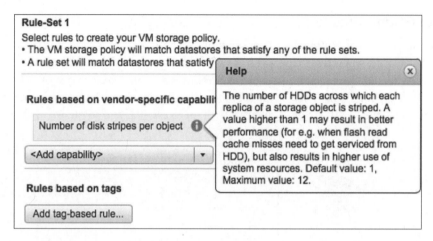

Rule-Set 1

Select rules to create your VM storage policy.
• The VM storage policy will match datastores that satisfy any of the rule sets.
• A rule set will match datastores that satisfy

Rules based on vendor-specific capabili

Number of disk stripes per object

<Add capability>

Help   (×)

The number of HDDs across which each replica of a storage object is striped. A value higher than 1 may result in better performance (for e.g. when flash read cache misses need to get serviced from HDD), but also results in higher use of system resources. Default value: 1, Maximum value: 12.

Rules based on tags

Add tag-based rule...

Figure 5-15   Number of disk stripes per object

Stripe Width Configuration Error

You may ask yourself what happens if a vSphere administrator requests the VSAN cluster to meet an SW policy setting that is not available or achievable. Figure 5-16 shows the resulting error. Basically, the deployment of the VM fails, stating that there were not sufficient magnetic disks found to meet the requirements of the defined policy.

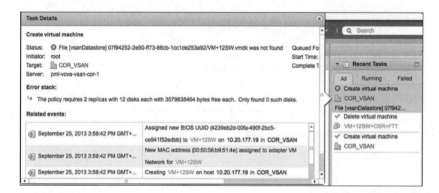

Figure 5-16   Task failed: Only found 0 such disks

Stripe Width Chunk Size

A question that then often arises after the SW discussion is whether there is a specific segment size. In other words, when the stripe width is defined using the VM storage policies, which increment do the components use to grow? VSAN uses a stripe segment size of 1MB. As depicted in Figure 5-17, "1MB stripe segment 1" will go to esxi-02, and when the next 1MB is written to, the "1MB stripe segment 2" will go to esxi-03, and so on.

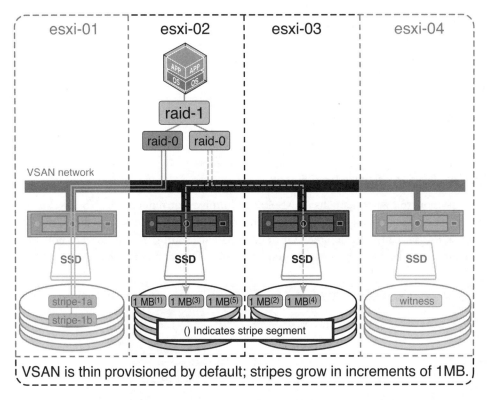

Figure 5-17   VSAN I/O flow: 1MB increment striping

Stripe Width Best Practice

After reading this section, you should more clearly understand that increasing the stripe width could potentially complicate placement. VSAN has a lot of logic built in to handle smart placement of objects. We recommend not increasing the stripe width *unless* you have identified a pressing performance issue such as read cache misses or during destaging.

Remember that all I/O should go to the flash layer first. All writes certainly go to flash first, and are later destaged to magnetic disks. For reads, the operation is first attempted on the flash layer. If a read cache miss occurs, the block is read from magnetic disk. Therefore, if all of your reads are being satisfied by the flash layer, there is no point in increasing the stripe width as it does not give any benefits. Doing the math correctly beforehand is much more effective, leading to proper sizing of the flash-based cache, rather than trying to increase the stripe width after the VM has been deployed!

Flash Read Cache Reservation Policy Setting

This policy setting is the amount of flash capacity reserved on the SSD as read cache for the storage object. It is specified as a percentage of the logical size of the storage object. As previously mentioned, this is specified as a percentage value (%) with up to four decimal places. This fine granular unit size is needed so that administrators can express sub 1 percent units. Take the example of a 1TB VMDK. If we limited the read cache reservation to 1 percent increments, this would mean cache reservations in increments of 10GB, which in most cases is far too much for a single VM.

Note that you do not have to set a reservation to get cache. The reservation should be set to 0 unless you are trying to solve a real performance problem.

In the initial version of VSAN, there is no proportional share mechanism for this resource, which is what vSphere administrators will be familiar with from other vSphere features.

Object Space Reservation Policy Setting

All objects deployed on VSAN are thin provisioned by default. The object space reservation capability defines the percentage of the logical size of the storage object that may be reserved during initialization. To be clear, the OSR is the amount of space to reserve specified as a percentage of the total object address space. You can use this property for specifying a thick provisioned storage object.

If OSR is set to 100 percent, all the storage capacity requirements of the VM are reserved up front. Note that although the object itself will still be thin provisioned, the space it can claim is reserved explicitly for this object so that the VSAN datastore cannot run out of disk space for this VM.

You may remember that certain storage objects (notably VM namespace and VM Swap) do not adhere to certain policy settings. One of these is object space reservation. Let's take a look at these two special objects.

VM Home Namespace Revisited

The VM namespace on VSAN is a *256GB thin object*. The namespace is a per-VM object. As you can imagine, if we allocated policy settings to the VM Home namespace, such as proportional capacity and flash read cache reservation, much of the magnetic disk and flash resources could be wasted. To that end, the VM Home namespace has its own special policy, as follows:

> Number of disk stripes per object: 1
>
> Flash read cache reservation: 0 percent
>
> Force provisioning: Enabled
>
> Object space reservation: 0 percent (thin)

The FTT policy setting is the only setting inherited from the VM storage policy. So, if a customer creates a VM storage policy with an FTT setting, the VM Home namespace will be deployed with the ability to tolerate the number failures specified in that policy.

Swap Revisited

The VM Swap follows much the same conventions as the VM Home namespace. It has the same default policy as the VM Home namespace, which is 1 disk stripe, and 0 percent read cache reservation and 0 percent object space reservation. There is one additional point in relation to FTT. The VM swap has an FTT setting of 1. It does not inherit the FTT from the VM storage policy.

However, VM Swap does not have its own namespace, so is not limited in the way the VM Home namespace is limited by the 256GB thin object.

The default values for VM Swap cannot be overridden by a policy either.

How to Examine the VM Swap Storage Object

As we have seen, the VM Swap is one of the objects that make up the set of VM objects, along with the VM Home namespace, VMDKs, and snapshot delta. Unfortunately in VSAN, you will not see the VM Swap file represented in the list of VM objects in the UI. This leads inevitably to the question regarding how you go about checking and verifying the policy and resource consumption of a VM's swap object.

This is in fact quite tricky, because even if you try to use the RVC command, `vsan.vm_object_info`, you only get information about VM Home namespace, VMDKs, and deltas. Chapter 10 covers RVC commands in extensive detail. Again, there is no information displayed for the VM Swap. To get information about the VM Swap, you first of all have to retrieve the UUID information from the VM's swap descriptor file. One way of doing this is to SSH on to an ESXi host that is participating in the VSAN cluster and use the cat command in the ESXi shell to display the contents of the VM Swap descriptor file. You are looking for the objectID entry. Here is an example:

```
# cat win1-6e39614a.vswp
# Object DescriptorFile
version = "1"
objectID = "vsan://c7c0a552-7851-b20b-8d05-1cc1de253a92"
.

.
```

Once you have the descriptor, this can then be used in RVC to display information about the actual swap object. The command to do this is vsan.object_info. This RVC command takes two arguments. The first argument is the cluster, and the second argument is the UUID:

```
/localhost/CH-Datacenter/computers> ls
0 CH-Cluster (cluster): cpu 86 GHz, memory 45 GB
/localhost/CH-Datacenter/computers> vsan.object_info 0 c7c0a552-7851-b20b-
8d05-1cc1de253a92
DOM Object: c7c0a552-7851-b20b-8d05-1cc1de253a92 (owner: 10.20.177.17,
policy: hostFailuresToTolerate = 1, forceProvisioning = 1,
proportionalCapacity = 100)
Witness: 048fa852-ac82-539b-a3ed-1cc1de253a92 (state: ACTIVE (5),
host: 10.20.177.19, md: naa.5000c5002bd78a5f, ssd: naa.50015178f35d87ac)
RAID_1
Component: fc8ea852-0603-7190-4bf6-1cc1de253a92 (state: ACTIVE (5),
host: 10.20.177.18, md: naa.5000c5002bd62be3, ssd: naa.50015178f35d86ee)
Component: 4d6aa852-0238-f7e6-c93c-1cc1de253a92 (state: ACTIVE (5),
host: 10.20.177.17, md: naa.5000cca00b33fc20, ssd: naa.50015178f35d8e33)
/localhost/CH-Datacenter/computers>
```

Now that we have the VM Swap object info, we can see a number of things:

- NumberOfFailuresToTolerate for VM Swap is set to 1. This gives us a RAID-1 (mirror) configuration for VM Swap.

- forceProvisioning for VM Swap is set to 1. This means that even if the current policy cannot be met we should always provision the VM Swap object.

- ProportionalCapacity for VM Swap is set to 100 percent. This means that the space needed for swap is indeed fully reserved.

What can be deduced from this is that from a space utilization standpoint, the VM Swap of a VM deployed on VSAN will consume (Configured memory – Memory reservation)

* (FTT + 1) amount of space on disk. In most environments, this basically means that on disk you will consume twice the provisioned VM memory, because the majority of customers do not set reservations.

Of course, the plan is to eventually get this information more easily accessible, but for now, this method should allow you to gather this information should you need it. The VM Swap (.vswp) is an important consideration when sizing your VSAN storage, so make sure to consider this. Chapter 9, "Designing a VSAN Cluster," provides a formula to do so.

Delta Disk / Snapshot Caveat

For the most part, a delta VMDK (or snapshot, as it's often referred to) will always inherit the policy associated with the base disk. In this first release of VSAN, a vSphere administrator can also specify a VM storage policy for a linked clone. In the case of linked clones, the policy is applied just to the linked clone (top-level delta disk), not the base disk. This is not visible through the UI, however. Both VMware Horizon View and VMware vCloud Director use this capability through the vSphere API.

Now that you know that you can reserve space and disks are thin provisioned, you are probably wondering where you can find out how much space a VM consumes and how much is reserved.

Verifying How Much Space Is Actually Consumed

When you select the VSAN datastore in the UI, then the Monitor tab, and then click **Storage Reports**, you can get a nice view of how much space is being consumed by each of the VMs, as illustrated in Figure 5-18. Note that the default view does not automatically show these columns. You have to add these columns to the view via the user interface.

VM	Space Used	% Space	Virtual Disk	% Virtual	Swap	Other VM Space	% Other VM S.	Shared Space	% Shared Space	Provisioned Space	Uncommitted Space
win1	5.42 GB	0.31	5.42 GB	0.31	0 B	287.2 KB	0.00	0 B	0.00	22.21 GB	16.79 GB
150GB+100OSR+SW=1	150 GB	8.45	150 GB	8.45	0 B	131.17 KB	0.00	0 B	0.00	154.23 GB	4.23 GB
SW=12VM	2 MB	0.00	2 MB	0.00	0 B	1.97 KB	0.00	0 B	0.00	154.23 GB	154.22 GB
COR_VSAN-VRA	12 GB	0.68	12 GB	0.68	0 B	316.94 KB	0.00	0 B	0.00	16.25 GB	4.25 GB
FTT=0,SW=4	1.99 KB	0.00	0 B	0.00	0 B	1.99 KB	0.00	0 B	0.00	44.23 GB	44.23 GB
150GB-VM	251.27 KB	0.00	0 B	0.00	0 B	251.27 KB	0.00	0 B	0.00	154.23 GB	154.23 GB
150GB-OSR-VM	150 GB	8.45	150 GB	8.45	0 B	1.99 KB	0.00	0 B	0.00	154.23 GB	4.23 GB
300GB-OSR-SW2-VM	300 GB	16.91	300 GB	16.91	0 B	2.01 KB	0.00	0 B	0.00	304.23 GB	4.23 GB

Figure 5-18   How much space is being consumed on the VSAN datastore

There are a few interesting pieces of output here with regard to object space reservation (OSR). As stated, all VMs deployed to VSAN are thin in nature. In the example in

Figure 5-18, we deployed a VM called 150GB-VM that did not use OSR. You can see that the size of the virtual disk for this VM is 0 bytes.

In a second example, we deployed a VM called 150GB-OSR-VM, which has 100 percent OSR. In this example, you can see that the virtual disk size is 150GB.

Force Provisioning Policy Setting

We have already mentioned this capability various times: force provisioning. If this parameter is set to a nonzero value, the object will be provisioned even if the policy specified in the VM storage policy is not satisfied by the datastore. However, if there is not enough space in the cluster to satisfy the reservation requirements of at least one replica, the provisioning will fail even if force provisioning is turned on!

Now that we know what the various capabilities do, let's take a look how VSAN leverages these in failure scenarios.

Witnesses and Replicas: Failure Scenarios

Failure scenarios are often a hot topic of discussion when it comes to VSAN. What should one configure, and how do we expect VSAN to respond? This section runs through some simple scenarios to demonstrate what you can expect of VSAN in certain situations.

The following examples use a four-host VSAN cluster. We will examine various *number of failures to tolerate* and *stripe width* settings and discuss the behavior in the event of a host failure. You should understand that the examples shown here are for illustrative purposes only. These are simply to explain some of the decisions that VSAN *might* make when it comes to object placement. VSAN may choose any configuration as long as it satisfies the customer requirements (that is, number of failures to tolerate and stripe width). For example, with higher numbers of number of failures to tolerate and stripe width, we have placement choices to use more or less witnesses and more or less hosts than shown in the examples that follow.

Example 1: Number of Failures to Tolerate = 1 and Stripe Width = 1

In this first example, the stripe width is set to 1. Therefore, there is no striping per se, simply a single instance of the object. However, the requirements are that we must tolerate a single disk or host failure, so we must instantiate a replica (a RAID-1 mirror of the component). However a witness is also required in this configuration to avoid a split-brain situation. A split-brain is when esxi-01 and esxi-03 continue to operate, but no longer communicate to each another. Whichever of the hosts can communicate with the witness is the host that has the valid copy of the data in that scenario. Data placement in these configurations may look like Figure 5-19.

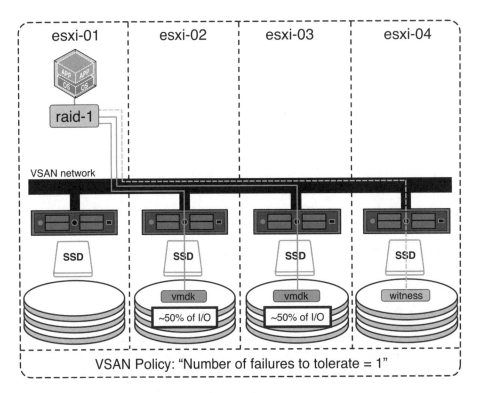

Figure 5-19   Number of failures to tolerate = 1

In Figure 5-19, the data remains accessible in the event of a host or disk failure. If esxi-04 has a failure, esxi-02 and esxi-03 continue to provide access to the data as a quorum continues to exist. However, if esxi-03 and esxi-04 both suffer failures, there is no longer a quorum, so data becomes inaccessible. Note that in this scenario the VM is running, from a compute perspective, on esxi-01, while the components of the objects are stored on esxi-02/03/04.

Example 2: Number of Failures to Tolerate = 1 and Stripe Width = 2

Turning to another example, this time the stripe width is increased to 2. This means that each component must be striped across two spindles at minimum; however, VSAN may decide to stripe across magnetic disks on the same host or across magnetic disks on different hosts. Figure 5-20 shows one possible distribution of storage objects.

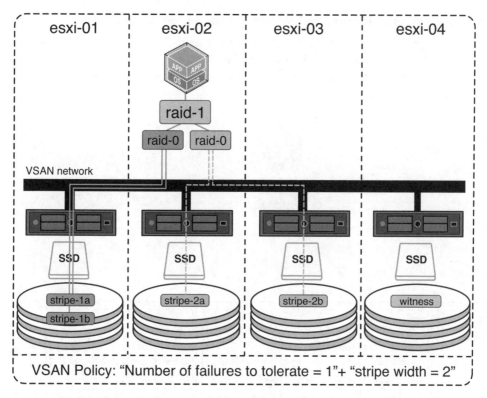

Figure 5-20 Number of failures to tolerate = 1 and stripe width = 2

As you can see, VSAN in this example has chosen to keep the components for the first stripe (RAID-0) on esxi-01 but has placed the components for the second stripe across esxi-02 and esxi-03. Once again, with number of failures to tolerate set to 1, we mirror using RAID-1. In this configuration, a witness is also used. Why might a witness be required in this example? Consider the case where esxi-01 has a failure. This impacts both the components on esxi-01. Now we have two components failed and two components still working on esxi-02 and esxi-03. In this case, we still require a witness to attain quorum.

Note that if one component in each of the RAID-0 configuration fails, the data would be inaccessible because both sides of the RAID-1 are impacted. Therefore, a disk failure in esxi-01 and a disk failure in esxi-02 can make the VM inaccessible until the disk faults are rectified. Because a witness contains no data, it cannot help in these situations. Note that this is more than one failure, however, and our policy is set to tolerate only one failure.

Example 3: Number of Failures to Tolerate = 2 and Stripe Width = 2

In this last example, the number of failures to tolerate is set to 2, meaning another replica is required. And because each replica is made up of two striped components, an additional two components must be deployed on the VSAN datastore. Again, a possible deployment might look like Figure 5-21.

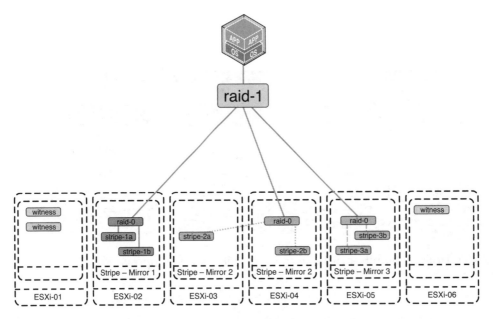

Figure 5-21   Number of failures to tolerate = 2 and stripe width = 2

The components per stripe width have been explained previously, and should be clear. Similarly, the fact that there is now a third RAID-0 replica configured should also be self-explanatory at this stage. But what about the fact that there are now three witnesses? Well, consider the situation where both esxi-02 and esxi-05 suffer a failure. In that case, four components are lost. To have a quorum majority, the two remaining components would require five objects to achieve a majority. This is why there are three witnesses in this configuration. Losing two hosts would still allow the data to be accessible!

What if a failure occurs? How does VSAN respond to this?

Recovery from Failure

When a failure has been detected, VSAN will determine which objects had components on the failed device. Depending on the type of failure, VSAN will take immediate action or wait for some period of time (60 minutes). The distinction here is if VSAN knows what has happened to a device. For instance when a host fails VSAN typically does not know why this happened, or even what has happened exactly. Is it a host failure, a network failure, is it transient or permanent, and so on. Should this occur, the affected components are said to be in an "*absent*" state. Let's say that we have suffered a permanent host failure in this scenario.

As soon as VSAN realizes the component is absent, a timer of 60 minutes will start. If the component comes back within those 60 minutes, VSAN will synchronize the replicas. If the component doesn't come back, VSAN will create a new replica, as demonstrated in Figure 5-22.

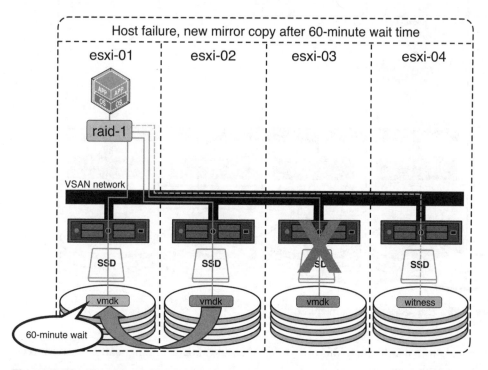

Figure 5-22   Host failure: 60-minute delay

Note that you can decrease this time-out value by changing the advanced setting called *VSAN.ClomRepairDelay* on each of your ESXi hosts in the Advanced Settings section. If you want to change this advanced setting, we highly recommend ensuring consistency across all ESXi hosts in the cluster by scripting the required change and to monitor on a regular basis for consistent implementation to avoid inconsistent behavior. (Consult the official VSAN documentation or VMware support before changing this ESXi advanced setting.)

As mentioned, in some scenarios VSAN responds to a failure immediately. This depends on the type of failure and a good example is a magnetic disk or flash device failure. In many cases, the controller or device itself will be able to indicate what has happened and will essentially tell VSAN that it is unlikely that the device will return within a reasonable amount of time. VSAN will then respond by marking all impacted components (VMDK in Figure 5-23) as *"degraded,"* and VSAN immediately creates a new mirror copy.

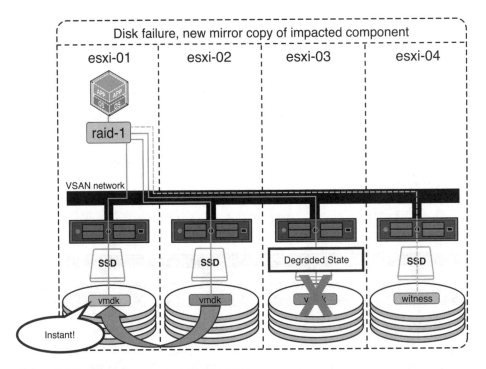

Figure 5-23   Disk failure: Instant mirror copy

Of course, before it will create this mirror VSAN will validate whether sufficient resources exist to store this new copy.

If a recovery occurs before the 60 minutes has elapsed or before the creation of the replica has completed, VSAN will decide whether it makes sense to complete the creation of the replica or if synchronizing the "old" components makes more sense. All of this falls under the concept *reconfiguration*.

Reconfiguration can take place on VSAN for a number of reasons. First, a user might choose to change an object's policy and the current configuration might not conform to the new policy, so a new configuration must be computed and applied to the object. Second, a disk or node in the cluster might fail. If an object loses one of the components in its configuration, it may no longer comply with its policy.

Reconfiguration is probably the most resource-intensive task because a lot of data will need to be transferred in most scenarios. To ensure that regular VM I/O is not impacted by reconfiguration tasks, VSAN has the ability to throttle the reconfiguration task to the extent that it does not impact the performance of VMs.

Now that you have seen how VSAN can respond to failure scenarios and handles split-brain scenarios, you might be wondering whether you can use VSAN to create a stretched cluster solution. Let's take a closer look at that.

What About Stretching VSAN?

The question keeps on coming up over and over again: vSphere Metro Storage Cluster (vMSC) using VSAN, can we do it? If you look at what VSAN is and does, it makes sense for people to ask this question. It is a distributed storage solution with a synchronous distributed caching layer that allows for high resiliency. You can specify the number of copies required of your data and VSAN will take care of the magic for you, if a component of your cluster fails, VSAN can respond to it accordingly.

Let's take a look at what the ideal scenario would look like for VSAN in a stretched environment when FTT = 1 has been defined. The scenario shown in Figure 5-24 is what you want VSAN to do when it comes to placement of components.

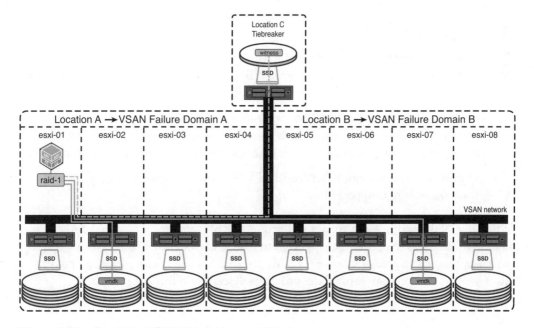

Figure 5-24   Stretching VSAN: What you would like to see

Now let it be clear, Figure 5-24 shows what you would expect VSAN to do in a stretched environment, but unfortunately *not* what VSAN does in its current form. If you look at the diagram in Figure 5-25, it becomes clear why it might not be such a great idea to use VSAN for this use case at this point in time.

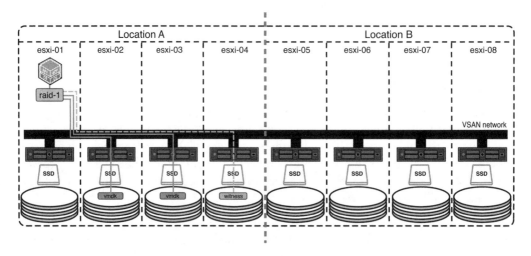

Figure 5-25   Stretching VSAN: What we have today

The problem today is as follows:

- **Object placement**: You cannot control where the replica is stored. You will want that second mirror copy to be in Location B, but you cannot control it today because you cannot define "failure domains" within VSAN in version 1.0.

- **Witness placement**: Essentially, you want to have the ability to have a third site that functions as a tiebreaker when there is a partition/isolation event. Today, witness components can be placed anywhere by VSAN and placement cannot be controlled.

- **Support**: VMware has not tested/certified VSAN over distance extensively, which means that it is not supported.

At the time of this writing, the answer to the question of whether we can use VSAN to build a vMSC is this: No, it is not supported to span a VSAN cluster over distance. This, of course, remains an area of interest for VMware's VSAN engineering team, and in the future we may see solutions around the problems described in this last section.

Summary

VSAN has a unique architecture that is future proof but at the same time extensible. It is designed to handle extreme I/O load and cope with different failure scenarios. Key, however, is policy-based management. Your decision making during the creation of policies will determine how flexible, performant, and resilient your workloads and VSAN datastore will be.

Chapter 6

VM Storage Policies and Virtual Machine Provisioning

This chapter looks at some sample virtual machine (VM) provisioning workflows. You have already learned the various VSAN capabilities that you can add to a VM storage policy and that VMs deployed on a VSAN datastore can use. This chapter covers how to create the appropriate VM storage policy using these capabilities, and also discusses the layout of these VM storage objects as they are deployed on the VSAN datastore.

Policy Setting: Number of Failures to Tolerate = 1

Let's begin by creating a very simple VM storage policy. Then we can examine what will happen if a VM is deployed to a VSAN datastore using this policy. Let's create the first policy to have a single capability setting of number of failures to tolerate set to 1. This means that any VMs deployed on the VSAN datastore with this policy will be configured with an additional mirror copy (replica) of the data so that if there is a single failure in the VSAN cluster, a full complement of the VSAN storage objects is still available. Let's see this in action, but before we do, let's visualize the expected results as shown in Figure 6-1.

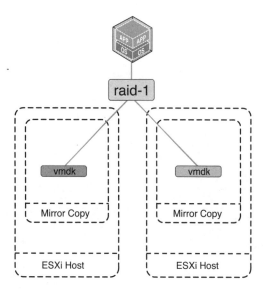

Figure 6-1   VSAN I/O flow: Number of failures to tolerate set to 1

In this VSAN environment, there are a number of ESXi hosts. Each ESXi host has a single disk group with a single solid-state disk (SSD) and a single magnetic disk. The VSAN cluster has been enabled, and the ESXi hosts have formed a single VSAN datastore. To this datastore, we will deploy a new VM, as demonstrated in Figure 6-2.

Let's start the process by revisiting the creation of a VM storage policy. This procedure was discussed in significant detail in Chapter 4, "VM Storage Policies on VSAN," where you also learned the various capabilities that you could use for VMs deployed on the VSAN datastore. As you might recall from Chapter 4, the five capabilities that can be present in a VM storage policy are as follows:

- Number of failures to tolerate
- Number of disk stripes per object
- Flash read cache reservation
- Object space reservation
- Force provisioning

We will keep this first VM storage policy simple, with just a single capability, number of failures to tolerate set to 1.

To begin, click the icon in the VM storage policies page in the vSphere Web Client to create a new policy. This will open the Create New VM Storage Policy screen, as shown in Figure 6-2.

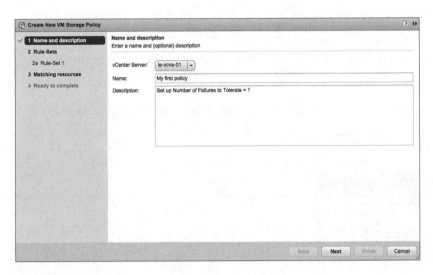

Figure 6-2   Create a VM storage policy

The next screen displays information about rule-sets. Rule-sets are a way of grouping multiple rules together. In this way, VMs can be deployed on different datastores, depending on which selection criteria are satisfied. For the purposes of this exercise, we are creating only a single rule-set. The wizards display additional information about rule-sets, as shown in Figure 6-3.

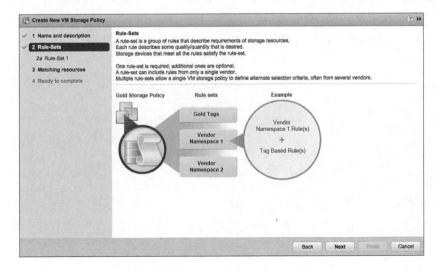

Figure 6-3   Rule-sets

On the next screen, we can begin to add our rule-set for VSAN. First is to change the vendor from None to VSAN, as shown in Figure 6-4. This will add an additional item to the <Add capability> drop-down. If you click **<Add capability>**, the list of capabilities supported by VSAN is shown.

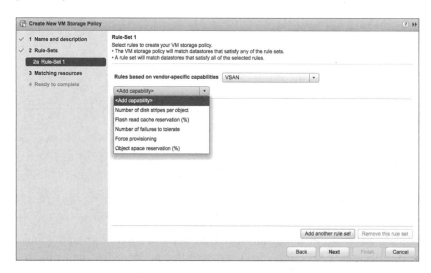

Figure 6-4   VSAN capabilities

For our first policy, the capability that we want to add is number of failures to tolerate, and we will set this to 1, as shown in Figure 6-5.

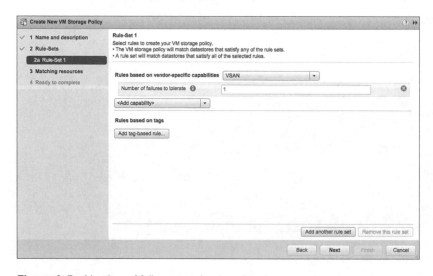

Figure 6-5   Number of failures to tolerate set to 1

There are a number of other features on this part of the wizard, namely Add tag-based rules and Add another rule set buttons. These are beyond the scope of this book, but you can find additional information in the official vSphere documentation.

Clicking **Next** moves the wizard on to the Matching resources window, and at this point the VSAN datastore should be displayed, as shown in Figure 6-6. This means that the contents of the VM storage policy (that is, the capabilities) are understood by the VSAN datastore.

CAUTION

Note that just because the VSAN datastore is shown in the Matching resources window, it does not mean that the VSAN datastore can provision VMs. It could be that the policy contains an unrealistic stripe width or failures to tolerate (FTT) setting that cannot be met by the VSAN cluster. This screen simply means that VSAN understands the policy contents. This is an important distinction.

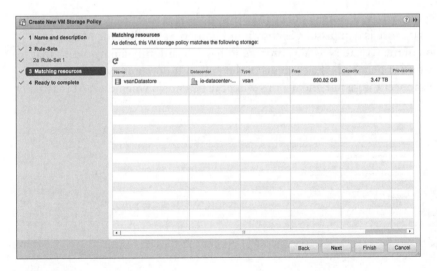

Figure 6-6 Matching resources

Review your policy and click **Finish** to create it. Congratulations. You have created your first VM storage policy. We will now go ahead and deploy a new VM using this policy. The process for deploying a new VM is exactly the same as before. The only difference is at the storage-selection step. By default, no VM storage policy is selected; it is set to None, as shown in Figure 6-7.

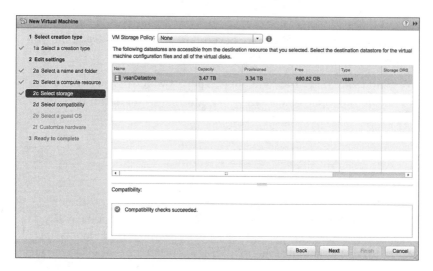

Figure 6-7   No policy selected

However, when our new VM storage policy (**My first policy**) is selected, you can see that the VSAN datastore is compatible, as shown in Figure 6-8. Just like the Matching resources section of the Create New VM Storage Policy Wizard, this simply means that the VSAN datastore understands the contents of the policy. It does not mean that the VSAN cluster can meet the requirements; this will only be known when the VM is actually deployed.

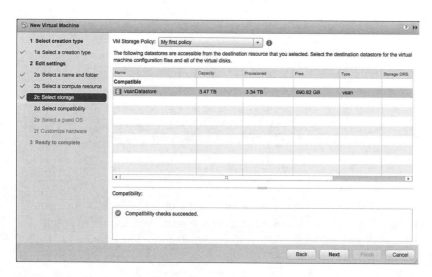

Figure 6-8   My first policy is selected, and the VSAN datastore is compatible.

Once the VM has been deployed, we navigate to the VM view by clicking **Manage**, and then selecting **VM Storage Policies**, as shown in Figure 6-9. From here, we can see the layout of the VM storage object's VM Home namespace, and VM disk files (VMDKs). The VM Home namespace is where the .vmx file and other configuration files required by a VM reside. These storage objects that make up a VM on the VSAN datastore are discussed in detail in Chapter 5, "Architectural Details."

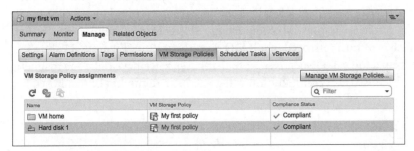

Figure 6-9   Compliance status is Compliant.

As you can see, both objects are compliant. In other words, they meet the capabilities defined in the VM storage policy. This means that this VM can tolerate a failure in the VSAN cluster and still have a full complement of the storage objects available. If we now select the Physical Disk Placement tab for either of the objects (VM Home or Hard Disk), we can see that there is a RAID-1 (mirror) configuration around the components. See Figure 6.10.

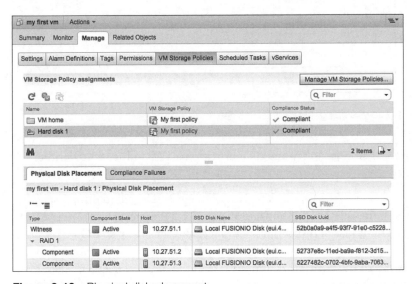

Figure 6-10   Physical disk placement

Policy Setting: Failures to Tolerate = 1, Stripe Width = 2

Let's try another VM storage policy setting that adds another capability. In this case, we will use a cluster with more resources than the first example to facilitate the additional requirements. This time we will explicitly request a number of failures to tolerate set to 1 and a number of disk stripes per object set to 2. Let's build out that VM storage policy and deploy a VM with that policy and see how it affects the layout of the various VM storage objects. In this scenario, we expect a RAID-1 configuration mirrored by a RAID-0 stripe configuration, resulting in four disk components. There are two components in each RAID-0 stripe, which is in turn mirrored in a RAID-1 configuration. Figure 6-11 shows how this will look from a logical perspective. Note that because we have only one magnetic disk per ESXi host, each RAID-0 configuration will go across a minimum of two hosts.

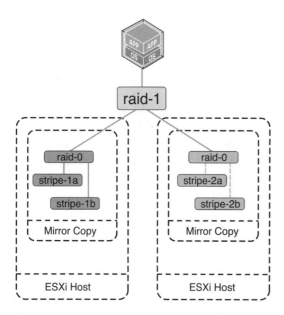

Figure 6-11   VSAN I/O flow: striping, two hosts

Now, let's create the VM storage policy and then provision a VM and see whether the result matches theory.

When creating the new policy, the vendor VSAN is once again selected to display specific capabilities of VSAN in the rule-sets as shown in Figure 6-12. To meet the necessary VM requirements, we select number of disk stripes per object and set this to 2, and we set number of failures to tolerate to 1. The number of disk stripes defined is a minimum number, so depending on the size of the virtual disk and the size of the physical magnetic disk, a virtual disk might end up being striped across multiple disks or hosts.

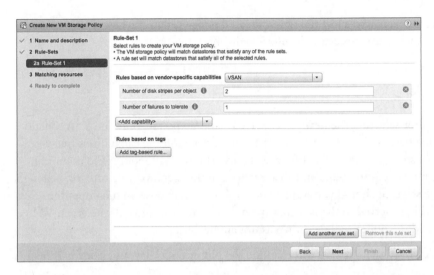

Figure 6-12 VM storage policy with failures to tolerate = 1 and stripe width = 2

Now that we have created a new VM storage policy, let's take a look at the VM provisioning workflow, beginning with Figure 6-13.

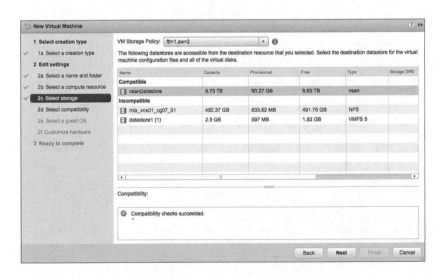

Figure 6-13 The VSAN datastore is compatible for policy ftt=1,sw=2.

In this example, we explicitly select the newly created policy called ftt=1,sw=2. Now you see that the available datastores are split into two distinct categories:

- Compatible

- Incompatible

As you can see, after selecting the newly created VM storage policy, only the VSAN datastore is compatible because it is the only one that can understand the capabilities that were placed in the VM storage policy. The other datastores (local VMFS and NFS) do not understand the policy requirements and so are placed in the incompatible category, though these can still be selected should you want to do so. If you do choose an incompatible datastore, you will be alerted to the fact that the datastore does not match the given VM storage policy, and the policy will be shown as not applicable.

After we have deployed the VM, we will examine the physical disk layout again, as shown in Figure 6-14.

Figure 6-14 Physical disk placement for policy of ftt=1,sw=2

As you can see in Figure 6-14, a RAID-1 configuration has been created, adhering to the number of failures to tolerate requirement specified in the VM storage policy. However, now you see that additionally each replica is made up of a RAID-0 stripe configuration, and each stripe contains two components, adhering to the number of disk stripes per object requirement of 2.

We also have a witness disk created. Now it is important to point out that the number of witness disks is directly related to how the components are distributed across the hosts and disks in the cluster. If this were a three-node cluster, a number of additional witness disks might have been necessary to ensure that greater than 50 percent of the components of this VM's objects remained available in the event of a failure, especially a host failure. In this case, which is leveraging an eight-node VSAN cluster, because the components are spread out across unique ESXi hosts, it is sufficient to create a single witness disk and keep greater than 50 percent of the components available when there is a failure in the cluster.

An interesting point to note is that the VM Home namespace does not implement the number of disk stripes per object requirement. The VM Home namespace only implements the number of failures to tolerate requirement. Therefore, if the VM Home namespace is examined, we see that the components are not in a RAID-0 configuration, as shown in Figure 6-15.

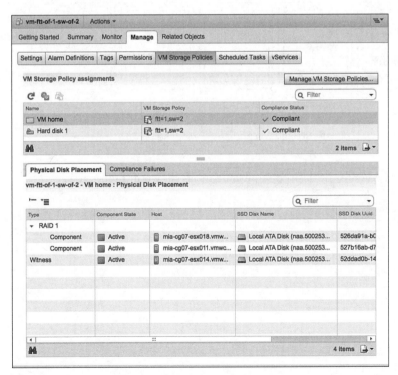

Figure 6-15   The VM Home namespace does not implement stripe width capability.

Policy Setting: Failures to Tolerate = 2, Stripe Width = 2

In this next example, we create another VM storage policy that has the number of disk stripes per object set to 2 and the number of failures to tolerate also set to 2. This implies that any VM deployed with this policy on the VSAN cluster should be able to tolerate up to two different failures, be they host, network, or disk failures. Considering the "two-host failure" capability specified and the number of disk stripes of 2, the expected disk layout is as shown in Figure 6-16.

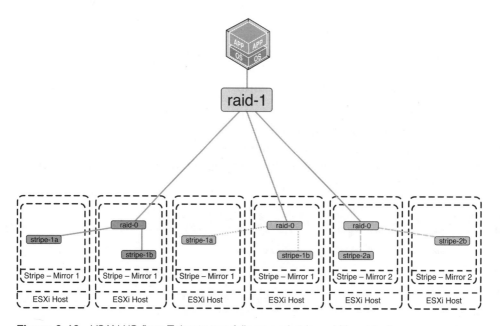

Figure 6-16   VSAN I/O flow: Tolerate two failures and stripe width set to 2

First, the policy is created with the desired requirements, as shown in Figure 6-17.

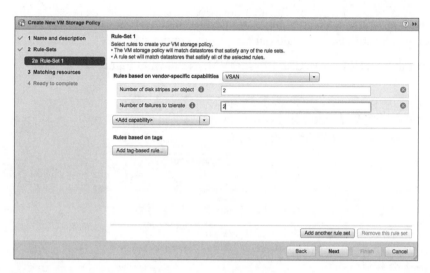

Figure 6-17   Failures to tolerate = 2, stripe width = 2.

Next we deploy a new VM with this new policy, and as expected the VSAN datastore is the only one that shows up as compatible when the VM storage policy ftt=2,sw=2 is selected, as shown in Figure 6-18.

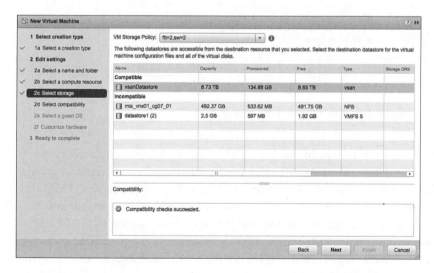

Figure 6-18   The VSAN datastore is compatible with the ftt=2,sw=2 policy.

Now that we have provisioned a VM, the physical disk placement can be examined to see how the VM storage objects have been laid out across hosts and disks.

First, let's look at the VMDK or hard disk 1 of this VM, as shown in Figure 6-19.

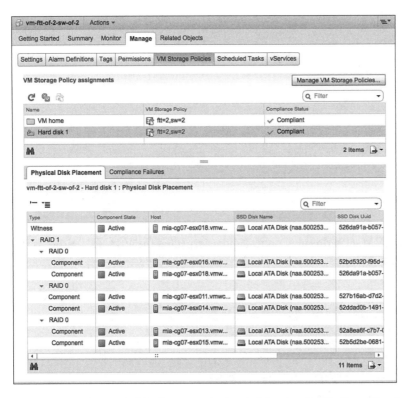

Figure 6-19   Physical disk placement for hard disk using the ftt=2,sw=2 policy

Now we see that for the virtual disk of this VM, VSAN has implemented an additional RAID-0 stripe configuration. For RAID-0 stripe configurations, all components in at least one of the RAID-0 stripe configuration must remain intact. That is why a third RAID-0 stripe configuration has been created. You might assume that if the first component in the first RAID-0 stripe configuration was lost, and the second component of the second RAID-0 stripe configuration was lost, VSAN might be able to use the remaining components to keep the storage object intact. This is not the case. Therefore, to tolerate two failures in the cluster, a third RAID-0 stripe configuration is necessary because two failures might take out the other two RAID-0 stripe configurations. This is also why all of these RAID-0 configurations are mirrored in a RAID-1 configuration. As you can see in Figure 6-19, components are stored on six different ESXi hosts in this eight-node VSAN cluster:

mia-cg07.esx11, mia-cg07.esx13, mia-cg07.esx14, mia-cg07.esx15, mia-cg07.esx16, and mia-cg07-esx018.

Next, let's look at the VM Home namespace, as shown in Figure 6-20.

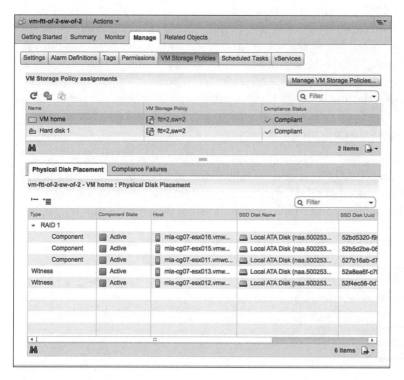

Figure 6-20 Physical disk placement for VM Home with the ftt=2,sw=2 policy

Previously, it was stated that the VM Home namespace does not implement the number of disk stripes per object policy setting, but that it does implement the number of failures to tolerate. There is no RAID-0 configuration, but we can now see that there are three replicas in the RAID-1 mirror configuration to meet the number of failures to tolerate set to 2 in the VM storage policy. What can also be observed here is an increase in the number of witness disks. Remember that greater than 50 percent of the components of the VM Home namespace object must be available for this object to remain online. There-fore, if two replicas were lost, there would still be one replica (that is, copy of the VM Home namespace data) available and two witness disks; therefore, greater than 50 percent of the components would still be available if two failures took out two replicas of this configuration.

Policy Setting: Failures to Tolerate = 1, Object Space Reservation = 50 Percent

This next scenario explores a different capability. As explained in previous chapters, all objects deployed on VSAN are thinly provisioned by default. This means that they initially consume no disk space, but grow over time as the guest OS running inside of the VM requires additional space. Using the object space reservation policy setting in the VM storage policy, however, a VM can be deployed with a certain percentage of its disk space reserved in advance. By default, object space reservation is 0 percent, which is why VMs deployed on the VSAN datastore are thin. If you want to have all the space reserved for a VM (that is, a "thick" disk), you can do this by setting the object space reservation to be 100 percent. We will go for somewhere in between.

Let's start with an example that reserves 50 percent of the disk space at VM deployment time, as shown in Figure 6-21. The percentage value refers to the size of the VMDK. If the VMDK is 40GB at deployment time, the amount of space reserved with an object space reservation value of 50 percent should reserve 20GB of disk space.

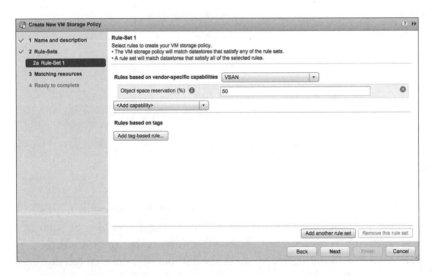

Figure 6-21   Object space reservation

Once the policy has been created, the VM may be deployed with the correct policy chosen, as shown in Figure 6-22.

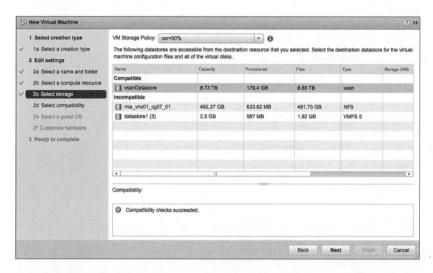

Figure 6-22   The VSAN datastore understands the object space reservation requirement.

The VSAN datastore understands the policy setting and is shown as compatible, whereas the other datastores are marked as incompatible. Now, the more observant of you might have noticed that we did not select a requirement of number of failures to tolerate. Surely we should have done that to ensure that the VM is highly available. Well, the point is that a number of failures to tolerate setting of 1 is always inferred, even if it is not explicitly specified. Therefore a number of failures to tolerate setting of 1 is implemented if a policy does not specify this requirement. To confirm, the physical disk placement views can be used to check whether a RAID configuration is indeed in place. Only if FTT is explicitly set to 0 in the policy will you not have a RAID-1 configuration.

First, we verify the RAID-1 configuration in the VM Home namespace view, as shown in Figure 6-23.

Figure 6-23   VM Home: The number of failures to tolerate is inferred even if not specified in the policy.

We can also confirm that the hard disk also has a mirrored configuration to meet a number of failures to tolerate policy setting even though it was not explicitly placed in the policy, as shown in Figure 6-24.

Figure 6-24   VMDK: The number of failures to tolerate is inferred even if not specified in the policy.

However, let's return to the initial additional requirement we specified. That requirement was to reserve 50 percent of the disk space required by our VM. To see how much space the VMDK is consuming, navigate to **Datastore > Manage > Files** using the vSphere Web Client. The VM was initially rolled out with a 40GB VMDK, and now we have requested an object space reservation of 50 percent, as shown in Figure 6-25.

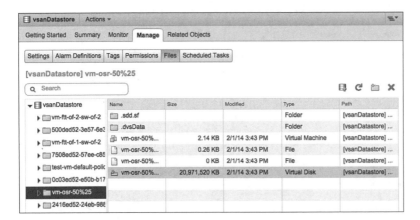

Figure 6-25   Object space reservation = 50 percent reserves 20GB out of 40GB.

As stated, we can see that the 40GB VM hard disk file deployed with this VM has reserved 20GB of disk space, equal to the 50 percent that was requested in the VM storage policy for this VM.

Policy Setting: Failures to Tolerate = 1, Object Space Reservation = 100 Percent

Let's look at one final policy. This is to reserve the full 100 percent of our VMDK. The same steps are followed as before, which is to create a policy that contains an object space reservation requirement, but this time the value is 100 percent rather than 50 percent, as shown in Figure 6-26. This means, as you might have already guessed, that we reserve all of the VM's disk space up front, similar to a thick format VM disk file.

As per the steps that have already been covered in the previous section, the policy requires only an object space reservation setting, but this time set to 100 percent. As before, a number of failures to tolerate setting of 1 is implied, even though it isn't explicitly stated in the policy.

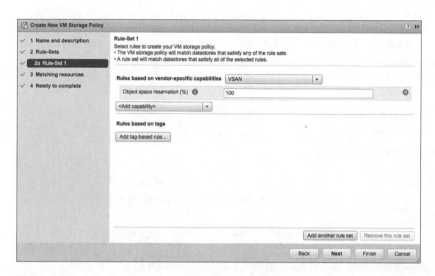

Figure 6-26   Object space reservation = 100 percent.

Once again, we select this policy during VM deployment. We can verify that the VSAN datastore is compatible with our policy selection, as shown in Figure 6-27.

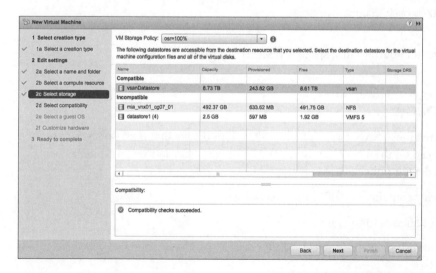

Figure 6-27   The VSAN datastore is compatible with the VM storage policy.

The next step is to determine how much disk space the VMDK file is actually reserving. Once again, you can use the **Datastore > Manage > Files** view to see how much space has been reserved up front for this VMDK, as shown in Figure 6-28. Because the object space reservation value was set to 100 percent, we should expect the full 40GB to be reserved.

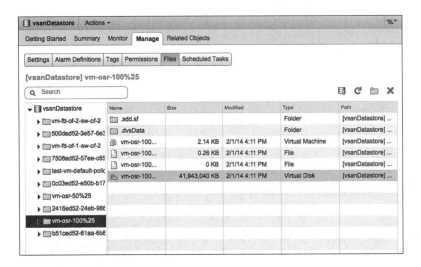

Figure 6-28   40GB of disk space is reserved.

As expected, the full 40GB of disk space is reserved up front.

Default Policy

As you might imagine, VSAN has a default policy. This means that if no policy is chosen for a VM deployed on the VSAN datastore (VM storage policy left set to None, as per Figure 6-29), a default policy is used for the VM.

The default policy contains the following capabilities:

- Number of failures to tolerate = 1

- Number of disk stripes per object = 1

- Flash read cache reservation = 0 percent

- Object space reservation = not used

- Force provisioning = disabled

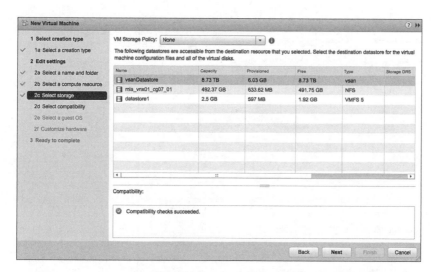

Figure 6-29 No policy selected results in the default policy being used.

When the VM is deployed, the first thing you will notice is that the VM storage policy is set to None, as shown in Figure 6-30. You will also notice that the number of failures to tolerate value of 1 is implemented when the objects are examined via the physical disk placement. As you can see in this figure, even though the policy is set to None, a RAID-1 configuration is in place for the VM objects. This means that even if you deploy a VM without a policy, VSAN will automatically provide availability via the default policy.

As shown in Figure 6-30, there is no VM storage policy associated with this VM. However, if we look at the VM Home, we can see that it is automatically deployed with a RAID-1 configuration, which is a mirror copy of the data. The two components that make up the RAID-1 mirror are placed on two different ESXi hosts, namely mia-cg07.esx17 and mia-cg07-esx015. This means that if one of the ESXi hosts fails, there is still a full copy of the data available. Another point to make is related to the witness disk. This is placed on a different ESXi host (mia-cg07-esx013) from the data components, too. This is to ensure that greater than 50 percent of the components remain available should a host failure occur on any single ESXi hosts in the cluster. The witness acts as a vote in this configuration. It allows the VM Home object to remain available in the event of a failure in the cluster.

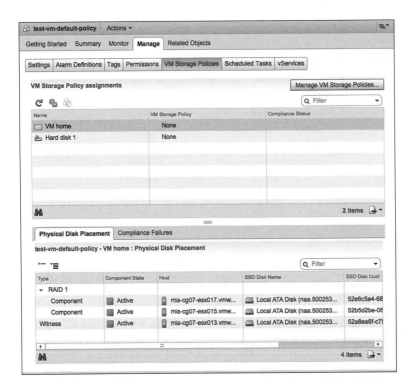

Figure 6-30   Number of failures to tolerate = 1 is part of the default policy.

Let's take a look at the hard disk/VMDK next. This is what the VMDK looks like when deployed to the VSAN datastore with a default policy. Because there is only a single VMDK on this VM, it is referred to as hard disk 1 in the user interface in this example. As Figure 6-31 shows, the two components that make up the RAID-1 mirror are placed on two different ESXi hosts, namely mia-cg07.esx12 and mia-cg07-esx013. The witness is placed on ESXi host mia-cg07-esx016.

As expected, all components, including the witness, are stored on different hosts to ensure availability.

One final note about the default policy, and that is the object space reservation setting. This is not included in the default policy. Instead, the Create VM wizard settings of thick and thin disks are implemented. If no changes are made to the Create VM wizard settings during deployment, a lazy zeroed thick (LZT) VMDK will be deployed on the VSAN datastore, similar to having an object space reservation of 100%.

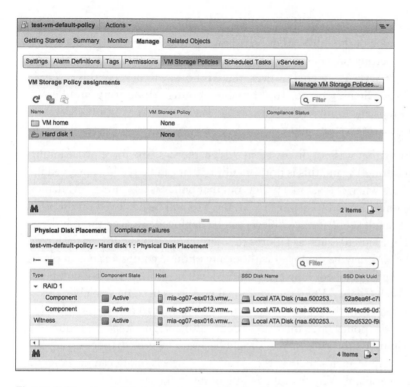

Figure 6-31   Hard disk 1 layout using default policy

Although the default policy exists, VMware recommends that administrators create their own policy and not rely on the default policy for deployments. VMware also cautions against editing the default policy; the recommendation is that if you need to change the default policy, it is much simpler to build a policy via VM storage policies in vCenter to meet those requirements. Also note that editing the default policy can only be done at the command line of the ESXi host, and this editing process needs to be repeated on every ESXi host in the cluster. This can lead to user errors, and so should be avoided if at all possible.

Summary

This completes the coverage of VM storage policy creation and VM deployments on the VSAN datastore. One policy setting that we did not include in this chapter was the flash read cache reservation. This is simply because this setting is not visible from the UI from a VM layout perspective in the vSphere Web Client. However, it is configured as a percentage value once again, in exactly the same way as object space reservation is configured, as a percentage value of the full VMDK size. For example, if 1 percent is the flash read cache reservation setting on a 40GB VMDK, this will reserve 400MB of flash read cache for that particular VM. As stated, however, there is no way to observe this reservation in the vSphere Web Client. Chapter 10, "Troubleshooting, Monitoring, and Performance," will show how an administrator can use the Ruby vSphere Console (RVC) to examine flash read cache reservation values.

The other policy setting that was not discussed in this chapter was the force provisioning vSphere Replication setting. Again, this is not something that can be readily observed in the vSphere Web Client when it is set in a policy and that policy is used for a VM deployment. If force provisioning is used to deploy a VM, the VM will be deployed on the VSAN datastore as long as one full set of storage objects can be deployed. So even though the policy may contain requirements such as failures to tolerate, or stripe width, or flash read cache reservation, the VM may be deployed without any of these configurations in place when force provisioning is specified. However, the VM will be shown as out of compliance in the vSphere Web Client. When the additional resources become available, this VM will be reconfigured using the additional resources to bring it to compliance. VSAN automatically enforces the policy once the resources are available; no steps are required by the administrator to initiate this process. You should be aware by now that deploying VMs that do not have their requirements met via the use of force provisioning can be dangerous and may result in an unavailable VM should a failure occur in the cluster.

What you will have noticed is that there are a few behaviors with VM storage policies that might not be intuitive, such as the default policy settings, the fact that a number of failures to tolerate set to 1 is implicitly included in a policy, and that some virtual storage objects implement only some of the policy settings. Chapter 5 explained these nuances in greater detail.

## Chapter 7

Management and Maintenance

This chapter covers the common VSAN management and maintenance procedures and tasks. It also provides some generic workflows and examples related to day-to-day management.

Host Management

VMware VSAN is a scale-out and scale-up storage architecture. This means that it is possible to seamlessly add extra storage resources to your VSAN cluster. These storage resources can be magnetic disks, complete disk groups including solid-state disks (SSDs), but also additional hosts containing storage capacity. Those who have been managing vSphere environments for a while will not be surprised that VSAN is extremely simple; adding storage capacity can truly be as simple as adding a new host to a cluster. Let's look at some of these tasks more in depth.

Adding Hosts to the Cluster

Adding hosts to the VSAN cluster is quite straightforward. Of course, you must ensure that the host meets VSAN requirements or recommendations such as a 1Gb dedicated network interface card (NIC) port (10GbE being recommended) and at least one SSD and one magnetic disk drive (HDD) if the host is to provide additional storage capacity. Also, pre-configuration steps such as a VMkernel port for VSAN communication should be considered, although these can be done after the host is added to the cluster. After the host has successfully joined the cluster, you should observe the size of the VSAN datastore grow according to the size of the additional magnetic disk in the new host. Remember that the SSD does not add anything to the capacity of the VSAN datastore. Just for completeness' sake, these are the steps required to add a host to a VSAN cluster using the vSphere Web Client:

1. Right-click the cluster object and click **Add Host**.

2. Fill in the IP address or host name of the server, as shown in Figure 7-1.

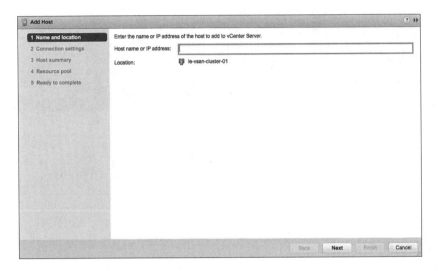

Figure 7-1   Adding a host to the cluster

3. Fill in the user account (root typically) and the password.

4. Accept the **SHA1 thumbprint** option.

5. Click **Next** on the Host Summary screen.

6. Select the license to be used.

7. Enable lockdown mode if needed and click **Next**.

8. Click **Next** in the Resource Pool section.

9. Click **Finish** to add the host to the cluster.

That is it; well, if you have your cluster configured to automatic mode, of course. If you do not have it configured to automatic mode, you will need to create a disk group manually. You will learn how to do that later in this chapter.

Removing Hosts from the Cluster

Should you want to remove a host from a cluster, you must first ensure that the host is placed into maintenance mode, which is discussed in further detail in the next section. After the host has been successfully placed into maintenance mode, you may safely remove it from the VSAN cluster. To remove a host from a cluster using the vSphere Web Client, follow these steps:

1. Right-click the host and click **Enter Maintenance Mode** and select the appropriate VSAN migration option from the screen in Figure 7-2, and then click **OK**.

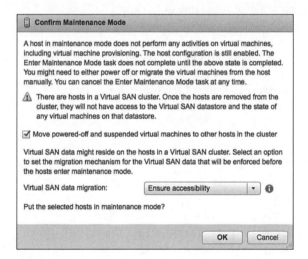

Figure 7-2   Enter maintenance mode

2. Now all the virtual machines (VMs) will be migrated (vMotion) to other hosts.

3. When migrations are completed, depending on the selected VSAN migration option, VSAN components may also be copied to other hosts.

4. When maintenance mode has completed, right-click the host again and select **Remove from Inventory** under All vCenter Actions.

5. Read the text presented twice, and click **Yes** when you understand the potential impact.

ESXCLI VSAN Cluster Commands

There are no specific host commands for VSAN. There is a namespace in ESXCLI for the VSAN, however. Using these command-line interface (CLI) commands, you can enable a host to join or leave a cluster. These are the basic commands as part of `esxcli vsan cluster`:

```
~ # esxcli vsan cluster
Usage: esxcli vsan cluster {cmd} [cmd options]

Available Commands:
  get      Get the information of the VSAN cluster that this host is joined to.
  join     Join the host to a given VSAN cluster.
  leave    Leave the VSAN cluster the host is currently joined to.
  restore  Restore the persisted VSAN cluster configuration.
~ #
```

One command that we have used regularly during troubleshooting exercises is the `get` command. The `get` command allows you to get cluster configuration information on the command line, which can be used to compare hosts against each other; for instance:

```
~ # esxcli vsan cluster get
Cluster Information
   Enabled: true
   Current Local Time: 2013-03-18T12:09:11Z
   Local Node UUID: 511b62c3-96e6-434e-6839-1cc1de253de4
   Local Node State: MASTER
   Local Node Health State: HEALTHY
   Sub-Cluster Master UUID: 511b62c3-96e6-434e-6839-1cc1de253de4
   Sub-Cluster Backup UUID: 511cc68b-352a-5cae-cf67-1cc1de252264
   Sub-Cluster UUID: 523845c8-73c9-5d99-0393-9ef20a328714
   Sub-Cluster Membership Entry Revision: 10
   Sub-Cluster Member UUIDs: 511b62c3-96e6-434e-6839-1cc1de253de4,
      511cc68b-352a-5cae-cf67-1cc1de252264,
      511cd526-5682-3688-8206-1cc1de253a92
   Sub-Cluster Membership UUID: 56092451-245f-9c0c-29f6-1cc1de253de4
```

Maintenance Mode

The previous section briefly touched on maintenance mode when removing an ESXi host from a VSAN cluster. With VSAN, maintenance mode includes new functionality that we will elaborate on here. In the past, when an ESXi host was placed in maintenance mode, it was all about migrating VMs from that ESXi host; however, when you implement VSAN, maintenance mode provides you with the option to migrate data as well. The VSAN maintenance mode options relate to data evacuation, as follows:

- **Ensure Accessibility**: This option evacuates enough data from the host entering maintenance mode to ensure that all VM storage objects are accessible after the host goes down. This is not full data evacuation. Instead, VSAN examines the storage objects that could end up without quorum or data availability when the host is placed into maintenance mode and makes enough copies of the object available to alleviate those issues. VSAN (or to be more precise, Cluster Level Object Manager [CLOM]) will have to successfully reconfigure all objects that would become inaccessible because of the lack of availability of those component(s) on that host. An example of when this could happen is when VMs are configured with "failures to tolerate" set to 0. Ensure Accessibility is the default option of the maintenance mode workflow and the recommended option by VMware.

- **Full Data Migration**: This option is a full data evacuation and essentially creates replacement copies for every piece of data residing on disks on the host being placed into maintenance mode. VSAN does not necessarily copy the data from the host entering maintenance mode; however, it can and will also leverage the hosts holding the replica copy of the object to avoid creating a bottleneck on the host entering maintenance mode. In other words, in an eight-host cluster, when a host is placed in maintenance mode using full data migration, then potentially all eight hosts will contribute to the re-creation of the impacted components. The host does not successfully enter maintenance mode until all affected objects are reconfigured and compliance is ensured when all of the component(s) have been placed on different hosts in the cluster.

- **No Data Migration**: This option does nothing with the storage objects. If the host is powered off after entering maintenance mode, the situation is equivalent to the host crashing.

Note that if a host enters maintenance mode, VSAN still operates, accesses, and serves data on that host. Only when the host is removed from the cluster or is powered off will VSAN stop using the host (or, of course, when you have decided to do a full data migration, when the data migration has been completed, and the "old" components have been removed).

Figure 7-3 shows which options can be selected when a host or hosts are placed into maintenance mode, with Ensure Accessibility being the default preselected data migration suggestion.

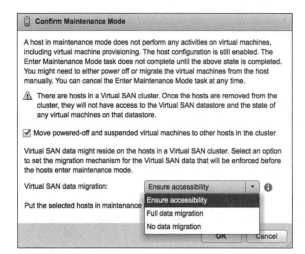

Figure 7-3   Maintenance mode options

Recommended Maintenance Mode Option for Updates and Patching

It is best to draw a comparison to a regular storage environment first. When you do upgrades, you typically do these upgrades in a rolling fashion, meaning that if you have two controllers, one will be upgraded while the other handles I/O. In this scenario, you are also at risk. The big difference is that as a virtualization administrator *you have a bit more flexibility*, and you *expect certain features* to work as expected, such as vSphere High Availability (HA), for instance. You need to ask yourself what level of risk you are *willing* to take, and what level of risk you *can* take.

From a VSAN perspective, when it comes to placing a host into maintenance mode, you will need to ask yourself the following questions:

- **Why am I placing my host in maintenance mode?** Am I going to upgrade my hosts and expect them to be unavailable for just a brief period of time? Am I removing a host from the cluster altogether? This will play a big role in which maintenance mode data migration option you should use.

- **How many hosts do I have?** When using three hosts, the only option you have is Ensure Accessibility because VSAN always needs three hosts to store (two replicas and one witness).

- **How long will the move take?**

  - What types of disks have I used (SAS versus SATA)?

- Do I have 10GbE or 1GbE?

- How big is my cluster?

- **Do I want to move data from one host to another to maintain availability levels?** Only stored components need to be moved, not the "raw capacity" of the host! That is, if 6TB of capacity is used out of 8TB, 6TB will be moved.

- **Do I just want to ensure data accessibility and take the risk of potential downtime during maintenance?** Only components of those objects at risk will be moved. For example, if only 500GB out of the 6TB used capacity is at risk, that 500GB will be moved.

There is something to say for all maintenance mode data migration options. When you select Full Data Migration, to maintain availability levels, your "maintenance window" will be stretched, as you could be copying terabytes over the network from host to host. It could potentially take hours to complete. If your ESXi upgrade including a host reboot takes about 20 minutes, is it acceptable to wait for hours for the data to be migrated? Or do you take the risk, inform your users about the potential downtime, and as such do the maintenance with a higher risk but complete it in minutes rather than hours?

To be honest, it is impossible for us to give you advice on what the best approach is for your organization. We do feel strongly that for normal software or hardware maintenance tasks, it will be acceptable to use the Ensure Accessibility maintenance mode data migration option. You should still, however, discuss *all* approaches with your storage team and look at their procedures. What is the agreed service level agreement (SLA) with your business partners and what fits from an operational perspective?

Disk Management

One of the design goals for VSAN, as already mentioned, is the ability to scale out the storage capacity. This requires the ability to add new disks, replace disks with a larger capacity disk, or simply replace failed disks. This next section discusses the procedures involved in doing these tasks in a VSAN environment.

Adding a Disk Group

Chapter 2, "VSAN Prerequisites and Requirements for Deployment," demonstrated how to add a disk group; however, for completeness, here are the steps again:

1. Click your VSAN cluster in the left pane.

2. Click the **Manage** tab on right side.

3. Click **Settings** and **Disk Management**.

4. As shown in Figure 7-4, select a host in the cluster and click the icon with the green plus sign (+).

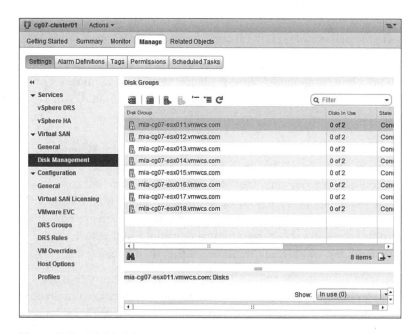

Figure 7-4   VSAN disk management

5. Select all magnetic disks and the flash device that needs to be part of this disk group and click **OK**.

Now a disk group is created; this literally takes seconds.

Note that, if desired, you can also create new disk groups on all hosts simultaneously. By simply not selecting a host when clicking the new disk group icon, it becomes possible to add a new disk group to all hosts in the cluster.

Removing a Disk Group

Before you start with this task, we want to recommend placing the ESXi host with the disk group that you want to remove in maintenance mode. This is not a required step for deleting a disk group, but we believe that most administrators would like to move the VM components currently in this disk group to other disk groups in the cluster before deleting the disk group. If you don't do this step, and evacuate the data, you may be left with degraded components that are no longer highly available while VSAN reconfigures these components. Therefore, it is recommended entering maintenance mode first. If you are planning on doing a full data migration maintenance mode, you should validate first whether sufficient disk space is available within the cluster to do so.

When you complete this step, the host is now in maintenance mode, as shown in Figure 7-5, and you should be able to remove the disk group. However, the icon to remove the disk group may not be visible in the Disk Groups view depending on how VSAN has been configured.

Disk Groups				
Disk Group	Disks In Use	State	Status	Network Partition Group
▾ 🗄 10.27.51.1	2 of 2	Maintenance M...	Healthy	Group 1
🗄 Disk group (010000000031323034443036383949494445249...	2		Healthy	
▾ 🗄 10.27.51.2	2 of 2	Connected	Healthy	Group 1
🗄 Disk group (010000000031323130443039313344944445249...	2		Healthy	
▾ 🗄 10.27.51.3	3 of 3	Connected	Healthy	Group 1
🗄 Disk group (010000000031323431443030353134494445249...	3		Healthy	
▾ 🗄 10.27.51.4	3 of 3	Connected	Healthy	Group 1
🗄 Disk group (010000000031323313044303932354944445249...	3		Healthy	

Figure 7-5 VSAN disk groups

When VSAN is configured initially, a decision is made about how disks are added to the VSAN datastore. This can be done fully automated, "automatic" mode, or in a manual fashion, "manual" mode. By default, VSAN is configured to automatic mode, which means that if we remove a disk group, VSAN immediately claims the disks again, and as such the option to remove a disk group is not presented to the user. When it is desired to remove a disk group, you will need to place the VSAN cluster in manual mode for the Remove the Disk Group icon to appear. This can simply be done through the VSAN cluster settings, as shown in Figure 7-6.

Figure 7-6 VSAN cluster mode

When the VSAN is placed in manual mode, return to the Disk Management view and you should see that the Remove the Disk Group icon (it has the red *X*) is now visible when you select the disk group on the host that is in maintenance mode. You can now proceed with removing the disk group.

Adding Disks to the Disk Group

If your VSAN was configured in automatic mode, adding disks to the disk group is not an issue. New or existing disks are automatically claimed by the VSAN cluster and are used to provide capacity to the VSAN datastore.

However, if your cluster was created in manual mode, you will need to add new disks to the disk groups to increase the capacity of the VSAN datastore. This can easily be done via the vSphere Web Client. Navigate to the VSAN cluster, select the **Manage** tab, and then the **VSAN Disk Management** section. Next, new disks can be "claimed" for a disk group. If your disks do not show up, be sure to do a rescan on your disk controller. Selecting a host and clicking the **Claim Disks** item will display a list of all of the ESXi hosts in the VSAN cluster and the available disks in each host. An alternative method is available, and this allows you to add disks to a disk group on a per-host basis when you select a particular disk group. Depending on the method chosen, simply select the disks that you want to add to the VSAN cluster and click **OK**. Figure 7-7 shows a number of disks available in a four-node cluster that have been selected for claiming.

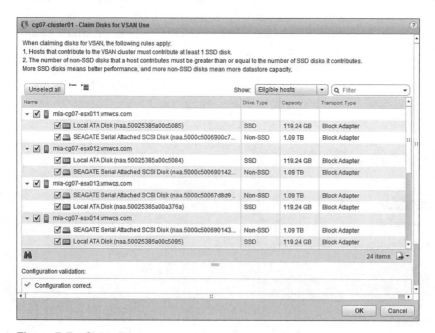

Figure 7-7   Claim disks

Removing Disks from the Disk Group

Just like removing disk groups discussed previously, disks can be removed from a disk group in the vSphere Web Client only when the cluster is placed in manual mode. If the cluster is in automatic mode, the VSAN cluster will simply reclaim the disk you've just removed. When the cluster is in manual mode, navigate to the Disk Management section of the VSAN cluster, select the disk group, and an icon to remove a disk becomes visible in the user interface (UI)—a disk with a red *X*—as shown in Figure 7-8. Note that this icon is *not* visible when the cluster is in automatic mode.

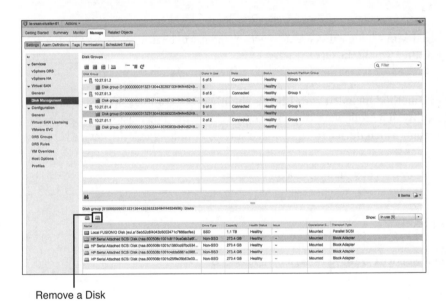

Remove a Disk

Figure 7-8   Remove a disk from a disk group

Wiping a Disk

In some cases, other features or operating systems may have used magnetic disks and flash devices before VSAN is enabled. In those cases, VSAN will not be able to reuse the devices when the devices still contain partitions or even a file system. Note that this has been done intentionally to prevent the user from selecting the wrong disks. If you want to use a disk that has been previously used, you can wipe the disks manually.

There are two commonly used methods to wipe a disk before VSAN is used:

- Using the command `partedUtil`, a disk partition management utility,which is included with ESXi

- Booting the host with the gparted bootable ISO image

The gparted procedure is straightforward. You can download the ISO image from http://gparted.org/, boot the ESXi host from it and it is simply a matter of deleting all partitions on the appropriate disk and clicking **Apply**.

> **WARNING**
>
> The tasks involved with wiping a disk are destructive, and it will be nearly impossible to retrieve any data after wiping the disk.

The `partedUtil` method included with ESXi is slightly more complex because it is a command-line utility. The following steps are required to wipe a disk using `partedUtil`. If you are not certain which device to wipe, make sure to double-check the device ID using `esxcli storage core device list`:

```
~ # partedUtil get  /dev/disks/naa.500xxxxxx
15566 255 63 250069680
1 2048 6143 0 0
2 6144 250069646 0 0


~ # partedUtil getptbl /dev/disks/naa.500xxxxxx
gpt
15566 255 63 250069680
1 2048 6143 381CFCCC728811E092EE000C2911D0B2 vsan 0
2 6144 250069646 AA31E02A400F11DB9590000C2911D1B8 vmfs 0
~ #


~ # partedUtil delete /dev/disks/naa.500xxxxxx 1
~ # partedUtil delete /dev/disks/naa.500xxxxxx 2
```

If you are looking for more guidance about the use of `partedUtil`, read the following VMware Knowledge Base (KB) article: http://kb.vmware.com/kb/1036609.

ESXCLI VSAN Disk Commands

From the ESXCLI, a number of disk-related activities might be done. First, you can get and set the manual or automated mode of the cluster. The remaining commands in ESXCLI for VSAN storage relate to disks and disk groups. You can add, remove, or list the disks in a disk group. This will list both SSDs and magnetic disks. The following output of `esxcli vsan storage list` highlights for the two devices whether it is a flash device and of which disk group they are part:

```
~ # esxcli vsan storage list
naa.5000c5002bd7526f
   Device: naa.5000c5002bd7526f
   Display Name: naa.5000c5002bd7526f
   Is SSD: false
   VSAN UUID: 52db9f60-57b8-ad88-70eb-889f3c72b5e1
   VSAN Disk Group UUID: 521f9dda-efda-4718-e75d-aec63eb6fbd4
   VSAN Disk Group Name: naa.500253825000c296
   Host UUID: 519f364d-ef04-8d94-8ad4-1cc1de252264
   Cluster UUID: 520bff2a-badc-0cdd-7be7-70e5e5ae032f
   Used by this host: true
   In CMMDS: true
   Checksum: 11848694795517181960
   Checksum OK: true
naa.500253825000c296
   Device: naa.500253825000c296
   Display Name: naa.500253825000c296
   Is SSD: true
   VSAN UUID: 521f9dda-efda-4718-e75d-aec63eb6fbd4
   VSAN Disk Group UUID: 521f9dda-efda-4718-e75d-aec63eb6fbd4
   VSAN Disk Group Name: naa.500253825000c296
   Host UUID: 00000000-0000-0000-0000-000000000000
   Cluster UUID: 00000000-0000-0000-0000-000000000000
   Used by this host: true
   In CMMDS: true
   Checksum: 12800345249350977942
   Checksum OK: true
```

As previously mentioned, it is also possible to remove a magnetic disk or a flash device from a disk group through the CLI; however, this should be done with absolute care and preferably through the UI, as shown on the previous pages.

Failure Scenarios

We have already discussed some of the failure scenarios in Chapter 5, "Architectural Details," and explained the difference between *absent* components and *degraded* components. From an operational perspective, though, it is good to understand how a magnetic disk, SSD, or host failure impacts you. Before we discuss them, let's first shortly recap the two different failure states, because they are fundamental to these operational considerations:

- **Absent**: VSAN does not know what has happened to the component that is missing. A typical example of this is when a host has failed. When this happens, VSAN waits for 60 minutes by default before new replica components are created.

- **Degraded**: VSAN knows what has happened to the component that is missing. A typical example of when this can occur is when an SSD or a magnetic disk has died. When this happens, VSAN instantly spawns new components to make all impacted objects compliant again with their selected policy.

Now that you know what the different states are, let's look again at the different types of failures, or at least the "most" common and what the impact is.

Magnetic Disk Failure

A disk failure is probably the most common failure that can happen in any storage environment, and VSAN is no different. The reason for this is simple: moving parts. The question, of course, is this: How does VSAN handle disk failure? What if it is doing a write or read to or from that disk?

If a read error is returned from a storage component, VSAN checks to see whether a replica component exists and reads from that instead. Every object by default is created with number of failures to tolerate set to 1, which means that there are always two identical copies of your object available. There are two separate scenarios when it comes to reading data. The first one is where the problem is recoverable, and the second one is an irrecoverable situation. When the issue is recoverable, the I/O error is reported to the object owner. The object owner will then initiate a component re-creation, and when that is completed, the errored component is deleted. However, if for whatever reason, no replica component exists (an unlikely scenario and something an administrator would have had to create a policy specifically for), VSAN will report an I/O error to the VM.

Write failures are also propagated up to the object owner, which again initiates a component re-creation on different disks in the VSAN cluster. When the component re-creation is completed, the cluster directory (Cluster Monitoring, Membership, and Directory Service [CMMDS]) is updated. Note that the flash device (which has no error) continues to service reads that are in cache.

The vCenter Web Client today does not provide an indication of how much data needs to be synced when a component or components are being created as a result of a failure; however, a very useful `vsan.resync_dashboard` Ruby vSphere Console (RVC) command does allow you to verify:

```
/localhost/CH-Datacenter/computers/cluster> vsan.resync_dashboard
2013-12-12 16:56:58 +0000: Querying all VMs on VSAN ...
2013-12-12 16:56:58 +0000: Querying all objects in the system from 10.20.177.18 ...
2013-12-12 16:56:59 +0000: Got all the info, computing table ...
+--------------------------------------------------------------+-----------------+---------------+
| VM/Object                                                    | Syncing objects | Bytes to sync |
+--------------------------------------------------------------+-----------------+---------------+
| win1                                                         | 1               |               |
| [vsanDatastore] 9a3f9352-346a-f78d-3360-1cc1de253de4/win1-000001.vmdk |       | 48.00 GB      |
+--------------------------------------------------------------+-----------------+---------------+
| Total                                                        | 1               | 48.00 GB      |
+--------------------------------------------------------------+-----------------+---------------+
/localhost/CH-Datacenter/computers/cluster>
```

Flash Device Failure

What about when the flash device becomes inaccessible? When a flash device becomes inaccessible, all the magnetic disks backed by that flash device are also made inaccessible. A flash device failure is the same as a failure of all the magnetic disks behind the flash device. In essence, when a flash device fails, the whole disk group is considered to be degraded. If there is spare capacity in the VSAN cluster, it tries to find another host or disk and starts reconfiguring the storage objects.

Therefore, from an operational and architectural decision, depending on the type of hosts used, it could be beneficial to create multiple smaller disk groups versus a single large disk group because a disk group should be considered to be a failure domain, as shown in Figure 7-9.

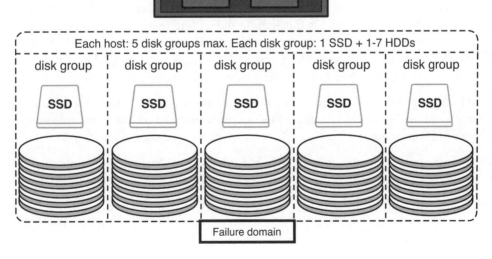

Figure 7-9 VSAN disk groups

Host Failure

Assuming VSAN VM storage policies have been created with the number of failures to tolerate at least set to 1, a host failure in a VSAN cluster is similar to a host failure in a cluster that has a regular storage device attached. The main difference, of course, being that the VSAN host that has failed contains components of objects that will be out of sync when the host returns. Fortunately, VSAN has a mechanism that syncs all the components as soon as they return.

In the case of a host failure, after 60 minutes VSAN will start re-creating components because the likelihood of the host returning within a reasonable amount of time is slim. When the reconstruction of the storage objects is completed, the cluster directory (CMMDS) is updated.

If the host that originally failed recovers and rejoins the cluster, the object reconstruction status is checked. If object reconstruction has completed on another node or nodes, no action is taken. If object resynchronization is still in progress, and it is deemed quicker to synchronize the components of the originally failed host, the components of the original host are made a replica, and the more recent (but unsynchronized) copies are discarded. Otherwise, the original components on the originally failed host are discarded.

You probably are wondering by now how this resynchronization of VSAN components actually works. VSAN maintains a bitmap of changed blocks in the event of components of an object being unable to synchronize due to a failure on a host, network, or disk. This allows updates to VSAN objects composed of two or more components to be reconciled after a failure. Let's use an example to explain this. If a host with replica A of object X has been partitioned from the rest of the cluster, the surviving components of X have quorum and data availability, so they continue functioning and serving writes and reads. While A is "absent," all writes performed to X are persistently recorded in a bitmap by VSAN. If the partitioned host with replica A comes back and VSAN decides to reintegrate it with the remaining components of object X, the bitmap is used to resynchronize component A.

When a host has failed, all VMs that were running on the host at the time of the failure will be restarted by vSphere HA. vSphere HA can restart the VM on any available host in the cluster whether or not it is hosting VSAN components, as shown in Figure 7-10.

In the event of an isolation of a host, vSphere HA can and will also restart the impacted VMs. As this is a slightly more complex scenario, let's take a look at it in more depth.

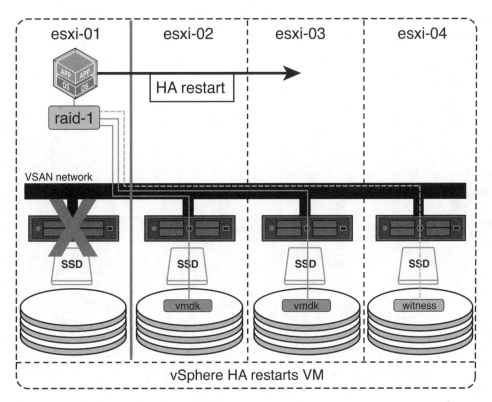

Figure 7-10   VSAN 1 host failed, HA restart

Network Partition

A network partition could occur when there is a network failure. In other words, some hosts can end up on one side of the cluster, and the remaining hosts on another side. VSAN will surface warnings related to network misconfiguration in the event of a partition.

After explaining the host and disk failure scenarios in the previous sections, it is now time to describe how isolations and partitions are handled in a VSAN cluster. Let's look at a typical scenario first and explain what happens during a network partition based on this scenario.

In the scenario depicted in Figure 7-11, VSAN is running a single VM on ESXi-01. This VM has been provisioned using a VM storage policy that has number of failures to tolerate set to 1.

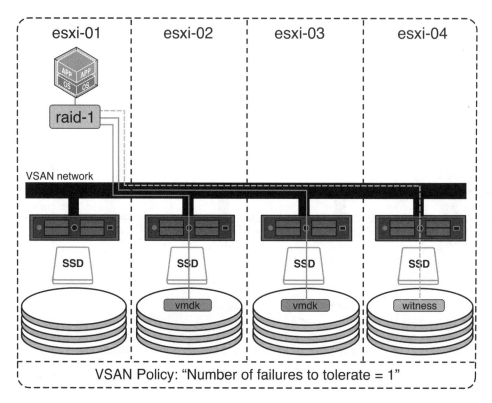

Figure 7-11   VSAN I/O flow: Failures to tolerate = 1

Because VSAN has the capability to run VMs on hosts that are not holding any active storage components of that VM, this question arises: What happens in the case where the network is isolated? As you can imagine, the VSAN network plays a big role here, made even bigger when you realize that it is also used by HA for network heartbeating. Note that the vSphere HA network is automatically reconfigured by VSAN to ensure that the correct network is used for handling these scenarios. Should this situation occur, the following steps describe how vSphere HA and VSAN will react to an isolation event:

1. HA will detect there are no network heartbeats received from esxi-01.

2. HA master will try to ping the slave esxi-01.

3. HA will declare the slave esxi-01 is unavailable.

4. VM will be restarted on one of the other hosts (esxi-03, in this case, as shown in Figure 7-12).

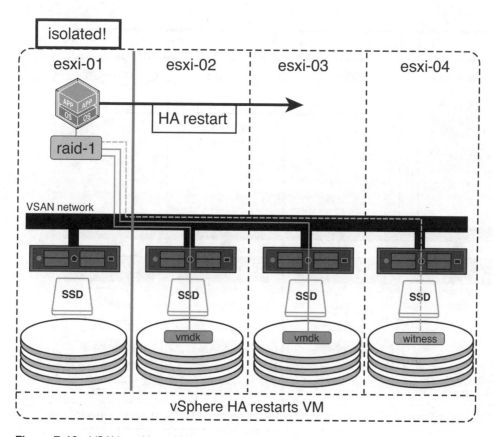

Figure 7-12 VSAN partition with one host isolated: HA restart

Now this question arises: What if something has gone horribly bad in my network and esxi-01 and esxi-02 end up as part of the same partition? What happens then? Well, that is where the witness comes in to play. Refer to Figure 7-13 first; that will make it a bit easier to understand.

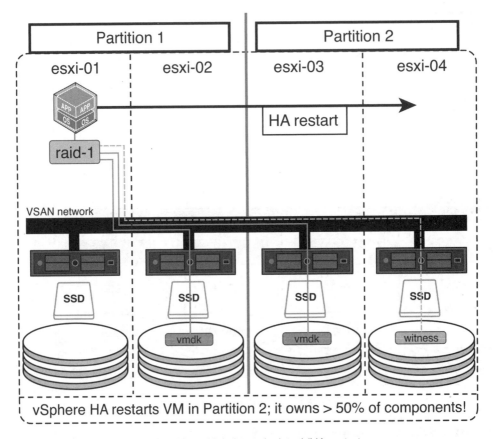

Figure 7-13   VSAN partition with multiple hosts isolated: HA restart

Now this scenario is slightly more complex. There are two partitions, one of which is running the VM with its virtual machine disk (VMDK), and the other partition has a VMDK replica and a witness. Guess what happens? Right, VSAN uses the witness to see which partition has quorum, and based on that result, one of the two partitions will win. In this case, Partition 2 has more than 50 percent of the components of this object and therefore is the winner. This means that the VM will be restarted on either esxi-03 or esxi-04 by vSphere HA. Note that the VM in Partition 1 will be powered off only if you have configured the isolation response to do so.

TIP

We would like to stress that this is highly recommended! (Isolation response > power off.)

But what if esxi-01 and esxi-04 were isolated, what would happen then? Figure 7-14 shows what it would look like.

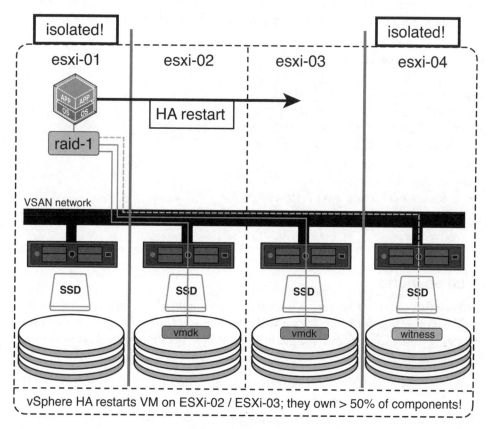

Figure 7-14   VSAN 2 hosts isolated: HA restart

Remember the rule we discussed earlier?

The winner is declared based on the percentage of components available within that partition.

If the partition has access to more than 50 percent of the components (of an object), it has won. For each object, there can be at most one winning partition. This means that when esxi-01 and esxi-04 are isolated, either esxi-02 or esxi-03 can restart the VM because 66 percent of the components of the object reside within this part of the cluster.

To prevent these scenarios from occurring, it is most definitely recommended to ensure the VSAN network is made highly available through NIC teaming and redundant network switches, as discussed in Chapter 3, "VSAN Installation and Configuration."

If vCenter is unavailable for whatever reason and you would like to retrieve information about the VSAN network, you can do so through the CLI of ESXi. From the CLI, an administrator can examine or remove the VSAN network configuration. In the following example, you can see the VMkernel network interface used for cluster communication, and also the IP protocol used:

```
~ # esxcli vsan network list
Interface
    VmkNic Name: vmk2
    IP Protocol: IPv4
    Interface UUID: 06419f51-ec79-0b57-5b3e-1cc1de252264
    Agent Group Multicast Address: 224.2.3.4
    Agent Group Multicast Port: 23451
    Master Group Multicast Address: 224.1.2.3
    Master Group Multicast Port: 12345
    Multicast TTL: 5
~ #
```

Disk Full Scenario

Another issue that can occur is a disk full scenario. You might ask, "What happens when the VSAN datastore gets full?" To answer that question, you should first ask the question, "What happens when an individual magnetic disk fills up?" because this will occur before the VSAN datastore fills up.

Before explaining how VSAN reacts to a scenario where a disk is full, it is worth knowing that VSAN will try to prevent this scenario from happening. VSAN balances capacity across the cluster and can and will move components around, or even break up components, when this can prevent a disk full scenario. Of course, the success of this action is entirely based on the rate at which the VM claims and fills new blocks and at which VSAN can relocate existing components. Simply put, the law of physics applies here.

In the event of a disk's reaching full capacity, VSAN pauses (technically called *stun*) the VMs that are trying to write data and require additional new disk space for these writes; those that do not need additional disk space continue to run as normal. Note that VSAN-based VMs are deployed thin by default and that this only applies when new blocks need to be allocated to this thin-provisioned disk. When this occurs, the error message shown in Figure 7-15 appears on the VM's summary screen.

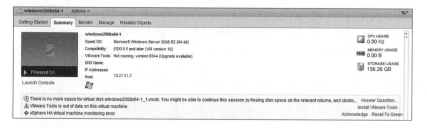

Figure 7-15 No More Space message

This is identical to the behavior observed on Virtual Machine File System (VMFS) when the datastore reached capacity. When additional disk capacity is made available on the VSAN datastore, the stunned VMs may be resumed via the vSphere Web Client. Administrators should be able to see how much capacity is consumed on a per-disk basis via the **Monitor > Virtual SAN > Physical Disks** view, as shown in Figure 7-16.

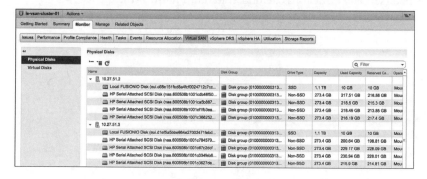

Figure 7-16 Monitoring physical disks

Thin Provisioning Considerations

By default, all VMs provisioned to a VSAN datastore are thin provisioned. The huge advantage of this is that VMs are not taking up any unused disk capacity. It is not uncommon in datacenter environments to see 40 percent to 60 percent of unused capacity within the VM. You can imagine that if a VM were thick provisioned, this would drive up the cost, but also make VSAN less flexible in terms of placement of components.

Of course, there is an operational aspect to thin provisioning. There is always a chance of filling up a VSAN datastore when you are severely overcommitted and many VMs are claiming new disk capacity. This is not different in an environment where Network File

System (NFS) is used, or VMFS with thin provisioned VMs. The Web Client interface fortunately has many places where capacity can be checked, of which the Summary tab shown in Figure 7-17 is an example.

Figure 7-17   Capacity of VSAN datastore

And, of course, when certain thresholds are reached, vCenter Server will raise an alarm to ensure that the administrator is aware of the potential problem that may arise when not acted upon. By default, this alarm is triggered when the 75 percent full threshold is exceeded with an exclamation mark (severity warning), and another alarm is raised when 85 percent is reached (severity critical), as demonstrated in Figure 7-18.

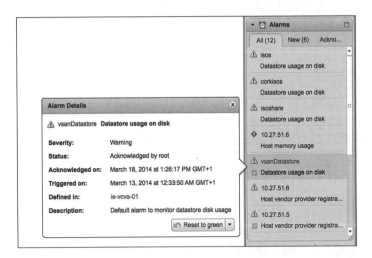

Figure 7-18   Datastore usage warning

vCenter Management

vCenter Server is an important part of most vSphere deployments because it is the main tool used for managing and monitoring the virtual infrastructure. In the past, new features introduced to vSphere often had a dependency on vCenter Server to be available, like for instance, vSphere Distributed Resource Scheduler (DRS). If vCenter Server was available, that service would also be temporarily unavailable; in the case of vSphere DRS, this meant that no load balancing would occur during this time.

Fortunately, VSAN does not rely on vCenter Server in any shape or form, not even to make configuration changes or to create a new VSAN cluster. Even if vCenter Server goes down, VSAN continues to function, and VMs are not impacted whatsoever when it comes to VSAN functionality. If needed, all management tasks can be done through ESXCLI (or RVC for that matter); and in case you are wondering, yes, this is fully supported by VMware.

You might wonder at this point why VMware decided to align the VSAN cluster construct with the vSphere HA and DRS construct, especially when there is no direct dependency on vCenter Server and no direct relationship. There are several reasons for this, so let's briefly explain those before looking at a vCenter Server failure scenario.

The main reason for aligning the VSAN cluster construct with the vSphere HA and DRS cluster construct is user experience. Today, when VSAN is configured/enabled, it takes a single click in the cluster properties section of the vSphere Web Client. This is primarily achieved because a compute cluster already is a logical grouping of ESXi hosts.

This not only allows for ease of deployment, but also simplifies upgrade workflows and other maintenance tasks that are typically done within the boundaries of a cluster. On top of that, capacity planning and sizing for compute is done at cluster granularity; by aligning these constructs, storage can be sized accordingly.

Last but not least: availability. vSphere HA is performed at cluster level, and it is only natural to deal with the new per-VM accessibility consideration within the cluster because vSphere HA at the time of writing does not allow you to fail over VMs between clusters. In other words, life is much easier when vSphere HA, DRS, and VSAN all share the same logical boundary and grouping.

vCenter Server Failure Scenario

What if you would lose the vCenter Server? What will happen to VSAN, and how do you rebuild this environment? Even though VSAN is not dependent on vCenter Server, other components are. If, for instance, vCenter Server fails and a new instance needs to be created from scratch, what is the impact on your VSAN environment?

After you rebuild a new vCenter, you need to redefine a VSAN-enabled cluster and add the hosts back to the cluster. Until you complete this last step, you will be receiving a "configuration issue" warning because the VSAN cluster will not have a matching vSphere cluster (with matching membership) in the vCenter inventory.

One additional consideration, however, is that the loss of the vCenter server will also mean the loss of the VM storage policies that the administrator has created. Storage policy–based management (SPBM) will not know about the previous VM storage policies and the VMs to which they were attached. VSAN, however, will still know exactly what the administrator had asked for and keep enforcing it. Today, there is no way in the UI to export existing policies, but in vSphere 5.5 an application programming interface (API) for VM storage policies has been exposed.

One important thing to note about the VM storage policy API is that it is exposed as a separate API endpoint on vCenter Server and it will not be accessible through the normal vSphere API. To consume this API, you must connect to the SPBM server that requires an authenticated vCenter Server session. This API can be leveraged to export and import these policies. You can find an example of how to retrieve information about current VM storage policies in the following article by William Lam: http://www.virtuallyghetto.com/2013/11/restoring-vsan-vm-storage-policy.html. Leveraging this example and the public SPBM APIs, it is possible to develop export and import scripts for your VM storage policies.

Running vCenter Server on VSAN

A common support question relates to whether VMware supports the vCenter Server that is managing VSAN to run in the VSAN cluster. The concern would be a failure scenario where the access to the VSAN datastore is lost and thus VMs, including vCenter Server, can no longer run. The major concern here is that no vCenter Server (and thus no tools such as RVC) is available to troubleshoot any issues experienced in the VSAN environment. Fortunately, VSAN can be fully managed via ESXCLI commands on the ESXi hosts. So, to answer the initial question, yes, VMware will support customers hosting their vCenter Server on VSAN (as in it is supported), but obviously in the rare event where the vCenter Server is not online and you need to manage or troubleshoot issues with VSAN, the user experience will not be as good. This is a decision that should be given some careful consideration.

Bootstrapping vCenter Server

If you can run vCenter Server on ESXi, how do you get it up and running in a greenfield deployment? Typically in greenfield deployments, no external storage is available, so VSAN needs to be available before vCenter Server can be deployed.

William Lam of virtuallyghetto.com has described a procedure that allows you to do exactly that. For the full procedure and many more articles on the topic of automation and

VSAN, check out William Lam's website (virtuallyghetto.com), who kindly gave us permission to leverage his content. For your convenience, we have written a short summary of the steps required to "bootstrap" vCenter Server on a single-server VSAN datastore:

1. Install ESXi 5.5 onto your physical hosts. Technically, one host is needed to begin the process, but you will probably want to have two additional hosts ready unless you do not care about your vCenter Server being able to recover if there are any hardware issues.

2. You must modify the default VSAN storage policy on the ESXi host in which you plan to provision your vCenter Server. You must run the following two ESXCLI commands to enable "force provisioning":

```
esxcli vsan policy setdefault -c vdisk -p
  "((\"hostFailuresToTolerate\" i1) (\"forceProvisioning\" i1))"
esxcli vsan policy setdefault -c vmnamespace -p

  "((\"hostFailuresToTolerate\" i1) (\"forceProvisioning\" i1))"
```

3. Confirm you have the correct VSAN default policy by running the following ESXCLI command:

```
~ # esxcli vsan policy getdefault
Policy Class  Policy Value
____          _____

cluster       (("hostFailuresToTolerate" i1))
vdisk         (("hostFailuresToTolerate" i1) ("forceProvisioning" i1))
vmnamespace   (("hostFailuresToTolerate" i1) ("forceProvisioning" i1))
vmswap        (("hostFailuresToTolerate" i1) ("forceProvisioning" i1))
```

4. You must identify the disks that you will be using on the first ESXi host to contribute to the VSAN datastore. You can do so by running the following ESXCLI command:

```
esxcli storage core device list
```

5. To get specific details on a particular device such as identifying whether it is an SSD or regular magnetic disk, you can specify the -d option and the device name:

```
esxcli storage core device list -d <disk identifier>
```

6. After you have identified the disks you will be using, make a note of the disk names as they will be needed in the upcoming steps. In this example, we have only a single SSD and single magnetic disk.

7. Before we can create our VSAN datastore, we need to first create a VSAN cluster. One of the parameters that is needed when going through this "bootstrapping" method without a vCenter Server is a unique UUID to identify the VSAN cluster. The UUID is in the format of *nnnnnnnn-nnnn-nnnn-nnnn-nnnnnnnnnnnn*, where *n* is a hexadecimal value. You can either make one up or you can find a free online UUID generator here: http://www.uuidgenerator.net/.

8. To create a VSAN cluster, we will use the following ESXCLI command and specify the UUID from the previous step for the -u option:

```
esxcli vsan cluster join -u <UUID>
```

9. After the VSAN cluster has been created, you can retrieve information about the VSAN cluster by running the following ESXCLI command:

```
esxcli vsan cluster get
```

10. Next we need to add the disks from our ESXi host to create our single-node VSAN datastore. To do so, we need the disk device names from our earlier step for both SSD and HDDs and to run the following ESXCLI command:

```
esxcli vsan storage add -d <HDD-DISK-ID> -s <SSD-DISK-ID>
```

The -d option specifies regular magnetic disks, and the -s option specifies an SSD disk. If you have more than one magnetic disk, you will need to specify multiple -d entries. You can also take a look at the disks being contributed to the VSAN datastore by running the following ESXCLI command:

```
esxcli vsan storage list
```

11. To save us one additional step, you can also enable the VSAN traffic type on the first ESXi host using ESXCLI, and you can also do this for the other two hosts in advance. This step does not necessarily have to be done now because it can be done later when the vCenter Server is available and using the vSphere Web Client. You will need to either create or select an existing VMkernel interface to enable the VSAN traffic type, and you can do so by running the following ESXCLI command:

```
esxcli vsan network ipv4 add -i <VMkernel-Interface>
```

12. At this point, you now have a valid VSAN datastore for your single ESXi host. You can verify this by logging in to the vSphere C# client, and you should see the VSAN datastore mounted to your ESXi host. You can now deploy the vCenter Server Appliance 5.5 OVA/OVF onto the VSAN datastore and power on the VM.

After deploying your vCenter Server, you should add the remaining hosts to the cluster as soon as possible. Also, you need to create a new VM storage policy, and it is recommended to attach this policy to the vCenter Server VM and ensure that the vCenter Server VM becomes compliant with this new policy.

Summary

As demonstrated throughout the chapter, VSAN is easy to scale out and up. Even when configured in manual mode, adding new hosts or new disks is still only a matter of a few clicks. For those who prefer the command line, ESXCLI is a great alternative to the vSphere Web Client. For those who prefer PowerShell, VMware has released a fling that provides additional cmdlets that enable you to manage VSAN using VMware PowerCLI. You can find more information about this at https://labs.vmware.com/flings/powercli-extensions.

## Chapter 8

Interoperability

This chapter focuses on how VSAN integrates with other core vSphere features and VMware products. If there is incompatibility or additional considerations, these are highlighted in the appropriate sections. Every effort has been made to ensure that the interoperability of components discussed in this chapter are correct, but VMware may make product changes and updates at any time. Therefore, we highly recommend referring to the official VSAN and related product documentation as well as the VSAN and related product release notes for the most up-to-date information. VMware also has an interoperability guide/matrix online, which we also urge you to reference. You can find the interoperability guide here:

http://partnerweb.vmware.com/comp_guide2/sim/interop_matrix.php

You can find details on how to navigate the *VMware Product Compatibility Guide* in VMware KB article 2006028.

Note that VMware now has a vast portfolio of software products and features and continues to release new products and features on a regular basis. This chapter is not all encompassing, but does look at those products and features that we have identified an interest in through various conferences and conversations with customers and partners. As always, official VMware documentation is the source of truth, because supportability and interoperability will no doubt change over time. We strongly recommend reading the release notes for each product to check for any nuances related to deploying the product with VSAN.

vMotion

The vSphere vMotion feature allows for the live migration of virtual machines (VMs) between hosts without any downtime to the applications and guest OS running inside the VM. This feature is fully supported for VMs that have been deployed to and reside on a VSAN datastore. VSAN provides the same vMotion experience as traditional SAN or NAS datastores, and all ESXi hosts in the cluster share the datastore. As mentioned previously, there is no data locality with this release of VSAN. In other words, a VM's compute may reside on one ESXi host in a VSAN cluster, and that VM's data may reside on completely different ESXi hosts in the VSAN cluster. This means that a vMotion of a VM between hosts in a VSAN cluster only ever needs to worry about moving the compute of a VM; it never needs to concern itself with data migration. Administrators can migrate running VMs between all ESXi hosts in a VSAN cluster, including those hosts that do not provide local storage to the VSAN datastore, but still access the VSAN datastore.

There is one additional behavior to highlight when comparing the vMotion of a VM on a VSAN datastore and the vMotion of a VM on a traditional datastore. In the presence of a network partition on a VSAN cluster, seeing the VSAN datastore from a partitioned ESXi host does not necessarily mean that the host has access to all of the storage objects that belong to the VM. Now if you attempt to vMotion a VM, vMotion will check whether the destination ESXi host can access the VM's storage objects, and if it cannot, the vMotion operation will fail, and the VM will remain running on the original ESXi host.

Of course, network partitions in a VSAN cluster also play a major role in vSphere High Availability (HA) behavior, as you will learn about in detail later in this chapter.

Storage vMotion

Because all VMs deployed on a VSAN cluster share the same distributed datastore, there is no Storage vMotion operation per se. That is, there is no way to move the storage objects of a VM around the cluster. VSAN has its own algorithms for initial placement of VM objects.

However, because ESXi hosts participating in a VSAN cluster might also have storage from other sources, such as network-attached storage (NAS) or storage-area networks (SANs), you might ask whether it is possible to live migrate a VM from a VSAN datastore to a Virtual Machine File System (VMFS) or Network File System (NFS) datastore presented to the same ESXi host, and vice versa. This live migration of VMs between different datastore types, including VSAN, is fully supported. The following are the possible storage vMotion scenarios that are supported:

- VMFS to VSAN

- NFS to VSAN

- VSAN to VMFS

- VSAN to NFS

In vSphere 5.5, the vSphere migration mechanism (vMotion) was enhanced to allow both the VM's compute *and* storage to be migrated from one ESXi host and datastore to another ESXi host and datastore without any downtime. Effectively, this enables the live migration of VMs across hosts over the network without the need to have shared storage. VMs can also be migrated between different clusters. vSphere administrators can also migrate VMs between different VSAN-enabled clusters leveraging the enhanced vMotion feature.

vSphere HA

vSphere HA is fully supported on a VSAN cluster to provide additional availability to VMs deployed in the cluster; however, a number of significant changes have been made to vSphere HA to ensure correct interoperability with VSAN.

> **NOTE**
>
> Although VSAN supports 32 nodes in this initial release, and although VSAN supports 100 VMs per ESXi host in the VSAN cluster, vSphere HA can only protect a total of 2,048 virtual machines per datastore. This means that if you push VSAN to its limit of 3,200 VMs, vSphere HA will not be in a position to protect all of these VMs. If you require vSphere HA to protect all 3,200 VMs in this example, one possibility to mitigate this limitation is to build multiple smaller clusters.

vSphere HA Communication Network

In non-VSAN deployments, vSphere HA agents communication takes place over the management network. In a VSAN environment, vSphere HA agents communicate over the VSAN network. The reasoning behind this is that in the event of a network failure we want vSphere HA and VSAN hosts to be part of the same partition. This avoids possible conflicts when vSphere HA and VSAN observe different partitions when a failure occurs, with different partitions holding subsets of the storage components and objects. The VSAN clustering agent, Cluster Monitoring, Membership, and Directory Service

(CMMDS), provides a consistent view of the partitions in a VSAN cluster, which allows VSAN to reach accurate decisions about the accessibility of objects for different VMs, and thus which VMs to restart in a given partition (that is, the partition in which the VM is accessible and has quorum).

vSphere HA in VSAN environments by default continues to use the management network's default gateway for isolation detection. We suspect that most VSAN environments will more than likely have the management network and the VSAN network sharing the same physical infrastructure (especially in 10GbE environments). However, if the VSAN and management networks are on a different physical infrastructure, it is recommended to change the default vSphere HA isolation address from the management network to the VSAN network. By default, the isolation address is the default gateway of the management network as previously mentioned. VMware's recommendation when using vSphere HA with VSAN is to use an IP address on the VSAN network for isolation. To prevent vSphere HA from using the default gateway and to use an IP address on the VSAN network, the following settings must be changed in the advanced options for vSphere HA:

- das.useDefaultIsolationAddress=false
- das.isolationAddress0=<ip address on VSAN network>

However, if there is no suitable isolation address on the VSAN network (because VSAN requires an L2 network and there might not be a gateway, for example), then leave the isolation address on the management network as per the default. More details around the use of vSphere HA advanced settings can be found in the following KB: http://kb.vmware.com/kb/2033250.

One other notable difference relates to network reconfiguration. If changes are made at the VSAN layer to the VSAN networks, this is not automatically detected by vSphere HA. Therefore, a vSphere HA cluster reconfiguration must be manually initiated by the vSphere administrator for these changes to be detected.

vSphere HA Heartbeat Datastores

Another noticeable difference with vSphere HA on VSAN is that the VSAN datastore cannot be used for datastore heartbeats. These heartbeats play a significant role in determining VM ownership in the event of a vSphere HA cluster partition with traditional SAN or NAS datastores. This feature is very advantageous when vSphere HA is deployed on traditional shared storage (SAN/NAS) because it allows some level of coordination between partitions. Because VSAN does not have shared datastores, this feature is not available to VSAN deployments. vSphere HA does not use the VSAN datastore for heart-beating and won't let a user designate it as a heartbeat datastore. VSAN instead uses the clustering service over the network that allows for very fast failure detection.

Note, however, that if ESXi hosts participating in a VSAN cluster also have access to shared storage, either VMFS or NFS, these traditional datastores are used for vSphere HA heartbeats.

vSphere HA Metadata

vSphere HA needs to store the protection metadata for each VM in the cluster. On traditional datastores, this was stored in a folder on the root directory of each datastore and labeled .vSphere-HA. In VSAN, this is done somewhat differently. Instead of storing it in the root directory of a datastore, the vSphere HA protection information is now stored in the VM's namespace metadata, along with the usual set of VM configuration files.

vSphere HA Admission Control

There is another consideration to discuss regarding vSphere HA and VSAN interoperability. When configuring vSphere HA, one of the decisions that needs to be made is about admission control. Admission control ensures that vSphere HA has sufficient resources at its disposal to restart VMs after a failure by setting aside resources.

Note that VSAN is not admission control-aware when it comes to failure recovery. There is no way to automatically set aside spare resources like this on VSAN to ensure that over-commitment does not occur.

If a failure occurs, VSAN will try to use all the remaining space on the remaining nodes in the cluster to bring the VMs to a compliant state. Caution and advanced planning is imperative on VSAN with vSphere HA as multiple failures in the VSAN cluster may fill up all the available space on the VSAN datastore due to overcommitment of resources.

Recommended practice dictates that you take "rebuild capacity" into consideration when planning and designing a VSAN environment. In Chapter 9, "Designing a VSAN Cluster," you learn how to achieve this. For simplicity reasons, it is recommended to align this form of VSAN (manual) admission control with the selected vSphere HA admission control settings.

vSphere HA Recommended Settings

When a host isolation event occurs in a VSAN cluster with vSphere HA enabled, vSphere HA will apply the configured isolation response. With vSphere HA, you can select three different types of responses to an isolation event:

- Leave powered on
- Power off, then fail over
- Shut down, then fail over

The recommendation is to have vSphere HA automatically power-off the VMs running on that host when a host isolation event occurs. Therefore, the "isolation response" should be set to "Power off, then fail over" and not the default setting that is leave powered on.

Note that "Power off, then fail over" is similar to pulling the power cable from a physical host. The VM process is literally stopped—this is not a clean shutdown. In the case of an isolation event, however, it is unlikely that VSAN can write to the disks on the isolated host and as such powering off is recommended. If the ESXi host is partitioned, it is also unlikely the VM will be able to access a quorum of components of the storage object.

vSphere HA Protecting VSAN and Non-VSAN VMs

For a VSAN-based VM, information about whether it should be restarted is stored in the VM's Home namespace object. For a non–VSAN-based VM, (that is, a VM that resides on a SAN or NAS datastore), this information is stored in the protection list file on the VM's Home datastore.

The vSphere HA master updates and accesses the restart information in similar ways for both the VSAN VMs and the non-VSAN VMs.

When protecting a VM, if the VM is a non-VSAN VM, the protection list file on the VM's Home datastore is updated.

If it is a VSAN-based VM that is being protected, a protection key is added to the VM's Home namespace object metadata.

After a vSphere HA master is elected, the master needs to determine which VMs are protected. If there are both VSAN datastores and traditional SAN/NAS datastores, not only does the vSphere HA master read the protection list file on traditional datastores, but it also retrieves the vSphere HA protection key saved in the VM Home namespace object metadata.

Distributed Resource Scheduler

VSAN fully supports Distributed Resource Scheduler (DRS) for the initial placement of VMs based on CPU and memory resources. DRS can also be placed into fully automated mode so that in the event of a CPU/memory resource disparity, the VM's compute can be live migrated using vMotion to another host in the cluster. We already touched on this in the vMotion section; however, because VMs deployed on VSAN have their compute and storage completely decoupled (for example, the VM compute could be on ESXi host 1, the first copy of the VM's storage objects could be on ESXi host 2, and the second copy of the

VM's storage objects could be on ESXi host 3), vMotion operations (directed by DRS) can seamlessly move a VM between ESXi hosts in the VSAN cluster.

Storage DRS

Storage DRS (SDRS) is used for initial placement and on-going load balancing of VMs across multiple shared datastores. Because VSAN provides a single distributed datastore, initial placement and load balancing are not relevant from an SDRS perspective. The performance and availability are based on entries in the VM storage policy, and the decision on where to initially place a VM's objects and components by VSAN is determined by these requirements.

SDRS can continue to be used on VMFS and NFS datastores in a VSAN cluster if these datastore types are present. You cannot include the VSAN datastore in a datastore cluster, however.

Storage I/O Control

Storage I/O Control (SIOC) is not supported with VSAN for reasons similar to those discussed in the "Storage DRS" section. Through the requirements placed in the VM storage policies, VSAN will decide on the best way to place the object/components to meet those requirements. SIOC throttles queue depths across hosts that share the same SAN or NAS datastores when bottlenecks occur, so this feature is not relevant to VSAN "distributed" datastores because it uses local storage only. SIOC will be automatically disabled on VSAN. SIOC was built to detect and manage performance issues on storage that VMware did not control. VSAN has built-in decision-making algorithms for balancing VM storage objects and components.

If you navigate to the VSAN datastore, select the **Manage** tab, and under General, you will observe under Datastore Capabilities that Storage I/O Control is shown as Not supported, as shown in Figure 8-1.

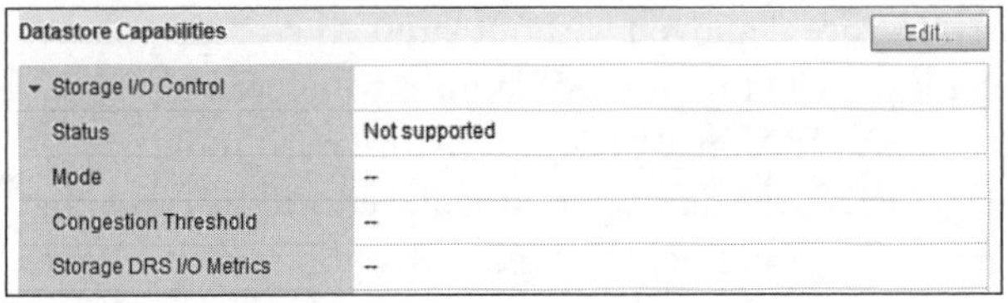

Figure 8-1   Storage I/O Control is not supported on VSAN.

Distributed Power Management

Distributed Power Management (DPM), a utility for powering down ESXi hosts in periods of low resource utilization, and powering them back up again when resources are needed, is incompatible with VSAN. It is automatically disabled. The reason for disabling DPM is that an ESXi host, even though it may have no running VMs, may still contain components of a VM's storage object (such as a RAID-0 stripe or a RAID-1 mirror). For that reason, you do not want the ESXi host to be placed into a standby/powered-off state. You will not be allowed to enable DPM on a VSAN-enabled cluster. If you do so, the error in Figure 8-2 will display.

Figure 8-2   DPM is not supported on VSAN.

VMware Data Protection

Both vSphere Data Protection (VDP) and VDP Advanced (VDPA) version 5.5.6 (released on March 11, 2014) are supported with VSAN. Earlier versions of VDP/VDPA do not work with VSAN. The VDP appliance can reside on the VSAN datastore, as well as have the capability to back up and restore VMs residing on the VSAN datastore. In fact, using VSAN to host your backup and restore infrastructure was one of the use cases identified for VSAN by the VSAN product team. The full complement of restore operations is also available, such as Restore to Original Location and Create New.

During the installation process, the administrator is prompted for a storage location for three 256GB virtual disks, which is where the backups are stored. The VSAN datastore may now be chosen during the installation, as shown in Figure 8-3.

The virtual machine disk objects (VMDKs) are deployed without any VM storage policy, which means that they inherit the default policy of number of failures to tolerate set to 1. Administrators planning to install VDP or VDPA on a VSAN datastore need to be aware that although 3 × 256GB are required by VDP, the actual space required will be twice that due to the number of failures to tolerate policy (and may be higher if a policy with a larger number of failures to tolerate setting is chosen). This is because the default policy will not use the object space reservation setting, but instead will use the traditional thin disk or thick disk method for deployment. By default, the disks will be deployed as thick if the default policy of None is used.

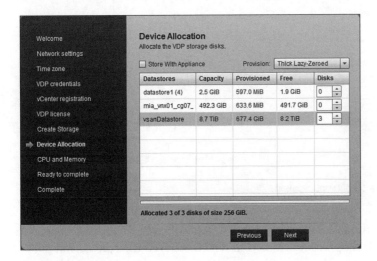

Figure 8-3 VDP can use VSAN for storage.

Backup VMs from a VSAN Datastore Using VDP

VMs residing on VSAN are backed up in exactly the same way as VMs on traditional datastores. There are no additional considerations to take into account for VMs residing on VSAN. Note that no VM storage policy information is backed up with the VM; therefore, when it comes to a restore, there is no policy information to restore with the VM, simply the VM data. The user may then choose which policy to associate with the VM on restore.

Restore VMs to a VSAN Datastore Using VDP

Restoring VMs that were backed up on a VSAN datastore is done in exactly the same way as restoring VMs that reside on traditional datastores. VMs may be restored using the "restore to original location" method or the "create new" method. When the "restore to original location" method is used, as shown in Figure 8-4, the VM is restored while maintaining its original VM storage policy. Therefore, there is no need to reapply any VM storage policy to the VM after it has been restored onto the VSAN datastore.

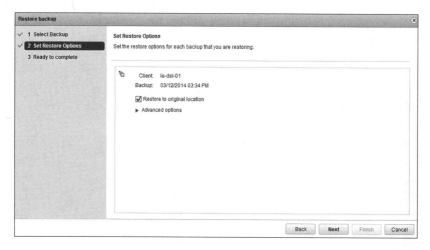

Figure 8-4   VDP can restore to original location.

When the "create new" method is used, the VM is restored without a VM storage policy because this data is not backed up with the VM. The VM is restored with the default policy (number of failures to tolerate=1). Therefore, the VM storage policy for the VM that is being restored would need to be reapplied to the VM once it has been restored onto the VSAN datastore. Notice in Figure 8-5 that the Advanced Options allow you to select an alternative datastore to restore to, if necessary.

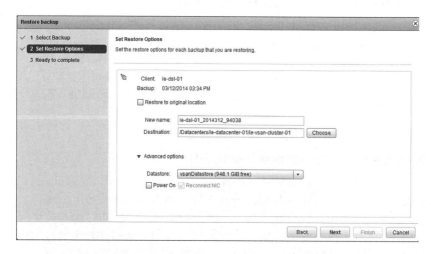

Figure 8-5   VDP can restore to a different location.

vSphere Replication

VMware fully supports vSphere Replication version 5.5.1 (released March 11, 2014) with VSAN to provide a disaster recovery (DR) solution. vSphere Replication supports the replication of VMs deployed on VSAN. In fact, vSphere Replication is agnostic to the underlying storage on which a VM resides. However, there are a number of considerations when replicating VMs on VSAN, especially in the area of VM storage policies.

Replicate to VSAN at a Recovery Site

In the case where vSphere Replication is replicating a VM that resides on traditional storage to a VSAN datastore at a recovery site, the Configure Replication wizard allows a VM storage policy to be selected for the VM that you want to have replicated when browsing for a target datastore for replication. When the policy is selected, possible target datastores are split into Compatible and Incompatible lists, as shown in Figure 8-6.

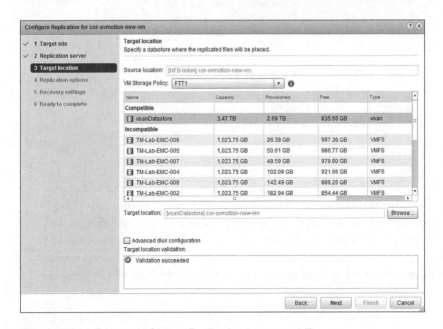

Figure 8-6   VSAN and vSphere Replication interoperability

Recover Virtual Machine

When it comes to the recovery of a VM, bringing the VM up on a VSAN datastore, the VM and its disks are associated with the VM storage policy specified during the "Configure Replication" steps. However, on initial recovery, the VMDKs are displayed as out of date, as shown in Figure 8-7.

Figure 8-7   Hard disk compliance status is out of date.

This is because the VM is initially configured with a default policy (number of failures to tolerate = 1). To bring the VM to compliance and reconfigure it to meet the policy requirement, administrators must click the icon to "Reapply VM storage policy to the selected VM." At this point, depending on the configuration that needs to be done to the VM storage components to become compliant, the VM hard disk(s) may be reported as not compliant. However, after the configuration is completed, the VM will be reported as compliant.

There is no way to automatically reprotect a VM that has been recovered (or automatically reverse replication) with vSphere Replication. This is not a limitation of VSAN but rather the way vSphere Replication operates. To do this automatically requires Site Recovery Manager (SRM) with vSphere Replication. In this case, SRM will break the replication and re-sync back in the other direction. To achieve this with vSphere Replication only, you will have to stop the replication when the VM is recovered, and then configure replication to go in the opposite direction.

Virtual Machine Snapshots

VSAN supports VM snapshots. Snapshot delta disks inherit the same VM storage policy as the VMDK against which the snapshot is taken. Therefore, if the VMs policy has number of failures to tolerate set to 1, the snapshot will have the same policy, and will have a replica created as per the policy requirement.

The vSphere Web Client user interface (UI) does not display the policy of a delta disk (snapshot) like it does for the VM Home namespace or the VM's disks; however, all delta disks in a snapshot chain inherit the same policy as their parent base disk.

The delta disk is itself another object in VSAN, and does not need to reside on the same magnetic disk as the base disk. When it is created, it may get created on the same magnetic disks or on different magnetic disks, depending on factors such as capacity. In any case, if the delta is provisioned on the same magnetic disks as the base disk and at any point a magnetic disk begins to reach its full capacity, VSAN can move some components to other magnetic disks seamlessly. Moving a component will typically have no noticeable performance impact because VSAN moves a component by creating the new component and resynchronizing it in the background while VM I/O continues to be serviced primarily from the flash device/solid-state disk (SSD).

VSAN does not have the ability to create a snapshot of the complete VSAN datastore.

vCloud Director

VSAN has been tested with vCloud Director 5.5.1 and can be used in place of traditional storage-area network (SAN) or network-attached storage (NAS) datastores. VSAN VM storage policies are also recognized by vCloud Director, and behave similarly to regular policies and datastores. Figure 8-8, taken from the VMware Compatibility Guide, shows the VSAN and vCloud Director interoperability matrix.

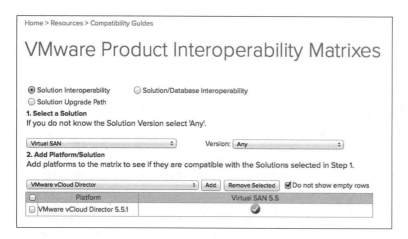

Figure 8-8   VSAN and vCloud Director interoperability matrix.

VMware Horizon View

One of the primary use cases for VSAN is VMware Horizon View, VMware's virtual desktop product. One of the major issues with virtual desktop infrastructure (VDI) deployments is the cost of storage that can meet the performance required by virtual desktops. In many cases, virtual desktop projects are canceled or put on hold because of either the cost of suitable storage or the poor performance of the existing storage infrastructure.

VMware Horizon View supports VSAN as a storage platform. The scale-out nature of VSAN, coupled with the performance provided by the SSD layer (all I/O goes to flash), makes VSAN a good solution for VMware Horizon View.

When used in conjunction with additional vSphere features such as vSphere Storage Accelerator (also known as Content Based Reach Cache [CBRC]), desktops deployed on VSAN via VMware Horizon View provide an excellent combination for customers interested in VDI.

VSAN Support for Horizon View

VMware released Horizon View version 5.3.1 (March 11, 2014) to support VSAN. There were no other new features in this release of Horizon View. The VSAN datastore can be used for either linked-clone desktop pools or full-clone desktop pools.

VM Storage Policies on VMware View

With Horizon View 5.3.1, disks associated with desktops are deployed with default VSAN policies. The default policy applies to both linked-clone desktop pools and full-clone desktop pools. The default policy for all virtual desktops deployed by Horizon View on the VSAN datastore is as follows:

- Number of disk objects to stripe: 1

- Number of failures to tolerate: 1

- Object space reservation: 0%

- Flash read cache reservation: 0%

In previous chapters, we advised against modifying the default policy. We mentioned that the only occasion where you might want to change the default policy was in a bootstrap situation where you might want to deploy vCenter when there was only a single node in the VSAN cluster. Now we discuss one other possible reason for editing the default policy. If customers want to use a different policy for the virtual desktops disks deployed via Horizon View 5.3.1, the only way to do this is to modify the default policy. This can only be done via the vSphere command-line interface (ESXCLI), as detailed in VMware KB article 2073795 (http://kb.vmware.com/kb/2073795).

In a future release of VMware Horizon View, we expect to see a way to create custom, configurable policies for each of the virtual desktop storage objects; however, this is not possible in the Horizon View 5.3.1 release.

View Configuration

When setting up a desktop pool in VMware View, there is no difference to how you typically set up any other pool. It is only when you get to the point where a datastore is selected that you select VSAN. Here a datastore must be chosen for the link clones in this desktop pool. In Figure 8-9, we have chosen the VSAN datastore.

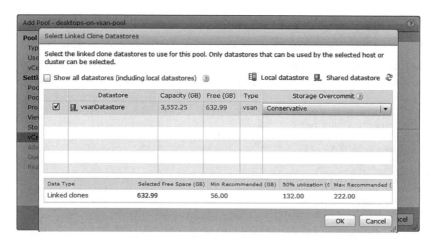

Figure 8-9   Use the vsanDatastore for linked clones.

When the desktop pool is created, we can now return to the vSphere Web Client to examine the deployed desktops.

First, it should be pointed out that desktop pools based on linked clones use a VM snapshot to create a replica object for linked clones. If the original VM (and snapshot delta) has a VM storage policy, the replica also has this policy associated with it. However, because the VM storage policies are not directly manageable in Horizon View version 5.3.1, the recommendation is to use default policies for everything, including the VM that will be used as the virtual desktop image. Figure 8-10 shows a replica object's VM storage policy, which is not using the default of None, but actually has a policy called FTT=1 associated with it.

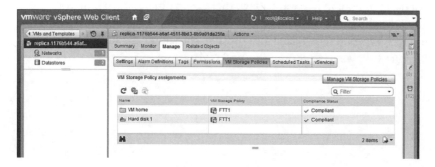

Figure 8-10   The replica inherits the VM storage policy from the original VM.

Now let's turn our attention to the desktops. Each desktop has four hard disks, each of which uses the default policy. The four hard disks are as follows:

1. OS disk that is cloned from the replica.

2. The user data disk or persistent disk (UDD for short) that holds Windows profiles so that they are not affected by View Composer operations such as refresh, recompose, and rebalance.

3. Internal disk that stores the computer account password to ensure connectivity to the domain when a desktop is refreshed. In addition, the configuration for Quickprep and Sysprep are stored in this disk.

4. The system disposable disk (SDD for short) that holds the Windows page files and temporary files (a nonpersistent disk that will be automatically deleted when a user's session ends).

By navigating to the VM storage policies in the vSphere Web Client, you can examine the VM storage policy of each desktop, as shown in Figure 8-11.

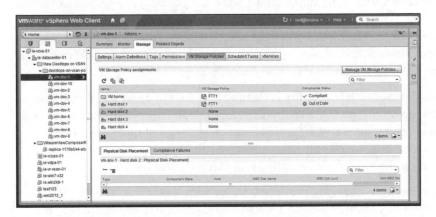

Figure 8-11   Desktop hard disks leverage the default VM storage policy.

Note that the default policy doesn't show up; it simply appears as None; however, if you examine any of the disks, you see the number of failures to tolerate attribute displayed as a RAID-1 configuration. In this case, hard disk 4 is displayed, as shown in Figure 8-12.

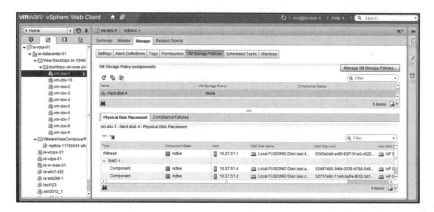

Figure 8-12   Default VM storage policy, shown as None, shows RAID-1 configuration

Changing the Default Policy

You have seen that with View 5.3.1 running on VSAN, it is "default" VSAN policies across the board. The base VM and associated snapshot should be deployed on the VSAN datastore with a default policy. The replica, when created, will inherit this default policy and thus the set of disks created for a desktop (OS disk, internal disk, persistent disk, disposable disk, checkpoint disk) will all inherit this same default policy.

The only way to change the default policy is via the ESXCLI, but again you should consider the fact that if you change the default policy, for example, reserve 10 percent of flash read cache, you are going to reserve 10 percent read cache for all of those disk objects, including the internal disk, which only has account info and Sysprep info. You might be better off allowing cache to be shared equally by all objects in this case.

So, keep this in mind when changing the default policy with View 5.3.1. We understand that a future version of VMware Horizon View will offer much greater control over the policies for each of the different desktop storage objects.

Other View Considerations

VSAN is compatible with the View Storage Accelerator/Content Based Read Cache (CBRC) feature of VMware View. VSAN provides one I/O caching layer and the View Storage Accelerator feature provides another content-based cache layer. The purpose of the View Storage Accelerator is to reduce input/output operations per second (IOPS) and to improve performance during boot storms.

Another consideration is that Horizon View and VSAN eliminate the need for the replica tiering feature provided by Horizon View. VSAN addresses the read caching requirements through the SSD layer, thus eliminating the need for replica tiering functionality in View. In fact, there is no support for replica tiering with View 5.3.1 when VSAN is the target datastore for desktop deployments.

One final consideration is that the SE Sparse Disk format is not supported on the VSAN datastore; therefore, only desktops deployed as full clones or as linked clones using the vmfsSparse format (also known as redo log format) are supported.

vCenter Operations

vCenter Operations version 5.8 (released on December 10, 2013) supports VSAN and can be used to examine some characteristics of the VSAN datastore. This version of vCenter Operations will treat the VSAN datastore just like any other traditional SAN or NAS datastore. One nice feature of vCenter Operations is its datastore relationship view. Here you can view all of the ESXi hosts and all of the VMs that are leveraging the VSAN datastore, as shown in Figure 8-13.

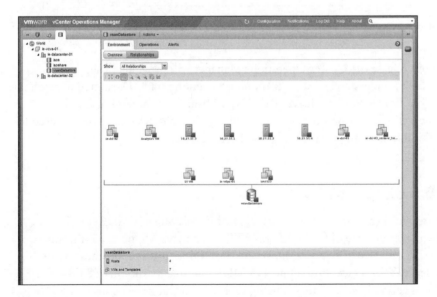

Figure 8-13   vCenter Operations 5.8 and VSAN datastore relationships view

As you might expect, however, not all the statistics from a regular datastore are visible for a VSAN datastore. In fact, vCenter Operations version 5.8, when used to examine a VSAN datastore, reports only capacity information, as shown in Figure 8-14. No disk I/O or workload metrics are reported. This is because these statistics are not surfaced up into vCenter Server in this initial release of VSAN, and thus are not consumable by vCenter Operations Manager.

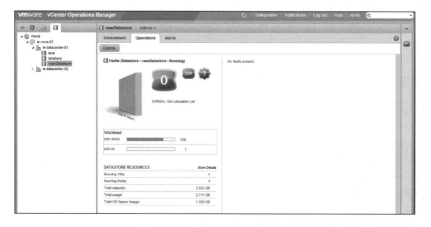

Figure 8-14   vCenter Operations Manager 5.8 reports only some VSAN datastore information.

A projected future release of vCenter Operations Manager will provide full support for VSAN and be able to understand all the VSAN objects, unique stats, distributed natures, content, and so on. For the initial release of VSAN, VMware recommends using the VSAN Observer utility that is part of the Ruby vSphere Console (RVC). This is covered in Chapter 10, "Troubleshooting, Monitoring, and Performance."

vSphere 5.5 62TB VMDK

vSphere 5.5 introduced support for larger virtual machine disk files (VMDKs). Prior to this release, the maximum size of a VMDK was 2TB – 512 bytes. vSphere 5.5 introduced support for VMDKs up to 62TB in size; however, VSAN does not support these new sizes in the initial release. VSAN currently supports VMDKs up to a maximum of 2TB – 512 bytes only. This is certainly an area that is being looked at for future versions of VSAN.

Fault Tolerance

There is no support for fault-tolerant VMs on VSAN in the initial release.

Stretched/vSphere Metro Storage Cluster

There is no support for stretched clusters or vSphere Metro Storage Cluster (vMSC) on VSAN in the initial release. We understand there are a number of requests for this functionality and believe that the VMware team is looking closely at this feature and the hope is that this can be supported in a future release.

PowerCLI

There is PowerCLI support for VSAN in the initial release. Support is provided via a PowerCLI for VSAN fling that is available on flings.vmware.com. Refer to Chapter 10 for more information on PowerCLI support and some guidance on how to use some of the PowerCLI cmdlets.

C# Client

The vSphere Web Client can only manage VSAN; the C# client cannot. This is true for many other new vSphere products and features. A VSAN cluster cannot be configured or managed via the older C# (thick) client; it can only be successfully configured and managed from the Web Client. VMware does not support the C# client for VSAN functionality.

vCloud Automation Service

vCloud Automation Service (vCAC) provides for centralized provisioning and management of vSphere infrastructures. From a VSAN integration standpoint, vCAC 6.0.1 can leverage the VSAN datastore, but any VMs deployed through vCAC will be deployed with a default VM storage policy. Changing the policies to specific VM requirements will have to be done outside of vCAC. Figure 8-15 shows the VMware product interoperability matrix for VSAN with vCAC.

Discussing how to integrate vCAC and VSAN is beyond the scope of this book; however, one of our VMware colleagues, Jad El-Zein, has written a very informative blog post that details what is achievable with the 6.0 release of vCAC and VM storage policies on top of VSAN. You can find that blog post at http://www.virtualjad.com/2014/03/using-vsan-storage-policies-in-vcloud.html.

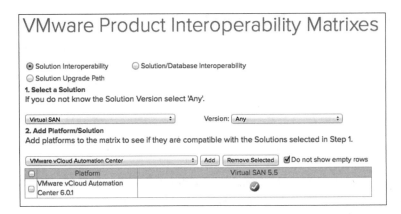

Figure 8-15   VSAN and vCloud automation center interoperability

Host Profiles

VSAN supports the Host Profiles feature. With host profiles, you can configure the first host that you plan to add to the VSAN cluster, take its host profile, and then use that configuration and apply it to the rest of the ESXi hosts that you plan on adding to the VSAN cluster. This can prove very useful if you are planning to build 8-node, 16-node, or even 32-node clusters. Figure 8-16 shows host profiles being used with hosts in a VSAN cluster.

Figure 8-16   VSAN and host profiles interoperability

Auto-Deploy

Auto-deploy, a mechanism for automating the deployment of ESXi hosts and which leverages host profiles extensively, is not supported with VSAN in this release.

Raw Device Mappings

There is no support for Raw Device Mappings (RDMs) on VSAN in this release.

vSphere Storage APIs for Array Integration

The vSphere Storage APIs for Array Integration (VAAI) are a set of API calls that can be used to offload certain common storage tasks to the storage array and free up resources on the ESXi hosts that would typically be consumed when doing these tasks. Typical offload tasks are zeroing blocks and clone operations. VAAI is not supported on VSAN in the initial release. If you navigate to the VSAN datastore, under the Manage tab, and under General, you will observe under Datastore Capabilities that Hardware Acceleration is shown as Not Supported on any host, as shown in Figure 8-17.

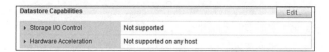

Figure 8-17   VAAI not supported on VSAN

Microsoft Clustering Services

Microsoft Clustering Services (MSCS) is not supported on top of VSAN. The main reason for this, as you have seen, is that there is no support for physical mode RDMs, which is a requirement for implementing MSCS nodes in VMs across ESXi hosts.

Summary

As stated earlier, VMware has a vast portfolio of software products and features and continues to release new products and features on a regular basis. Although we have tried to cover as many products and features as possible that we believe would be of most interest to you, there will be cases where interoperability between VSAN and a given product is not included. We would like to refer you to the official VMware documentation as the source of the most updated and accurate information. Because supportability and interoperability will no doubt change over time, we highly recommend reviewing the VMware documentation when upgrading existing environments.

Chapter 9

Designing a VSAN Cluster

This chapter walks you through all the steps required to enable you to design your perfect VSAN cluster. We will leverage all the insights provided throughout the various chapters to ensure that your VSAN cluster will meet your technical and business requirements. We do want to point out before we go through the various exercises that the *VMware Compatibility Guide* (VCG) contains a list of predefined configurations that are called VSAN Ready Nodes. If you are not interested in configuring your own server and selecting each hardware component by yourself, a VSAN Ready Node configuration by one of the currently listed hardware vendors (at the time of this writing, Cisco, IBM, Supermicro, and Dell) could be a great alternative.

Before running through three design exercises, we would like to discuss some constraints of VSAN 1.0.

Sizing Constraints

With VSAN 1.0, some constraints need to be taken into consideration when designing an environment. Some are straightforward, others are less obvious. A summary of the constraints of VSAN 1.0 is as follows:

- Maximum of 32 hosts per cluster
- Maximum of 100 virtual machines (VMs) per host
- Maximum of 3,200 VMs per cluster
- Maximum of 2,048 vSphere High Availability (HA) protected VMs on a VSAN datastore

- Maximum of 5 disk groups

- Maximum of 7 disks per disk group

- One flash device per disk group

- Maximum of 3,000 components per host

As said, the majority of these are straightforward. There are three worth explaining further:

- The maximum number of vSphere HA protected VMs on a VSAN datastore

- Number of hosts in a cluster

- The maximum number of components

The maximum number of vSphere HA protected VMs on a VSAN datastore is 2,048. This is not just a VSAN datastore limitation, but also applies to Virtual Machine File System (VMFS)- and Network File System (NFS)-based datastores. Note that there is no hard stop while powering on new VMs; when additional VMs above the limit of 2048 are powered-on on a VSAN datastore, these VMs will not be protected by vSphere HA.

The reason for this constraint is the so-called vSphere HA "power-on list" and the way HA is limited internally because of this. This list tracks all the VMs and their power state. This file has 2,048 slots to register VMs. When the number of slots is exceeded, any additional VM that is powered on cannot be registered and as such is not protected by vSphere HA.

The second thing that is worth mentioning is that in order to scale up from 16 hosts to 32 hosts, an advanced setting needs to be set on each of the ESXi hosts in the cluster. This option was disabled by default as in order to scale up to 32 hosts, VSAN requires an additional 150MB of memory per host. Note that a reboot is required for this setting to take effect. For more details we like to refer to KB article http://kb.vmware.com/kb/2073930. In short, on each host you will need to set the advanced setting through the user interface (UI) or through the command-line interface (CLI) as follows:

```
esxcli system settings advanced list -o /CMMDS/goto11
```

The third constraint that is worth discussing is the maximum number of components. The maximum number of components in VSAN 1.0 is 3,000 per host. Various types of objects may be found on the VSAN datastore that contain one or more components:

- VM namespace

- VM swap

- VM disk

- Virtual disk snapshot

As you are no doubt aware at this stage in the book, each VM has a namespace, a swap file, and typically a disk. It is important to understand that the number of failures to tolerate (FTT) plays a critical role as well when it comes to the number of components. The higher you configure FTT, the more components certain objects will have. Meaning that when you configured FTT to 1, this means your disk object will have two mirrors (or in other words, two components). This applies also to the stripe width. If it is increased to larger than 1, the number of components will also go up. Therefore, if a virtual machine disk (VMDK) object is striped across two disks, you will have two components. On top of that, the maximum size of a component is 256GB, meaning that if you have a 512GB virtual disk object, the object is configured with two 256GB components. This is important to realize when it comes to scaling and sizing.

Let's run through an exercise to show what the impact could be when changing the storage policies.

Failures to Tolerate = 1, Stripe Width = 1

This means that the minimal components count for each VM is six; however, if a VM is configured with two disks, the total component count is eight. If a snapshot gets created on that VM, the component count increases by another two per disk, resulting in 12 in total:

- 1 × VM namespace object = 2 components for resiliency

- 1 × VM swap object = 2 components for resiliency

- 2 × VM disk object = 4 components for resiliency

- 2 × VM snapshot file object for each disk = 4 components for resiliency

As demonstrated, the component count can go up quickly. If you want to run 100 VMs on a host with each VM having 5 disks and 5 VM snapshots while using a standard policy (number of failures to tolerate = 1), the component count will be as follows:

- 100 × VM namespace objects = 100 × 2 components = 200

- 100 × VM swap objects = 100 × 2 components = 200

- 100 × 5 VM disk objects = 500 × 2 components = 1,000

- 100 × 5 snapshot objects of each of the 5 VM disk objects =
  5 × 500 × 2 components = 5,000

As you can see, this results in more than 6,000 components, with "only" 5 disks and 5 snapshots. You may wonder whether it is possible to validate the current component count. In Chapter 10, "Troubleshooting, Monitoring, and Performance," you learn how to verify this using Ruby vSphere Console (RVC).

We will not run though this exercise for each of the following three scenarios, as we expect that the majority of environments will not come close, but we do believe that it is important to understand these constraints.

Flash to Magnetic Disk Ratio

During the beta of VSAN, the recommendation from VMware was a 10 percent ratio of flash versus magnetic disks from a capacity point of view. This recommendation has been changed over time and is now as follows:

> The general recommendation for sizing Virtual SAN's flash capacity is to have 10 percent of the anticipated consumed storage capacity before the number of failures to tolerate is considered.

Let's run through a short scenario to explain the impact. Let's assume we have the following in our environment:

- 100 VMs

- 50GB per VM

- 50 percent of VMDK consumed projected

With the old recommendation, this meant we suggested 10 percent of 100 VMs × 50GB × 2 (FTT=1) = 1000GB of flash capacity. Note that the consumed storage is not taken into consideration and we look at the total capacity including mirror objects. With the new recommendation, however, it means we suggest 10 percent of 100 VMs × (50 percent of 50GB) = 250GB of flash capacity. In this case, we do not take mirrors into account and on top of that take consumed disk space into account.

Let's assume we use the minimal number of hosts required, which is three. That means we need 330GB of flash capacity per host (1000GB / 3 hosts) in the old scenario. With the new formula, we would need only 85GB of flash capacity per host in a three-host cluster (250GB / 85GB). This, of course, will have its impact on performance, with less read cache and less write buffer capacity. Keep in mind that there is a 70/30 split between read cache and write buffering. What is the result of this changed recommendation exactly?

- 59.5GB versus 231GB read cache

- 25.5GB versus 99GB write buffer

In the exercises to come, we will use the "10 percent of anticipated consumed capacity" rule.

Designing for Performance

One critical aspect when designing a VSAN infrastructure is, of course, the performance aspect. During the various scenarios described in the examples that follow, our focus is on capacity sizing and partly performance. Where we talk about performance, we discuss the number of IOPS provided by magnetic disks, but not the numbers of input/output operations per second (IOPS) provided by flash.

As you have learned throughout the book by this point, VSAN heavily leans on flash devices to provide the required performance capabilities. Flash is leveraged both as a read cache and as a write buffer. Therefore, incorrectly sizing your flash capacity can have a great impact on your workload as shown in the previous section. The difference between a 59.5GB read cache or a 231GB read cache for 33 VMs is huge. Having ~ 1.8GB or 7GB per VM available does make a difference in terms of reducing the need to resort to magnetic disk. Not only will the size of the flash device make a difference to your VMs, so will the type of flash used.

At the end of the day, all the best practices mentioned are recommendations, and these will apply to the majority of environments; however, your environment may differ. You may have more demanding applications. What truly matters is the aggregate active (hot) data set of the applications executing in the cluster. In practice, you will have to estimate that. Unfortunately, at the time of this writing, no tools are available to help you with this; however, VMware is building tools that will be able to provide you with a more precise sizing of the cluster's flash requirements.

Chapter 2, "VSAN Prerequisites and Requirements for Deployment," listed the categories of flash devices that VMware uses to provide an idea around potential performance that can be achieved when using such a device.

The list of the designated flash device classes specified within the *VMware Compatibility Guide* is as follows:

- **Class A**: 2,500 to 5,000 writes per second

- **Class B**: 5,000 to 10,000 writes per second

- **Class C**: 10,000 to 20,000 writes per second

- **Class D**: 20,000 to 30,000 writes per second

- **Class E**: 30,000+ writes per second

Just to demonstrate the difference between the various devices, we will list the theoretical performance capabilities of some of the devices in the described classes:

- **FusionIO ioDrive2 800GB, 230k Random Write IOPS, 215k Random Read IOPS— using 4K blocks** (http://www.fusionio.com/data-sheets/iodrive2)

- **Intel S3700, 800GB, 36k Random Write IOPS, 75k Random Read IOPS— using 4K blocks** (http://www.intel.com/content/www/us/en/solid-state-drives/ solid-state-drives-dc-s3700-series.html)

- **Samsung SM1625 800GB, 23k Random Write IOPS, 100k Random Read IOPS— using 4K blocks** (http://www.samsung.com/global/business/semiconductor/ news-events/press-releases/detail?newsId=12244)

Now if you would have 400 VMs on four hosts, using a FusionIO flash card versus an Intel S3700 drive could make a substantial difference. Just imagine you have 2,000 VMs on 16 hosts. Of course, the price tag on these two examples also significantly varies, but it is a consideration that needs to be taken into account.

Impact of the Disk Controller

A question that often arises is what the impact of the disk controller queue depth is on performance of your VSAN environment. Considering the different layers of queuing involved, it probably makes the most sense to show the picture from VM down to the device, as illustrated in Figure 9-1.

Figure 9-1 shows that there are six different layers at which some form of queuing is done, although in reality there are even more buffers and queues (but we tried to keep it reasonably simple and depict the layers that potentially could be a bottleneck). Within the guest, the vSCSI adapter has a queue. Then the next layer is VSAN, which, of course, has its own queue and manages the I/O. Next the I/O flows through the multi-pathing layer to the various devices on the host. On the next level, a disk controller has a queue; potentially (depending on the controller used), each disk controller port has a queue. Last but not least, of course, each device (that is, disk) will have a queue.

If you look closely at Figure 9-1, you see that I/O of many VMs will all flow through the same disk controller and that this I/O will go to or come from one or multiple devices (usually multiple devices). This also implies that the first real potential "choking point" is the queue depth of the disk controller.

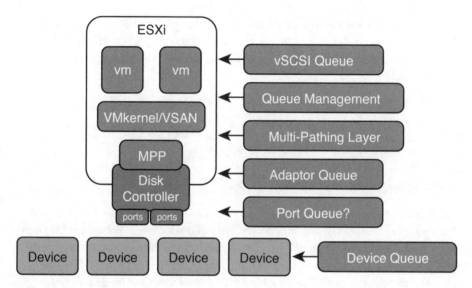

Figure 9-1 Different queuing layers

Assume you have 4 SATA disks, each of which has a queue depth of 32. Total combined, this means that in parallel you can handle 128 I/Os. Now what if your disk controller can handle only 64? This will result in 64 I/Os being held back by the VMkernel/VSAN. As you can see, it would be beneficial in this scenario to ensure that your disk controller queue can hold the same number of I/Os (or more) as your device queue can hold, allowing for VSAN to shape the queue anyway it prefers without being constrained by the disk controller itself.

When it comes to disk controllers, a huge difference exists in maximum queue depth value between vendors, and even between models of the same vendor. Just for educational purposes, Table 9-1 lists five popular disk controllers and their queue depth to show what the impact can be when making an "uneducated" decision.

Table 9-1 Disk Controller Queue Depth

Manufacturer	Disk Controller	Queue Depth
Dell	PERC H710 Adapter	975
HP	Smart Array P420i	1,020
Intel	C602 AHCI (Patsburg)	31 (per port)
LSI	2008	25
LSI	2308	600

For VSAN, it is recommended to ensure that the disk controller has a queue depth of at least 256. Now the disk controller is just one part of the equation, because there is also the device queue. We have looked at various controllers and devices, and here are the typical standards you will find:

```
mpt2sas_raid_queue_depth: int
    Max RAID Device Queue Depth (default=128)
mpt2sas_sata_queue_depth: int
    Max SATA Device Queue Depth (default=32)
mpt2sas_sas_queue_depth: int
    Max SAS Device Queue Depth (default=254)
```

We have highlighted the important parts here. As you can see, the controller in this case has three different queue depths depending on the type of device used. When a RAID configuration is created, the queue depth will be 128. When a SAS drive is directly attached, often referred to as VSAN SAS or pass-through, the queue depth will be 254. The one that stands out the most is the queue depth of the SATA device; this is by default only 32, and you can imagine this can once again become a choking point. However, fortunately, the shallow queue depth of SATA can easily be overcome by using NL-SAS drives (nearline serially attached SCSI) instead, which has a much deeper queue depth.

You can validate the queue depth of your controller using `esxcfg-info -s | grep "==+SCSI Interface" -A 18` as it will display a lot of information related to your SCSI interfaces including the queue depth.

Note that even the firmware and driver used can have an impact on the queue depth of your controller and devices. We highly recommend using the driver listed on the *VSAN Compatibility Guide* (http://www.vmware.com/resources/compatibility/search.php?deviceCategory=vsan) shown on the details page of a specific disk controller, as shown in Figure 9-2. In some cases, it has been witnessed that the queue depth increased from 25 to 600 after a driver update. As you can imagine, this can greatly impact performance.

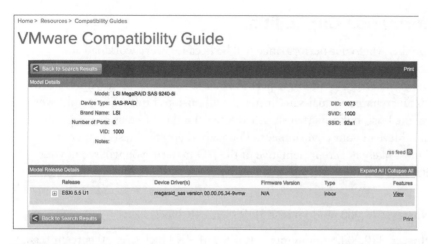

Figure 9-2 Device driver details

The question now that usually arises is this: What about NL-SAS versus SATA drives? Because NL-SAS drives are essentially SATA drives with a SAS connector, what are the benefits? NL-SAS drives come with the following benefits:

- Dual ports allowing redundant paths

- Ability to connect a device to multiple computers

- Full SCSI command set

- Faster interface compared to SATA, up to 20 percent, no STP (Serial ATA Tunneling Protocol) overhead

- Deeper command queue (depth)

From a cost perspective, the difference between NL-SAS and SATA is for most vendors negligible. For a 4TB drive, the cost difference on different websites at the time of this writing was on average $30. Considering the benefits, it is highly recommended to use NL-SAS over SATA for VSAN.

After reading this section, it should be clear that the disk controller is a critical component of any VSAN design because it can have an impact on how VSAN performs (and not just the disk controller, but even the firmware and device driver used). When deploying VSAN, it is highly recommended to ensure the driver installed is the version recommended in the *VSAN Compatibility Guide*, or upgrade to the latest version as needed.

VSAN Performance Capabilities

It is difficult to predict what your performance will be because every workload and every combination of hardware will provide different results. After the VSAN launch, VMware announced the results of multiple performance tests (http://blogs.vmware.com/vsphere/2014/03/supercharge-virtual-san-cluster-2-million-iops.html). The results were impressive, to say the least, but note that these exercises should not be used as a guarantee for what you can achieve in your environment. These are theoretical tests that are not necessarily (and most likely not) representative of the I/O patterns you will see in your own environment (and so results will vary). Nevertheless, we believe that the data is worth sharing:

- **16-host cluster**: 920,000 random read IOPS with 4K block size

- **16-host cluster**: 320,000 random mixed IOPS with 4K block size (70 percent read, 30 percent write)

- **32-host cluster**: 640,000 random mixed IOPS with 4K block size (70 percent read, 30 percent write)

- **32-host cluster**: 2 million random read IOPS with 4K block size

It proves that VSAN is capable of delivering a high-performance environment; however, the cost at which this comes is important to know. The configuration used to reach these numbers is as follows per host:

- Dell PowerEdge R720

- Dual Socket Host with eight-core Intel E5 2650 v2 2.6GHz processor

- 128GB memory (8 × 16GB DIMMs)

- 1 × Intel S3700 400GB

- 7 × 10K RPM 1.1 TB SAS magnetic disks

- LSI 9207-8i disk controller

- Intel 82599EB 10GbE

Some tweaks were done to optimize the environment for large-scale workloads with high outstanding I/O and to scale to 32 hosts. The following list describes these changes:

- Allowed VSAN to form 32-host clusters (advanced setting: /adv/CMMDS/goto11).

- The heap size for the vSphere network stack was increased to 512MB (advanced setting: /adv/Net/TcpipHeapMax).

- The boot time parameters for VMware Paravirtual SCSI (PVSCSI) to better support large-scale workloads with high outstanding I/O: `"vmw_pvscsi.cmd_per_lun=254 vmw_pvscsi.ring_pages=32"`. (PVSCSI adapters are virtual high-performance storage adapters that can result in greater throughput and lower CPU utilization.)

- All power-saving features were disabled.

- A single VSAN VMkernel port was used per host, with a dedicated 10GbE uplink.

Note that all performance tests and reference architectures by VMware that are publicly available have been done with 10GbE networking configurations. For our design scenarios, we will use 10GbE as the golden standard because it is heavily recommended by VMware and increases throughput and lowers latency. Different configuration options for networking, including the use of Network I/O Control, are discussed in Chapter 3, "VSAN Installation and Configuration."

VMware View Performance

Besides running through theoretic maximal performance capability, VMware has validated VSAN performance using View Planner and various cluster configurations ranging from 3 hosts up to 16 hosts. In this test, VSAN performance was compared to the performance of an all-flash array, and the number of desktops that could be run on the same number of hosts is compared to show the overhead of VSAN compared to that of hosts not running VSAN but connected to an external (all-flash) storage system:

> The host running the desktop VMs has 16 Intel Xeon E5-2690 cores running @ 2.9GHz. The host has 256GB physical RAM, which is more than sufficient to run 100 1GB Windows 7 VMs. For VSAN, each host has two disk groups where each disk group has one PCI-e solid-state drive (SSD) of 200GB and six 300GB 15k RPM SAS disks.

The View Planner benchmark results for a 3-host VSAN cluster was 305 desktops, 803 desktops on an 8-host cluster, and 1,615 desktops for a 16-host cluster, which shows that VSAN can scale linearly without a decline in response time. It is good to understand that compared to an all-flash array, VSAN did not introduce a significant overhead. On the same 8-host cluster using an all-flash array, the total number of desktops was 805, just 2 desktops more than on the VSAN-enabled cluster, which is negligible in our opinion.

More importantly, even when it comes to response times, VSAN is close to what an all-flash array offers, as shown in Figure 9-3. All-flash arrays, however, come at a much higher price. According to VMware, the VSAN configuration used comes in at around 25 percent of the cost of the all-flash array.

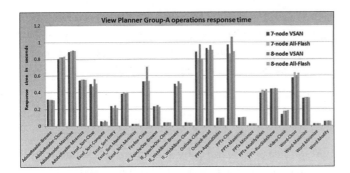

Figure 9-3   View operations response time

You can learn more about these tests on the VMware website:

- **VDI Benchmarking Using View Planner on VMware Virtual SAN Beta – Part 1**
  http://blogs.vmware.com/performance/2013/10/vdi-benchmarking-using-view-planner-on-vmware-virtual-san-vsan.html

- **VDI Benchmarking Using View Planner on VMware Virtual SAN Beta – Part 2**
  http://blogs.vmware.com/performance/2013/11/vdi-benchmarking-using-view-planner-on-vmware-virtual-san-part-2.html

- **VDI Benchmarking Using View Planner on VMware Virtual SAN Beta – Part 3**
  http://blogs.vmware.com/performance/2013/11/vdi-benchmarking-using-view-planner-on-vmware-virtual-san-part-3.html

- **VDI Benchmarking Using View Planner on VMware Virtual SAN GA (vSphere 5.5 U1)** http://blogs.vmware.com/performance/2014/03/vdi-performance-benchmarking-vmware-virtual-san-5-5.html

Now that we have looked at the constraints and some of the performance aspects, let's take a look at how we would design a VSAN cluster from a capacity point of view.

Design and Sizing Tools

Before we look at our first design, we would like to point you to various tools that can help with designing and sizing your VSAN infrastructure. The scenarios provided in this chapter were all developed using the VSAN Calculator, which you can find on http://vmwa.re/vsancalc. However, this calculator is not an official tool, but at the time of writing this chapter the only available solution.

VMware has since announced an official online calculator available through http://virtualsansizing.vmware.com, which is shown in Figure 9-4.

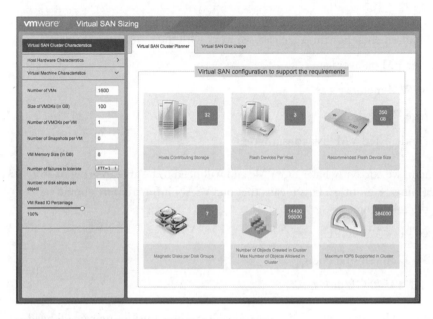

Figure 9-4   Official VMware VSAN sizing calculator

This official VMware VSAN sizing calculator enables you to create a design based on certain parameters such as the following:

- Number of VMs

- Size of VM disks (VMDKs)

- Number of VMDKs

- Number of snapshots

- Read versus write I/O ratio

We highly recommend that you use these tools to validate your design scenarios and decisions to ensure optimal performance and availability for your workloads, with virtualsansizing.vmware.com being the preferred solution as the official VMware-supported sizing calculator.

Scenario 1: Where to Start

When designing a VSAN environment, it is of great importance to understand the requirements of your VMs. The various examples here show what the impact can be of certain decisions you will need to make during this journey. As with any design, it starts with gathering requirements. For this scenario, we work with the following parameters:

- 1.5 vCPU per VM on average

- 5GB average VM memory size

- 54GB average VM disk size

- 50 percent anticipated VM disk consumption

In the environment, we currently have 173 VMs and will need to be able to grow to 250 VMs in the upcoming 18 months. This means that our VSAN infrastructure should be able to provide the following:

- 250 × 1.5 vCPU = 375 vCPUs

- 250 × 5GB = 1250 GB of memory

- 250 × 54GB = 13500 GB disk space

We will take the vCPU-to-core ratio of 5:1 into consideration. Considering we will need to be able to run 375 vCPUs, we will divide that by 5, resulting in the need for 75 cores.

Now let's look at the storage requirements a bit more in depth. Before we can calculate the requirements, we need to know what level of resiliency will be taken into account for these VMs. For our calculations, we will take a number of failures to tolerate setting of 1 into account. We also add an additional 10 percent disk space to cater for metadata and the occasional snapshot. If more disk space is required for snapshots for your environment, do not forget to factor this in when you run through this exercise.

The formula we will use taking the preceding parameters into account looks like the following:

(((Number of VMs * Avg VM size) + (Number of VMs * Avg mem size)) * FTT+1) + 10% slack space

We have included the average memory size because each VM will create a swap file on disk that is equal to the size of the VM memory configuration. Using our industry standard averages mentioned previously, this results in the following:

(((250 * 54) + (250 * 5)) * 2) = (13,500 + 1250) * 2 = 29500GB + 10% = 32450GB

Divide the outcome by 1,024 and round it up; a total combined storage capacity of 32TB is the outcome. Now that we know we need 32TB of disk capacity, 1250GB of memory and 75 cores, let's explore the hardware configuration.

Determining Your Host Configuration

We will start with exploring the most common scenario, a 2U host. For this scenario, we have decided to select the Dell R720XD, which is depicted in Figure 9-5. This server has been optimized for storage capacity and can be selected with either a 12 × 3.5-inch drive or 24 × 2.5-inch drive. The Dell R720XD is a dual-socket server and can hold up to 768GB of memory. The dual-socket can be configured with anything ranging from a 4-core to 12-core CPU. You can find more details on the Dell R720XD at http://www.dell.com/us/business/p/poweredge-r720xd/pd.

Figure 9-5   Dell R720XD server

Our requirements for the environment are as follows:

- 3 hosts minimum (according to VSAN)

- 32TB of raw disk capacity

- 75 CPU cores

- 1250GB of memory

- Minimal overcommitment in failure scenarios ($N + 1$ for high availability [HA])

As stated, the Dell R720XD can hold 12 cores per socket, at most resulting in a total of 24 cores per host in a dual-socket configuration. This means that from a CPU perspective, we will need roughly three hosts. However, because we have a requirement to avoid overcommitment in a failure scenario, we need a minimum of four hosts. From a memory perspective, each host can be provisioned with 768GB of memory. Considering we require 1250GB of memory, we could suffice with two hosts when it comes to memory. Because we need to take minimal overcommitment into consideration and optimal memory configurations, 512GB per host is what has been decided on.

Of course, price is always a consideration, and we urge you to compare prices based on CPU, memory, and disk configurations. We will not take pricing into account in this scenario, considering the ever-changing prices for compute components. In this scenario, we will go with *four hosts* because this is the maximum required from a CPU and memory point of view, and we will cater the disk design based on this outcome.

Storage sizing is a bit more delicate. Let's look at our options here. We know we need 32TB of storage, and we know that three hosts is the minimum number of hosts a VSAN cluster requires. Considering we have the option to go with either 3.5-inch drives or 2.5-inch drives, we will have a maximum of 96 × 2.5-inch drive slots or 48 × 3.5-inch drive slots total combined for our four hosts at our disposal. As each group of disks (seven at most) will require one flash device, this should be taken into account when deciding the type of disk.

One critical factor to consider is the number of IOPS provided by both magnetic disks and flash devices. Typical 3.5-inch 7200 RPM SATA drives can deliver roughly 80 IOPS, whereas a 2.5-inch 10K RPM SAS drive can deliver 150 IOPS. (IOPS numbers are taken from http://www.techrepublic.com/blog/the-enterprise-cloud/calculate-iops-in-a-storage-array/2182/#.) From a capacity perspective, SATA drives range from 1TB up to 4TB, whereas SAS drives are limited today to 1.2TB. We know we require 32TB, so let's do some quick math to show the potential impact a decision like this can have. We will use the extreme sides of the spectrum to show the largest contrast, meaning a large-capacity, slow SATA drive versus a small-capacity, relatively fast SAS drive:

- 32TB / 4TB = ~ 8 SATA magnetic disks = 640 IOPS from SATA-based magnetic disks.

- 32TB / 0.6TB = ~ 54 SAS magnetic disks = 8100 IOPS SAS-based from magnetic disks.

As you can see, a huge difference exists between the two extreme examples provided. Although VSAN has been designed to leverage your flash device as the primary provider of performance, it is an important design consideration because these IOPS are used when data needs to be destaged to magnetic disks or when a read cache miss occurs and the data block has to be retrieved from magnetic disk. In this scenario, we have decided to use SAS drives to provide a decent performance even when data does not reside in cache. The question that then comes up is why not use a 1.2TB drive for this configuration? The answer is simple as not every hardware vendor has the 1.2TB in its catalog available and the price is still relatively high. Let's do the math. In total, as described earlier, we need 54 × 600GB SAS drives across 4 hosts. This results in a total of 14 drives per host.

To ensure that our VSAN cluster provides an optimal user experience, we will use the rule of thumb of 10 percent flash of anticipated consumed VM disk capacity. In our scenario, we will have a maximum of 250 VMs. These VMs have a virtual disk capacity of 54GB, of which it is anticipated that 50 percent will be actually consumed. This results in the following recommendation from a flash capacity point of view:

10% of (250 VMs * (50% anticipated consumed of 54GB)) = 675GB

Considering we will require 4 hosts, this means it is recommended to have 675GB / 4 = ~169GB of flash capacity in each host. Note that in our configuration we are required to have a minimum of 2 disk groups per host, as a disk group has a maximum of 7 magnetic disks, and we have 14 drives in total per host. Each disk group will also need to have its own flash device. Using the *VMware Compatibility Guide*, we have determined that, for our Dell configuration, we could leverage the following flash devices when taking a performance requirement of a minimum of 20,000 writes per second. (Class D and E qualify for this.) The options we have at our disposal currently are as follows:

- 200GB SSD SAS Write Intensive (WI) 6Gbps 2.5in
- 400GB SSD SAS Write Intensive (WI) 6Gbps 2.5in

To provide 170GB of flash capacity per host, we need one 200GB flash device per host.

The final outstanding item is the disk controller. VMware recommends using a pass-through controller, and Dell offers two variants for the R720XD: the H310 and the H710P. The H310 is a standard pass-through controller. The H710P offers advanced functionality such as caching, self-encrypting drives, and other functionality. Considering VSAN provides its own caching logic, we've decided to go with the H310.

The final configuration is four Dell R720XD (2.5-inch drive slot) hosts consisting of the following:

- Dual-socket — 12-core E5-2695
- 512GB memory
- Disk controller: Dell H310
- 14 × 600GB SAS 10K RPM
- 1 × 200GB SSD SAS (WI)

Scenario 2

In this scenario, we take a slightly different approach than we did in scenario 1. We use a different type of host hardware form factor, and we use different sizing and scaling input. For this scenario, we will work with the following parameters:

- 2 vCPU per VM on average

- 6GB average VM memory size

- 40GB average VM disk size

- 100 percent anticipated consumed VM disk capacity

- Failures to tolerate = 2

In the environment, we currently have 80 VMs and need to be able to grow to 100 VMs in the upcoming 12 months. Therefore, our VSAN infrastructure should be able to provide the following:

- 100 × 2 vCPU = 200 vCPUs

- 100 × 6GB = 600GB of memory

- 100 × 40GB = 4000GB disk space

In our sizing exercise, we look at two different server platforms. Our VMs are not CPU intensive but rather memory intensive. We take a vCPU-to-core ratio of 8:1 into consideration. Considering that we will need to be able to run 200 vCPUs, we divide that by 8, resulting in the need for 25 cores.

Now let's look at the storage requirements a bit more in depth. Before we can calculate the requirements, we need to know what level of resiliency will be taken into account for these VMs. For our calculations, we will take once again a number of failures to tolerate setting of 1 into account, and we will also factor in the ability to rebuild storage objects upon failure. This ensures that after a failure of a host, our VMs will be fully protected, because spare disk capacity is available for this scenario. We will also add an additional 10 percent disk space to cater for metadata and the occasional snapshot.

The formula we will use taking the preceding parameters into account looks like the following:

((((Number of VMs * Avg VM size) + (Number of VMs * Avg mem size)) * FTT+1) + 10% slack space

We have included the average memory size because for each VM a swap file will be created on disk, which is the size of your memory configuration for that VM. Using our industry standard averages mentioned earlier, this results in the following:

((((100 * 40) + (100 * 6)) * 3) = (4000 + 600) * 3 = 13800 GB + 10% = 15180GB

Divide the outcome by 1,024 and round it up; a total combined storage capacity of 15TB is the outcome. Now that we know we need 15TB of disk capacity, 600GB of memory, and 25 cores, let's explore the hardware configuration.

Determining Your Host Configuration

For this scenario, we selected the Supermicro Twin Pro 2, shown in Figure 9-6. This server has a hyper-converged form factor, used by many of the current storage start-ups. It allows for four hosts in 2U each, with a max of 1TB of memory in a dual-socket configuration. It offers you 6 × 2.5-inch drive slots and dual 10GbE NIC ports per host.

Figure 9-6   Supermicro Twin Pro 2

Our requirements for the environment are as follows:

- 3 hosts minimum (according to VSAN)
- 15TB of raw disk capacity
- 25 CPU cores
- 600GB of memory
- Factor in rebuild disk capacity requirements

The Supermicro Twin Pro 2 comes with four nodes by default. In this exercise, we flip the capacity calculation upside down. Instead of calculating how many hosts we need based on the available capacity data, we calculate how much capacity each host needs.

From a CPU perspective, we divide the total number of required CPU cores by four, as we have four hosts in total. This results in 6.25 cores required per host. From a memory perspective, again the calculation is fairly straightforward: 600GB divided by 4 is 150GB at a minimum per host.

When it comes to storage sizing, we need to factor in rebuild disk capacity. We require a total of 15TB of raw disk capacity to ensure we can rebuild after a host has failed. We will divide 15TB by 3 hosts and equip all 4 hosts with 5TB because that will provide us with the additional capacity required to rebuild components and tolerate further failures when a failure has occurred. The Twin Pro 2 comes with 6 × 2.5-inch disk slots per host. When using an SSD disk, that leaves us with five disk slots for magnetic disks. To meet our required 5TB per host, that leaves us with one option for the disks:

> 1.2TB SAS 2.0 6.0Gbps 10000RPM

These 20 drives (5 drivers per host) will be able to produce roughly 3,000 IOPS.

To ensure our VSAN cluster provides an optimal user experience, we will use the rule of thumb of 10 percent flash capacity of anticipated VM disk capacity. In our scenario, we will have 100 VMs with 40GB each, of which we expect 100 percent to be consumed over time. This results in a recommendation of 400GB flash capacity, with hosts resulting in 100GB per host. Note that in our configuration we would only have one disk group per host because we do not exceed the disk group limitation of seven magnetic disks. Using the *VMware Compatibility Guide*, we have determined that our configuration could leverage the following flash device when taking a performance requirement of 30,000 writes per second (Class E qualifies for this) and a single disk slot constraint into account. The options we have at our disposal are limited, unfortunately, because the majority of high-performant devices only come in sizes of 200GB and up. Therefore, we have increased the maximum capacity to 200GB:

- Intel — S3700 200GB

- SanDisk SDLKOD6M-200G-BCA1 — 200GB

Each of the flash devices in the preceding list is more than capable of meeting our requirements.

The final outstanding item is the disk controller. The Supermicro comes with various types of disk controllers, of which the LSI 3008 provides pass-through capabilities. VMware recommends using a pass-through controller and therefore we will use the LSI 3008 and not the LSI 3108, which is also an option.

The final configuration is 1 × Supermicro Twin Pro 2 (four hosts), each host consisting of the following:

- Dual-socket quad-core Intel E5-2609 v2 2.50GHz

- 256GB of memory

- Disk controller: LSI 3008

- 5 × 1.2TB SAS 10K RPM

- 1 × 200GB SSD SAS

Scenario 3

In the previous two scenarios, we used fairly moderate numbers from a VM count perspective, resulting in small clusters. In this scenario, we require the ability to run 1,500 VMs within this environment. This imposes a couple of additional challenges, making the exercise different again from the previous two. For this scenario, we work with the following parameters:

- 1 vCPU per VM on average

- 6GB average VM memory size

- 50GB average VM disk size

- 75 percent anticipated consumed VM disk capacity

In the environment, we currently have 12 VMs, and need to be able to grow to 1,500 VMs in the upcoming 12 months. Therefore, our VSAN infrastructure should be able to provide the following:

1,500 × 1 vCPU = 1,500 vCPUs

1,500 × 6GB = 9000GB of memory

1,500 × 50GB = 75000GB disk space

We will take a vCPU-to-core ratio of 7:1 into consideration. Considering that we will need to be able to run 1,500 vCPUs, we will divide that by 7, resulting in the need for 215 CPU cores. The total combined required memory is 9000GB.

Now let's look at the storage requirements a bit more in depth. Before we can calculate the requirements, we need to know what level of resiliency will be taken into account for these VMs. For our calculations, we take once more a number of failures to tolerate setting of 1 into account, and we will also factor in the ability to rebuild storage objects upon failure. This ensures that after a failure of a host our VMs will be fully protected, because spare disk capacity is available for this scenario. We will also add an additional 10 percent disk space to cater for metadata and the occasional snapshot.

The formula we will use taking the preceding parameters into account looks like the following:

(((Number of VMs * Avg VM size) + (Number of VMs * Avg mem size)) * FTT+1) + 10% slack space

We have included the average memory size because for each VM, a swap file will be created on disk which is the size of your memory configuration for that VM. Using the industry standard averages previously mentioned, this results in the following:

((((1,500 * 50) + (1,500 * 6)) * 2) = (75,000 + 9000) * 2 = 168000GB + 10% = 184800GB

Divide the outcome by 1,024 and round it up; a total combined storage capacity of 181TB is the outcome. Now that we know we need 181TB of disk capacity, 9000GB of memory, and 215 CPU cores, let's explore the hardware configuration.

Determining Your Host Configuration

In this scenario, the customer has indicated that they have standardized their environment on HP hardware and a preferred configuration is the HP ProLiant DL380p Gen8 2U host, which is depicted in Figure 9-7. The DL380p can be configured with 2 processors (max 12 cores per CPU), 768GB of memory (24 DIMM slots), and has 25 disk slots.

Figure 9-7 HP DL380

Our requirements for the environment are as follows:

- 3 hosts minimum (according to VSAN)
- 181TB of raw disk capacity
- 215 CPU cores
- 9000GB of memory

As stated, the HP DL380p can hold 12 cores per socket at most, resulting in a total of 24 cores per host in a dual-socket configuration. Therefore, from a CPU perspective, we need roughly nine hosts at a minimum. From a memory perspective, each host can be provisioned with 768GB of memory. Considering that we require 9000GB of memory, we need 12 hosts when it comes to memory. Of course, price is always a consideration, and we urge you to compare prices based on CPU, memory, and disk configurations. We will not take pricing into account in this scenario, considering the ever-changing prices for compute components.

Let's look at our options for storage. We know we need 181TB of storage. We will look at a couple of options in terms of disk sizes and potential performance implication:

- 181TB = ~ 91 × 2TB = 7,280 IOPS

- 181TB = ~ 151 × 1.2TB = 22,650 IOPS

- 181TB = ~ 201 × 0.9TB = 30,150 IOPS

- 181TB = ~ 301 × 0.6TB = 45,150 IOPS

We know that each server can hold 25 × 2.5-inch drive or 12 × 3.5-inch drives. From a drive perspective, we would need 15 hosts at most if we use the 0.6TB drives. You may wonder why we end up with 15 hosts, because 301 / 25 is less than 15. We need to take into consideration that a number of slots will be used by SSDs; as you may recall from the previous examples, each disk group (with a maximum of seven) disks requires one SSD. If we create 3 disk groups of 7 magnetic disks, we would need 3 SSDs resulting in a total of 24 disk slots used. The total number of 301 magnetic disks divided by 21 slots per host assigned to magnetic disks is 14.3 hosts, and rounded up, results in 15 hosts.

Because we want the ability to both scale out and scale up, we will go with 20 hosts, and we will be leveraging 900GB drives. This leaves us with sufficient slots to increase storage capacity when required. In total, we require 181TB divided by 20 hosts, resulting in ~9TB per host. We will use twelve 900GB drives instead of using 11; we will use 12 to evenly balance out the number of disks per disk group to a total of 6 disks per disk group, thus configuring two disk groups per host.

Using the 10 percent flash capacity rule, we require 10 percent of 1,500 × (75% of 50GB), which is 5625GB of flash capacity in total. Considering that we will be using 20 hosts in our cluster, this results in ~280GB per host. Because typical flash devices come in sizes of 100, 200, 400, and 800GB, we have decided to leverage 200GB drives because we will need two drives for the two disk groups these servers will have. Because we have slightly over-provisioned our environment, there should be no performance penalty.

This is what each host configuration will look like for the 20 HPDL350p (25 SFF) hosts consisting of the following:

- Dual-socket 6-core E5-2630
- 512GB of memory
- Disk controller: HP H220i
- 12 × 900GB SAS 10K RPM
- 2 × 200GB SSD SAS (WI)

Summary

As this chapter has demonstrated, it is really important to select your hardware carefully. Selection of a disk type, for instance, can impact your potential performance. Other components, such as disk controllers, can have an impact on the operational effort involved with VSAN.

Think about your configuration before you make a purchase decision. As mentioned earlier, VMware offers a great alternative in the VSAN Ready Node program. These servers are optimized and configured for VSAN, taking away much of the complexity that comes with hardware selection.

Chapter 10

Troubleshooting, Monitoring, and Performance

This chapter discusses the extensive suite of tools available to you to monitor and trouble-shoot a VSAN environment, and also how to use these tools to investigate and quickly remedy issues on VSAN.

VSAN can leverage already-existing tools as well as some built-in tools specific to VSAN. This chapter covers the following tools:

- **ESXCLI**: The command-line interface (CLI) of the ESXi host

- **Ruby vSphere Console (RVC)**: A generic tool for managing vCenter instances, but that has also been extended to support VSAN

- **VSAN Observer**: A web-based performance utility that leverages RVC

- **ESXTOP**: ESXi host performance monitoring tool

It should also be noted that traditional monitoring utilities, such as the vSphere web client, can continue to be used for VSAN, including performance views of individual VMs, and their respective VMDKs.

ESXCLI

ESXi 5.5U1 introduces a new ESXi CLI (ESXCLI) namespace: esxcli vsan. This has a selection of additional namespaces that can be used for examining, monitoring, and configuring the VSAN cluster, as demonstrated here:

```
~ # esxcli vsan
Usage: esxcli vsan {cmd} [cmd options]
Available Namespaces:
  datastore              Commands for VSAN datastore configuration
  network                Commands for VSAN host network configuration
  storage                Commands for VSAN physical storage configuration
  cluster                Commands for VSAN host cluster configuration
  maintenancemode        Commands for VSAN maintenance mode operation
  policy                 Commands for VSAN storage policy configuration
  trace                  Commands for VSAN trace configuration
```

The sections that follow take a look at some of the options available.

esxcli vsan datastore

The esxcli vsan datastore namespace provides commands for VSAN datastore configuration. There is very little that can be done here in the initial release of VSAN other than get and set the name of the VSAN datastore. By default, the VSAN datastore name is vsanDatastore. If you do plan on changing the vsanDatastore name, you would have to repeat this command on each ESXi host in the cluster, so you are probably better off doing this at the cluster level via the vSphere Web Client. It is highly recommended that if you are managing multiple VSAN clusters from the same vCenter Server that the VSAN datastores are given unique, easily identifiable names:

```
~ # esxcli vsan datastore
Usage: esxcli vsan datastore {cmd} [cmd options]

Available Namespaces:
  name                 Commands for configuring VSAN datastore name.
```

```
~ # esxcli vsan datastore name
Usage: esxcli vsan datastore name {cmd} [cmd options]
Available Commands:
  get                  Get VSAN datastore name.
  set                  Configure VSAN datastore name. In general, Rename
                       should always be done at cluster level. Across a VSAN
                       cluster VSAN datastore name should be in sync.
```

```
~ # esxcli vsan datastore name get
  Name: vsanDatastore
```

esxcli vsan network

This namespace provides commands for VSAN network configuration. It is somewhat more useful than the previous *datastore* namespace as it allows you to list the current configuration, clear the current configuration, restore the VSAN network configuration (this is used during the boot process by ESXi, and is not meant for customer invocation), as well as remove an interface from the VSAN network configuration:

```
~ # esxcli vsan network
Usage: esxcli vsan network {cmd} [cmd options]
Available Namespaces:
  ipv4                  Commands for configuring IPv4 network for VSAN.
Available Commands:
  clear                 Clear the VSAN network configuration.
  list                  List the network configuration currently in use by
                        VSAN.
  remove                Remove an interface from the VSAN network
                        configuration.
  restore               Restore the persisted VSAN network configuration.
```

```
~ # esxcli vsan network list
Interface
   VmkNic Name: vmk6
   IP Protocol: IPv4
   Interface UUID: f4c8e352-f46e-c538-42ad-0011010700df
   Agent Group Multicast Address: 224.2.3.4
   Agent Group Multicast Port: 23451
   Master Group Multicast Address: 224.1.2.3
   Master Group Multicast Port: 12345
   Multicast TTL: 5
```

What is interesting to view here is the multicast information. If you cast your mind back to the requirements in Chapter 2, "VSAN Prerequisites and Requirements for Deployment," you might remember that there is a requirement to allow multicast traffic between ESXi hosts participating in the VSAN cluster.

Another interesting point to note is that VSAN supports only IPv4 at the moment. There is no support for IPv6 in this initial release. However, it is the multicast details that are of most interest. The Agent Group Multicast Port corresponds to the *cmmds* port that is opened on the ESXi firewall when VSAN is enabled. The first IP address, 224.2.3.4 is used for the master/backup communication, whereas the second address, 224.1.2.3, is used for the agents. esxcli vsan network list is a useful command to view the network configuration and status should a network partition occur.

Additional commands that can be useful for troubleshooting networking problems are as follows:

- `esxcli network diag ping`: Tests the responsiveness of a VMkernel port

- `esxcli network ip neighbor list`: Displays Address Resolution Protocol (ARP) cache entries for all other VSAN nodes on the network

- `esxcli network ip connection list`: Displays the User Datagram Protocol (UDP) connection information

- `tcpdump-uw`: Sniffs the network traffic

esxcli vsan storage

This namespace is used for storage configuration, and includes options on how VSAN should claim disks, as well as the ability to add and remove physical disks to VSAN.

The command `esxcli vsan storage automode` allows you to get or set the auto-claim option. If it is disabled, the cluster is in manual mode:

```
~ # esxcli vsan storage
Usage: esxcli vsan storage {cmd} [cmd options]
Available Namespaces:
  automode          Commands for configuring VSAN storage auto claim mode.
Available Commands:
  add               Add physical disk for VSAN usage.
  list              List VSAN storage configuration.
  remove            Remove physical disks from VSAN disk groups.


~ # esxcli vsan storage automode
Usage: esxcli vsan storage automode {cmd} [cmd options]
Available Commands:
  get                Get status of storage auto claim mode.
  set                Configure storage auto claim mode
```

To display the magnetic disks and solid-state disks (SSDs) that have been claimed and are in use by VSAN from a particular ESXi host, you may use the `list` option. In this particular configuration, there is only a single magnetic disk and a single SSD. Both have a `true` flag against the field `Used by this host`, indicating that they have been claimed by VSAN and the `Is SSD` field indicates the type of device (false for magnetic disks, true for solid state disks):

```
~ # esxcli vsan storage list
naa.5000c5006900c7cf
    Device: naa.5000c5006900c7cf
    Display Name: naa.5000c5006900c7cf
    Is SSD: false
    VSAN UUID: 526977e9-92fb-b7c1-0c88-4ed9ed73b0d1
    VSAN Disk Group UUID: 527b16ab-d7d2-ac98-229b-019ccdde17a3
    VSAN Disk Group Name: naa.50025385a00c5085
    Used by this host: true
    In CMMDS: true
    Checksum: 641692210327909576
    Checksum OK: true

naa.50025385a00c5085
    Device: naa.50025385a00c5085
    Display Name: naa.50025385a00c5085
    Is SSD: true
    VSAN UUID: 527b16ab-d7d2-ac98-229b-019ccdde17a3
    VSAN Disk Group UUID: 527b16ab-d7d2-ac98-229b-019ccdde17a3
    VSAN Disk Group Name: naa.50025385a00c5085
    Used by this host: true
    In CMMDS: true
    Checksum: 8907154225867547805
    Checksum OK: true
```

If you want to use ESXCLI to *add* new disks to a disk group on VSAN, you can use the add option. There is a different option to choose depending on whether the disk is a magnetic disk or an SSD (-d|--disks or -s|--ssd, respectively). Note that only disks that are empty and have no partition information can be added to VSAN.

There is also a remove option that allows you to remove magnetic disks and SSDs from disk groups on VSAN. It should go without saying that you need to be very careful with this command and removing disks from a disk group on VSAN should be considered a maintenance task. The remove option removes all the partition information (and thus all VSAN information) from the disk supplied as an argument to the command. Note that when an SSD is removed from a disk group, the whole disk group becomes unavailable.

If you have disks that were once used by VSAN and you now want to repurpose these disks for some other use (Virtual Machine File System [VMFS], Raw Device Mappings [RDM], or in the case of SSDs, vFRC [vSphere Flash Read Cache]), you can use the remove option to clean up any VSAN partition information left behind on the disk.

Additional useful commands for looking at disks and controllers include the following:

- `esxcli storage core adapter list`: Displays the driver and adapter description, which can be useful to check that your adapter is on the hardware compatibility list (HCL)

- `esxcfg-info -s | grep "==+SCSI Interface" -A 18`: Displays lots of information, but most importantly shows the queue depth of the device, which is very important for performance

- `esxcli storage core device smart get -d XXX`: Displays SMART statistics about your drive, especially SSDs. Very useful command to display Wear-Leveling information, and overall health of your SSD

- `esxcli storage core device stats get`: Displays overall disk statistics

esxcli vsan cluster

The `esxcli vsan cluster` command allows the ESXi host on which the command is run to get VSAN cluster information, as well as allow the ESXi host to leave or join a VSAN cluster. This can be very helpful in a scenario where vCenter Server is unavailable and a particular host needs to be removed from the VSAN cluster. The restore functionality is not intended for customer invocation and is used by ESXi during the boot process to restore the active cluster configuration from configuration file:

```
~ # esxcli vsan cluster
Usage: esxcli vsan cluster {cmd} [cmd options]

Available Commands:
   get              Get the information of the VSAN cluster that this host
                    is joined to.
   join             Join the host to a given VSAN cluster.
   leave            Leave the VSAN cluster the host is currently joined
                    to.
   restore          Restore the persisted VSAN cluster configuration.
```

A `get` option to this command is useful for gathering information about the local ESXi hosts (node) health, as well as its role in the cluster. In the following example, you can see that this ESXi host is an *agent* and its status is healthy. Other states, as was discussed in Chapter 5, "Architectural Details," are *master* and *backup*. These states relate to the role the host plays for the clustering service (CMMDS). Refer to Chapter 5 if you need a refresher on the various roles of hosts in VSAN:

```
~ # esxcli vsan cluster get
Cluster Information
   Enabled: true
   Current Local Time: 2014-02-08T10:11:15Z
   Local Node UUID: 52b20dab-3f82-819c-c5df-0011010700df
   Local Node State: AGENT
   Local Node Health State: HEALTHY
   Sub-Cluster Master UUID: 52b228a4-2235-2422-1b19-00110107007f
   Sub-Cluster Backup UUID: 52b20efb-e15b-01b9-fb23-00110107009f
   Sub-Cluster UUID: 52ce6421-83d3-6415-5e51-3c6e6ee31b62
   Sub-Cluster Membership Entry Revision: 9
   Sub-Cluster Member UUIDs:
      52b228a4-2235-2422-1b19-00110107007f,
      52b20efb-e15b-01b9-fb23-00110107009f,
      52b20e01-7cd7-b9b5-b704-0011010700af,
      52b22966-99f2-93fa-81d9-00110107003f,
      52b20d6c-9920-87ad-5d4d-0011010700bf,
      52b228ae-8a0d-2756-bf5d-00110107005f,
      52b20dab-3f82-819c-c5df-0011010700df,
      52cc513c-c042-9524-79d8-00110107001f
   Sub-Cluster Membership UUID: 76eae352-1441-9b05-9845-00110107007f
```

One additional useful piece of information from this output is the subcluster member UUIDs. There are eight entries in this field in total, indicating that this is an eight-node cluster. This is always useful to show how many nodes each host thinks is participating in the cluster when it comes to troubleshooting partition issues. If you want to display which host corresponds to which UUID, you can use the `esxcli system uuid get <uuid>` command.

esxcli vsan maintenancemode

`maintenancemode` is an interesting command option. You might think this would allow you to enter and exit maintenance, but it doesn't. All this option allows you to do is to cancel an in-progress VSAN maintenance mode operation. This could still prove very useful, though, especially when you have decided to place a host in maintenance mode and selected the Full Data Migration option and want to stop this data migration process (which can take a very long time) and instead use the Ensure Access option:

```
~ # esxcli vsan maintenancemode
Usage: esxcli vsan maintenancemode {cmd} [cmd options]
```

```
Available Commands:
  cancel                 Cancel an in-progress VSAN maintenance mode operation.
```

esxcli vsan policy

Virtual machine (VM) storage policies are something that we have covered in great detail in previous chapters of this book. Earlier, we looked at what would happen to a VM storage object if the VM were deployed without selecting a VM storage policy. VSAN associates a default storage policy with the VM's storage objects and this esxcli vsan policy namespace is one way to examine and modify this default storage policy:

```
~ # esxcli vsan policy
Usage: esxcli vsan policy {cmd} [cmd options]

Available Commands:
  cleardefault           Clear default VSAN storage policy values.
  getdefault             Get default VSAN storage policy values.
  setdefault             Set default VSAN storage policy values.


~ # esxcli vsan policy getdefault
Policy Class   Policy Value
------------   --------------------------------------------------------
cluster        (("hostFailuresToTolerate" i1))
vdisk          (("hostFailuresToTolerate" i1))
vmnamespace    (("hostFailuresToTolerate" i1))
vmswap         (("hostFailuresToTolerate" i1) ("forceProvisioning" i1))
```

Here we can see the different VM storage objects that make up a VM deployed on a VSAN datastore, and we can also see the default policy values. Although the policy value is called host failures to tolerate, it actually is the equivalent to the number of failures to tolerate in the vSphere Web Client. All the objects will tolerate at least one failure in the cluster and remain persistent. The class vdisk refers to VM disk objects (VMDKs). It also covers snapshot deltas. The class vmnamespace is the VM Home namespace where the configuration files, metadata files, and log files belonging to the VM are stored. The vmswap policy class is, of course, the VM swap. One final note for vmswap is that it also has a forceProvisioning value. This means that even if there are not enough resources in the VSAN cluster to meet the requirement to provision both VM swap replicas to meet the failures to tolerate requirement, VSAN will still provision the VM with a single VM swap instance. A detailed discussion on force provisioning can be found in the various chapters throughout this book.

If you do want to change the default policy to something other than these settings, there is a considerable amount of information in the help file about each of the policies. The command to set a default policy is as follows:

```
# esxcli vsan policy setdefault <-p|--policy> <-c|--policy-class>
```

Of course, we did not cover all of the five policy settings in the default, but you can certainly include any of the five policy settings in the default policy if you want. Take care with changing the default policy, as highlighted a number of times earlier in the book. Setting unrealistic default values for number of failures to tolerate or flash read cache reservation, for example, may lead to the inability to provision any VMs. Using the help output from the esxcli vsan policy setdefault command, further details are provided about the policy settings that are displayed here for your information:

- cacheReservation: Flash capacity reserved as read cache for the storage object. Specified as a percentage of the logical size of the object. To be used only for addressing read performance issues. Reserved flash capacity cannot be used by other objects. Unreserved flash is shared fairly among all objects. It is specified in parts per million. Default value: 0, Maximum value: 1000000.

- forceProvisioning: If this option is yes, the object will be provisioned even if the requirements specified in the storage policy cannot be satisfied by the resources currently available in the cluster. VSAN will try to bring the object into compliance if and when resources become available. Default value: No.

- hostFailuresToTolerate: Defines the number of host, disk, or network failures a storage object can tolerate. For n failures tolerated, n + 1 copies of the object are created, and 2n + 1 hosts contributing storage are required. Default value: 1, Maximum value: 3.

- stripeWidth: The number of magnetic disk drives across which each replica of storage object is striped. A value higher than 1 may result in better performance (for example, when flash read cache misses need to get serviced from magnetic disk), but there is no guarantee that performance will improve with an increased stripeWidth. Default value: 1, Maximum value: 12.

- proportionalCapacity: Percentage of the logical size of the storage object that will be reserved (thick provisioning) upon VM provisioning. The rest of the storage object is thin provisioned. Default value: 0%, Maximum value: 100%.

The other argument that needs to be included with the setdefault command is the -c|--policy-class option. This is the VSAN policy class whose default value is being set. The options are cluster, vdisk, vmnamespace, vmswap—one of which must be specified in the command.

In fact, with the release of VMware Horizon View version 5.3.1 and support for View desktops deployed on VSAN, desktop storage objects are deployed with the default policy; however, these defaults might not be suitable for every View deployment on VSAN. Although VMware strongly recommends that customers use the default policy with Horizon View 5.3.1, customers may modify the policy based on their requirements as discussed in Chapter 8, "Interoperability." The default policy may be modified using the ESXCLI command mentioned earlier.

Lastly, a word about `cluster`, which is one of the policy class options, but is not a VM storage object like `vmnamespace`, `vdisk`, or `vmswap`. This option is used as a catchall for any objects deployed on a VSAN datastore that are not part of a VM's storage objects. Although we don't envision non-VM storage object types being placed on the VSAN datastore, this is there as a "just in case."

esxcli vsan trace

`esxcli vsan trace` is a troubleshooting and diagnostic utility and should not be used without the guidance of VMware Global Support Services (GSS). It is designed to capture internal diagnostics from VSAN for further analysis. The options are shown here simply for completeness:

```
~ # esxcli vsan trace
Usage: esxcli vsan trace {cmd} [cmd options]


Available Commands:
  set               Configure VSAN trace. Please note: This command is not
                    thread safe.


~ # esxcli vsan trace set -h
Usage: esxcli vsan trace set [cmd options]


Description:
  set               Configure VSAN trace. Please note: This command is not
                    thread safe.


Cmd options:
  -f|--numfiles=<long>  Log file rotation for VSAN trace files.
  -p|--path=<str>       Path to store VSAN trace files.
  -r|--reset            When set to true, reset defaults for VSAN trace
                        files.
  -s|--size=<long>      Maximum size of VSAN trace files in MB.
```

Additional Non-ESXCLI Commands for Troubleshooting VSAN

In addition to the esxcli vsan namespace commands, there are a few additional CLI commands found on an ESXi host that may prove useful for monitoring and troubleshooting.

osls-fs

`osls-fs` is more of a troubleshooting command than anything else. It is useful for displaying the contents of the VSAN datastore. The command is not in your search path, but can be found in the following location. In this command, we are listing the contents of a VM folder on the VSAN datastore. This can prove useful if the datastore file view is not working correctly from the vSphere Web Client, or it is reporting inaccurate information for some reason or other:

```
~ # cd /vmfs/volumes/vsanDatastore
~ # /usr/lib/vmware/osfs/bin/osfs-ls win2k8x64-1_1/

.fbb.sf
.fdc.sf
.pbc.sf
.sbc.sf
.vh.sf
.pb2.sf
.sdd.sf
.6cc6d752-a00c-ad67-268e-0010185def78.lck
win2k8x64-1.vmdk
win2k8x64-1.nvram
win2k8x64-1.vmx
win2k8x64-1.vmxf
win2k8x64-1.vmsd
win2k8x64-1_2.vmdk
.dvsData
.f6ccd752-5843-0da9-4149-0010185def78.lck
win2k8x64-1_1.vmdk
vmware.log
.d8dad752-a897-8b6a-8a96-0010185def78.lck
```

cmmds-tool

`cmmds-tool` is another useful troubleshooting command from the ESXi host and can be used to display lots of VSAN information. It can be used to display information such as configuration, metadata, and state about the cluster, hosts in the cluster, and VM storage objects. Many other high-level diagnostic tools leverage information obtained via cmmds-tool. As you can imagine, it has a number of options:

```
~ # cmmds-tool
usage: cmmds-tool <cmd> <options>
commands:
    add                    Adds an entry from stdin. On successful exit the
                           entry is guaranteed to be in the directory
    delete                 Deletes matching entries. On successful exit the
                           entry will be deleted from the directory
    dump                   Dumps first matching entry to stdout
    find                   Finds matching entries
    wait                   Waits for a matching entry to appear
    waitdump               Waits for a matching entry to appear and dumps
                           the entry to stdout
    waitformembership      Waits for a membership entry to appear
    whoami                 Get the node's uuid as used in the sub-cluster
    amimember              Check if I am the member in the current sub-cluster
    readdump               Reads a cmmds directory dump from a file
                           (specified with -d/--dumpfile) and
                           o/p to stdout in a given format specified
                           using -f option.
options:
    -o/--owner=<uuid>:        Entry owner
    -u/--uuid=<uuid>:         Entry uuid
    -t/--type=<int>|<name>:   Entry type
    -r/--rev=<int>:           Entry revision (-1 for latest)
    -i/--timeout=<int>:       Max time for wait (0 for infinite wait)
    -f/--format=<fmt>:        Output format (fmt should be one of
                              json/python/simple. Default is 'simple'
    -d/--dumpfile=<file>:     Filename to read the cmmds dump from.
    -p/--print-dump-hdr:      When CMMDS dump is read off the file, should
                              the dump file header be printed as well
    -v/--verbose=<int>:       Verbosity level
    -h/--help:                Print this help text
```

The find option may be the most useful, especially when you want to discover information about the actual storage objects backing a VM. You can, for instance, see what the health is of a specific object. In this example, we want to find additional information about a disk object represented by UUID 52777432-f127-f001-d081-800a04cafb0e.

```
~ # cmmds-tool find -u 52777432-f127-f001-d081-800a04cafb0e
owner=52ca9e00-b362-a040-eb2a-984be1047ad4(Health: Healthy)
  uuid=52777432-f127-f001-d081-800a04cafb0e type=DISK rev=0
  [content = (1587068342272 1100 1+10000000 1200000000 1+0 13400000
  10 i10 i15 11600000 10 116777216 i0
  5214b1a5-b6b1-3a3a-f8b6-ee4ecc7a8d0e
  "52d7b4db-515e86a0-383a-001b21168828")], errorStr=(null)
owner=52ca9e00-b362-a040-eb2a-984be1047ad4(Health: Healthy)
  uuid=52777432-f127-f001-d081-800a04cafb0e type=HEALTH_STATUS rev=0
  [content = (i0 1319401449472)], errorStr=(null)
owner=52ca9e00-b362-a040-eb2a-984be1047ad4(Health: Healthy)
  uuid=52777432-f127-f001-d081-800a04cafb0e type=DISK_USAGE rev=645
  [content = (118874368 10 10 10 10)], errorStr=(null)
owner=52ca9e00-b362-a040-eb2a-984be1047ad4(Health: Healthy)

  uuid=52777432-f127-f001-d081-800a04cafb0e type=DISK_STATUS rev=645
  [content = (1430420688896 10 10 i10 18 10 1261888 10 10 10 10 10 10
  10 10 1+0 i4)], errorStr=(null)
```

There are, of course, many other options available to this command that can run. For example, a -o <owner> will display information about all objects of which <owner> is the owner. This can be a considerable amount of output.

Type is another option, and can be specified with a -t option. From the preceding output, types such as DISK, HEALTH_STATUS, DISK_USAGE, and DISK_STATUS can be displayed. Other types include DOM_OBJECT, DOM_NAME, POLICY, CONFIG_STATUS, HA_METADATA, HOSTNAME, and so on.

Here is the list of hostnames taken from a four-node cluster:

```
~ # cmmds-tool find -t HOSTNAME

owner=52caa324-d534-150c-d007-984be1047764(Health: Healthy)
  uuid=52caa324-d534-150c-d007-984be1047764 type=HOSTNAME rev=0
  [content = ("cs-tkmt-h03")], errorStr=(null)

owner=52ca9198-f7bf-3c3c-93c2-984be104893e(Health: Healthy)
  uuid=52ca9198-f7bf-3c3c-93c2-984be104893e type=HOSTNAME rev=0
  [content = ("cs-tkmt-h02")], errorStr=(null)

owner=52ca9e00-b362-a040-eb2a-984be1047ad4(Health: Healthy)
  uuid=52ca9e00-b362-a040-eb2a-984be1047ad4 type=HOSTNAME rev=0
  [content = ("cs-tkmt-h04")], errorStr=(null)
```

```
owner=52c6c45b-e7f4-31e0-7797-984be10a24d4(Health: Healthy)
  uuid=52c6c45b-e7f4-31e0-7797-984be10a24d4 type=HOSTNAME rev=0
  [content = ("cs-tkmt-h01")], errorStr=(null)
```

As you can see, this very powerful command enables you to do lots of investigation and troubleshooting from an ESXi host. In a scenario where a disk has failed in a large cluster, this command can prove helpful when trying to identify which storage objects have been impacted by this failure. Again, exercise caution when using this command. Alternatively, use only under the guidance of VMware support staff if you have concerns.

vdq

The vdq command serves two purposes and is really a great troubleshooting tool to have on the ESXi host. The first option to this command tells you whether disks on your ESXi host are eligible for VSAN, and if not, what the reason is for the disk being ineligible.

The second option to this command is that once VSAN has been enabled, you can use the command to display disk mapping information, which is essentially which SSD or flash devices and magnetic disks are grouped together in a disk group.

Let's first run the option to query all disks for eligibility fro VSAN use. This first output is from a host that does not have VSAN:

```
~ # vdq -q
[
    {
        "Name"      : "naa.600508b1001c1184075bd1f8c2c882ec",
        "VSANUUID"  : "",
        "State"     : "Ineligible for use by VSAN",
        "Reason"    : "Has partitions",
        "IsSSD"     : "0",
        "IsPDL"     : "0",
    },

    {
        "Name"      : "naa.6000d3100046c5000000000000000010",
        "VSANUUID"  : "",
        "State"     : "Ineligible for use by VSAN",
        "Reason"    : "Has partitions",
        "IsSSD"     : "0",
        "IsPDL"     : "0",
    },

]
```

In the preceding example, no disks are available for VSAN to use because they all contain preexisting partitions. Here is the output taken from a host that has VSAN already enabled:

```
~ # vdq -q
[
   {
      "Name"      : "mpx.vmhba32:C0:T0:L0",
      "VSANUUID"  : "",
      "State"     : "Ineligible for use by VSAN",
      "Reason"    : "Has partitions",
      "IsSSD"     : "0",
      "IsPDL"     : "0",
   },

   {
      "Name"      : "eui.48f8681115d6416c00247172ce4df168",
      "VSANUUID"  : "52b0a0a9-a4f5-93f7-91e0-c52287f74668",
      "State"     : "In-use for VSAN",
      "Reason"    : "None",
      "IsSSD"     : "1",
      "IsPDL"     : "0",
   },

   {
      "Name"      : "naa.600508b1001c530aff02e0c5c7971e1d",
      "VSANUUID"  : "52236e03-b7f5-10a7-88e3-f0b41fe207a8",
      "State"     : "In-use for VSAN",
      "Reason"    : "Non-local disk",
      "IsSSD"     : "0",
      "IsPDL"     : "0",
   },

]
```

As you can see, two disks have been claimed by VSAN, while a third disk is ineligible because it already has partitions. In this example, the ineligible disk is the ESXi host boot disk. It also points out which disk is an SSD (IsSSD) and whether the disk is in a permanent device loss state (IsPDL).

The second useful option to the command is to dump out the VSAN disk mappings; in other words, which flash devices and which magnetic disks are in a disk group. Here is a sample output (which includes the -H option to make it more human readable):

```
~ # vdq -i -H
Mappings:
   DiskMapping[0]:
          SSD:  eui.48f8681115d6416c00247172ce4df168
          MD:   naa.600508b1001c530aff02e0c5c7971e1d
```

This command shows the SSD relationship to magnetic disks (MD). This is very useful if you want to find out the disk group layout on a particular host from the command line. This command will quickly tell you which magnetic disks are fronted by which SSDs, especially when you have multiple disk groups defined on an ESXi host.

Although some of the commands shown in this section may prove useful to examine and monitor VSAN on an ESXi host basis, administrators ideally need something whereby they can examine the cluster as a whole. VMware recognized this very early on in the development of VSAN, and so introduced extensions to the Ruby vSphere Console (RVC) to allow a cluster-wide view of VSAN. The next topic delves into RVC.

Ruby vSphere Console

The previous section looked at ESXi host-centric commands for VSAN. This section covers a tool that enables you to take a cluster-centric view of VSAN. VMware vCenter Server 5.5 U1 contains a new component called the Ruby vSphere Console (RVC). The RVC is also included on the VMware vCenter Virtual Appliance (VCVA). As mentioned in the introduction, RVC is a programmable interface that allows administrators to query the status of vCenter, clusters, hosts, storage, and networking. For VSAN, there are quite a number of programmable extensions to display pretty much everything you need to know about a VSAN cluster. This section covers those VSAN extensions in RVC.

You can connect RVC to any vCenter Server. On the VCVA, you log in via Secure Shell (SSH) and run rvc <user>@<vc-ip>.

For Windows-based Virtual Center environments, you need to open a command shell and navigate to c:\Program Files\VMware\Infrastructure\VirtualCenter Server\support\rvc. Here, you will find an rvc.bat file that you may need to edit to add appropriate credentials for your vCenter Server (by default, Administrator@localhost). Once those credentials have been set appropriately, simply run the rvc.bat file, type your password, and you are connected.

After you log in, you will see a virtual file system, with the vCenter Server instance at the root. You can now begin to use navigation commands such as **cd** and **ls**, as well as tab completion to navigate the file system. The structure of the file system mimics the inventory items tree views that you find in the vSphere Client. Therefore, you can run cd *<vCenter Server>*, followed by cd *<datacenter>*. You can use ~ to refer to your current datacenter, and all clusters are in the "computers" folder under your datacenter. Note that when you navigate to a folder/directory, the contents are listed with numeric values. These numeric values may also be used as shortcuts. For example, in the vCenter folder in the example that follows, there is only one datacenter, and it has a numeric value of 0 associated with it. We can then cd to 0, instead of typing out the full name of the datacenter:

```
> ls
0 /
1 mia-cg07-vc01/
> cd 1
/mia-cg07-vc01> ls
0 mia-cg07-dc01 (datacenter)
/mia-cg07-vc01> cd 0
/mia-cg07-vc01/mia-cg07-dc01> ls
0 storage/
1 computers [host]/
2 networks [network]/
3 datastores [datastore]/
4 vms [vm]/
```

VSAN Commands

If you want to learn about any command, run *<command>* -help. You can also use help and help *<command-namespace>* (like help vm, help vm.ip) to learn more about commands. Because we are primarily interested in VSAN, let's take a look at what commands are available to us for monitoring and troubleshooting VSAN:

```
/mia-cg07-vc01/mia-cg07-dc01> help vsan
Commands:
enable_vsan_on_cluster: Enable VSAN on a cluster
disable_vsan_on_cluster: Disable VSAN on a cluster
cluster_change_autoclaim: Enable VSAN on a cluster
host_consume_disks: Consumes all eligible disks on a host
host_wipe_vsan_disks: Wipes content of all VSAN disks on a host
host_info: Print VSAN info about a host
cluster_info: Print VSAN info about a cluster
```

disks_info: Print physical disk info about a host

cluster_set_default_policy: Set default policy on a cluster

object_info: Fetch information about a VSAN object

disk_object_info: Fetch information about all VSAN objects on a given physical disk

cmmds_find: CMMDS Find

fix_renamed_vms: This command can be used to rename some VMs which get renamed by the VC in case of storage inaccessibility. It is possible for some VMs to get renamed to vmx file path. eg. "/vmfs/volumes/vsanDatastore/foo/foo.vmx". This command will rename this VM to "foo". This is the best we can do. This VM may have been named something else but we have no way to know. In this best effort command, we simply rename it to the name of its config file (without the full path and .vmx extension of course!).

vm_object_info: Fetch VSAN object information about a VM

disks_stats: Show stats on all disks in VSAN

whatif_host_failures: Simulates how host failures impact VSAN resource usage

observer: Run observer

resync_dashboard: Resyncing dashboard

vm_perf_stats: VM perf stats

enter_maintenance_mode: Put hosts into maintenance mode

lldpnetmap: Gather LLDP mapping information from a set of hosts

check_limits: Gathers (and checks) counters against limits

object_reconfigure: Reconfigure a VSAN object

obj_status_report: Print component status for objects in the cluster.

apply_license_to_cluster: Apply license to VSAN

check_state: Checks state of VMs and VSAN objects

reapply_vsan_vmknic_config: Unbinds and rebinds VSAN to its vmknics

recover_spbm: SPBM Recovery

To see commands in a namespace: help namespace_name

To see detailed help for a command: help namespace_name.command_name

All the commands shown here must be prefixed by vsan. Therefore, to run enable_vsan_on_cluster, you must use vsan.enable_vsan_on_cluster. Remember that there is command completion, so you only need to type the first couple of characters of each command and then use the Tab key to complete the command (or display which commands match your current types command).

Of course, there is another set of commands in RVC that is also of interest to VSAN administrators. These are the SPBM (Storage Policy Based Management) commands and are used for all things related to VM storage policies. Here is a list of SPBM commands in RVC:

```
/mia-cg07-vc01/mia-cg07-dc01> help spbm
Commands:
profile_delete: Delete a VM Storage Profile
profile_apply: Apply a VM Storage Profile. Pushed profile content to
  Storage system
profile_create: Create a VM Storage Profile
device_change_storage_profile: Change storage profile of a virtual disk
check_compliance: Check compliance
namespace_change_storage_profile: Change storage profile of VM
  namespace
vm_change_storage_profile: Change storage profile of VM namespace and
  its disks
device_add_disk: Add a hard drive to a virtual machine

To see commands in a namespace: help namespace_name
To see detailed help for a command: help namespace_name.command_name
```

We will return to SPBM commands shortly, but for the moment we will examine the VSAN commands in RVC and how they can help you with monitoring, troubleshooting, and resolving VSAN issues. You must use vsan. to precede all VSAN commands.

To get even more help on a particular command, simply precede the full command with help.

enable_vsan_on_cluster and disable_vsan_on_cluster

These commands do exactly what they say—enabling and disabling VSAN on the cluster. The only other way to do this is via the vSphere Web Client. You cannot do this via ESXCLI. With ESXCLI, you could get the ESXi host to join or leave the cluster, scaling it in or scaling it out, but there was no way to enable or disable the VSAN service on the cluster. The following commands (where 0 is a numeric representation of the cluster as shown in the ls output), allow you to do this:

```
/mia-cg07-vc01/mia-cg07-dc01/computers> ls
0 cg07-cluster01 (cluster): cpu 126 GHz, memory 696 GB
/mia-cg07-vc01/mia-cg07-dc01/computers> vsan.disable_vsan_on_cluster 0
```

Re-enabling VSAN is just as straightforward:

```
/mia-cg07-vc01/mia-cg07-dc01/computers> vsan.enable_vsan_on_cluster 0
```

host_info

In most cases, it is much easier to navigate to the particular object that you are interested in. If you use the vsan.host_info command, it is easier to navigate to the object in the inventory and then use the numeric shorthand value of the host in the command, as shown in the following example:

```
/mia-cg07-vc01/mia-cg07-dc01> ls
0 storage/
1 computers [host]/
2 networks [network]/
3 datastores [datastore]/
4 vms [vm]/
/mia-cg07-vc01/mia-cg07-dc01> cd 1
/mia-cg07-vc01/mia-cg07-dc01/computers> ls
0 cg07-cluster01 (cluster): cpu 126 GHz, memory 697 GB
/mia-cg07-vc01/mia-cg07-dc01/computers> cd 0
/mia-cg07-vc01/mia-cg07-dc01/computers/cg07-cluster01> ls
0 hosts/
1 resourcePool [Resources]: cpu 126.58/126.58/normal, mem 697.07/697.07/
normal
/mia-cg07-vc01/mia-cg07-dc01/computers/cg07-cluster01> cd 0
/mia-cg07-vc01/mia-cg07-dc01/computers/cg07-cluster01/hosts> ls
0 mia-cg07-esx011.vmwcs.com (host): cpu 2*8*2.39 GHz, memory 103.00 GB
1 mia-cg07-esx012.vmwcs.com (host): cpu 2*8*2.39 GHz, memory 103.00 GB
2 mia-cg07-esx013.vmwcs.com (host): cpu 2*8*2.39 GHz, memory 103.00 GB
3 mia-cg07-esx014.vmwcs.com (host): cpu 2*8*2.39 GHz, memory 103.00 GB
4 mia-cg07-esx015.vmwcs.com (host): cpu 2*8*2.39 GHz, memory 103.00 GB
5 mia-cg07-esx016.vmwcs.com (host): cpu 2*8*2.39 GHz, memory 103.00 GB
6 mia-cg07-esx017.vmwcs.com (host): cpu 2*8*2.39 GHz, memory 103.00 GB
7 mia-cg07-esx018.vmwcs.com (host): cpu 2*8*2.39 GHz, memory 103.00 GB
/mia-cg07-vc01/mia-cg07-dc01/computers/cg07-cluster01/
  hosts> vsan.host_info 0
VSAN enabled: yes
Cluster info:
  Cluster role: agent
  Cluster UUID: 52ce6421-83d3-6415-5e51-3c6e6ee31b62
  Node UUID: 52b20dab-3f82-819c-c5df-0011010700df
  Member UUIDs: ["52b228a4-2235-2422-1b19-00110107007f",
    "52b20efb-e15b-01b9-fb23-00110107009f", "52b20e01-7cd7-b9b5-b70
4-0011010700af", "52b22966-99f2-93fa-81d9-00110107003f",
    "52b20d6c-9920-87ad-5d4d-0011010700bf", "52b228ae-8a0d-2756-bf5
```

```
d-00110107005f", "52b20dab-3f82-819c-c5df-0011010700df",
    "52cc513c-c042-9524-79d8-00110107001f"]
Storage info:
  Auto claim: no
  Disk Mappings:
    SSD: Local ATA Disk (naa.50025385a00c5085) - 119 GB
    MD: SEAGATE Serial Attached SCSI Disk (naa.5000c5006900c7cf) - 1117 GB
NetworkInfo:
  Adapter: vmk6 (10.7.7.11)
```

In this example, we navigated to the host folder and then when we ran the command, we used the numeric value of 0 that represented the first host in the list, which is mia-cg07-vc01.vmwcs.com. This command shows us a combination of information around cluster, network, and storage. We can see the cluster role and members, the disk mappings showing one magnetic disk and one SSD, and networking information related to the VMkernel adapter being used for VSAN traffic on this host. This would have taken a few different esxcli commands to display, so immediately we can see the power of the RVC.

host_consume_disks and host_wipe_vsan_disks

These next commands are ways of telling a specific host in the VSAN cluster to claim any empty local disks that are not already claimed. This is done via the host_consume_disk command. Obviously, this would be with VSAN set up in manual mode; if VSAN were configured in automatic mode, empty, local disks would already be automatically claimed.

However, if you added new disks to a VSAN host, and these disks were already used for some other purpose, and had residual data or partition information on them, the command host_wipe_vsan_disks could be used to create a new, clean, empty disk drive that could be used by VSAN.

cluster_info

We now meet the first command to give us a cluster-centric view of VSAN. This is probably the best command to start with to get a big picture of the cluster configuration. Once again, navigate to the cluster object in the RVC inventory, or simply type the full path to the cluster object when you run the vsan.cluster_info command. This command is the equivalent of running the vsan.host_info command against every host in the cluster. Previously we saw that vsan.host_info display cluster, host, disk, and network info. Now we have a single command to display this information for every host. We won't list all eight hosts in this eight-node VSAN cluster, but you should still get the idea from the truncated output shown here:

```
/mia-cg07-vc01/mia-cg07-dc01/computers> vsan.cluster_info 0
Host: mia-cg07-esx011.vmwcs.com
  VSAN enabled: yes
  Cluster info:
    Cluster role: agent
    Cluster UUID: 52ce6421-83d3-6415-5e51-3c6e6ee31b62
    Node UUID: 52b20dab-3f82-819c-c5df-0011010700df
    Member UUIDs: ["52b228a4-2235-2422-1b19-00110107007f",
      "52b20efb-e15b-01b9-fb23-00110107009f", "52b20e01-7cd7-b9b5-b
704-0011010700af", "52b22966-99f2-93fa-81d9-00110107003f",
      "52b20d6c-9920-87ad-5d4d-0011010700bf", "52b228ae-8a0d-2756-b
f5d-00110107005f", "52b20dab-3f82-819c-c5df-0011010700df",
      "52cc513c-c042-9524-79d8-00110107001f"]
  Storage info:
    Auto claim: no
    Disk Mappings:
      SSD: Local ATA Disk (naa.50025385a00c5085) - 119 GB
      MD: SEAGATE Serial Attached SCSI Disk
        (naa.5000c5006900c7cf) - 1117 GB
  NetworkInfo:
    Adapter: vmk6 (10.7.7.11)

Host: mia-cg07-esx012.vmwcs.com
  VSAN enabled: yes
  Cluster info:
    Cluster role: agent
    Cluster UUID: 52ce6421-83d3-6415-5e51-3c6e6ee31b62
    Node UUID: 52b20d6c-9920-87ad-5d4d-0011010700bf
    Member UUIDs: ["52b228a4-2235-2422-1b19-00110107007f",
      "52b20efb-e15b-01b9-fb23-00110107009f", "52b20e01-7cd7-b9b5-b
704-0011010700af", "52b22966-99f2-93fa-81d9-00110107003f",
      "52b20d6c-9920-87ad-5d4d-0011010700bf", "52b228ae-8a0d-2756-b
f5d-00110107005f", "52b20dab-3f82-819c-c5df-0011010700df",
      "52cc513c-c042-9524-79d8-00110107001f"]
  Storage info:
    Auto claim: no
    Disk Mappings:
      SSD: Local ATA Disk (naa.50025385a00c5084) - 119 GB
      MD: SEAGATE Serial Attached SCSI Disk (naa.5000c500690142df)
        - 1117 GB
```

Ruby vSphere Console   243

```
NetworkInfo:
   Adapter: vmk6 (10.7.7.12)
```

Once again, you can see the cluster role and members, the disk mappings showing one magnetic disk and one SSD, and networking information related to the VMkernel adapter using for VSAN traffic on this host. We are sure that you will agree that this is a very useful command to get an overview of the cluster configuration.

disks.info

As previously mentioned, VSAN will only claim disks that are local and empty (in other words, have no existing partition table). If you find that VSAN is not claiming a disk for some reason, disks.info is a great command to check and see why not. This command will display whether a disk is already in use by VSAN, whether it is available for consuming by VSAN, or whether it is ineligible for use by VSAN. Typically, if the disk is ineligible, disks.info displays partition information if the disk is already partitioned. The output can be rather long to display due to some of the disk identifiers and the state of those disks in some cases, hence the reason we've not included the output of this command in the book.

cluster_set_default_policy

This book has previously discussed the concept of a default policy in great detail. In the previous ESXCLI section, we actually saw commands related to the default policy settings. You might remember that we stated that if you used the ESXCLI method of changing the default policy, this would have to be done on a per-host basis. Well, this command allows us to change the default policy across all the hosts in the cluster. Suppose, for instance, that the default policy setting did not meet your requirements. Perhaps you would prefer a default policy that had a higher number of failures to tolerate, or perhaps a higher stripe width. Or perhaps you want to reserve some read cache as part of the default policy. In that case, cluster_set_default_policy is the command you would use. First, you would need to create a policy that you want to use as the default. This will then be available under the vmprofiles (profiles was the original name for policies) folder of any VM that is using the policy. The cluster_set_default_policy command may then be pointed to that policy and this will become the new default policy for any VMs that are deployed without an explicitly associated VM storage policy.

object_reconfigure

You can use the RVC command vsan.object_reconfigure on already-existing VSAN objects to change their current VM storage policy setting and assign them a new policy. If perhaps you felt that you needed to add a stripe width or increase the number of failures to tolerate of a particular object, this command can do that for you.

object_info, disk_object_info, vm_object_info

These three RVC commands are grouped together as they are in some way related. They all involve displaying detailed information about objects in the cluster, be they disk, cluster, or VM objects. Let's begin with the vm_object_info command because this is possibly the more intuitive one of the three to begin with. To use this command, you simply navigate to a VM and provide it as the argument. In the example that follows, we navigated to a host that has a single VM and ran the command against it. What then happens is that RVC checks all ESXi hosts in the cluster to see which ESXi hosts contain objects related to this VM. At this point, you should be well aware of the fact that VSAN may not place a VM's storage objects on the same host as the VM compute. In fact, VM storage objects (including replicas) may be on completely different hosts in the VSAN cluster than the compute of said VM.

The output has been truncated for readability reasons:

```
/mia-cg07-vc01/mia-cg07-dc01/computers/cg07-cluster01/hosts/mia-cg07-esx011.vmwcs.com> cd vms
/mia-cg07-vc01/mia-cg07-dc01/computers/cg07-cluster01/hosts/mia-cg07-esx011.vmwcs.com/vms> ls
0 test-vm-default-policy: poweredOff
/mia-cg07-vc01/mia-cg07-dc01/computers/cg07-cluster01/hosts/mia-cg07-esx011.vmwcs.com/vms> vsan.vm_object_info 0
2014-02-08 11:15:16 +0000: Fetching VSAN disk info from mia-cg07-esx011.vmwcs.com (may take a moment) ...
2014-02-08 11:15:17 +0000: Fetching VSAN disk info from mia-cg07-esx012.vmwcs.com (may take a moment) ...
VM test-vm-default-policy:
  Namespace directory
    DOM Object: 0c03ed52-e50b-b174-4eea-0011010700df (owner: mia-cg07-esx015.vmwcs.com, policy: hostFailuresToTolerate = 1)
      Witness: 0c03ed52-8b83-33b6-898a-0011010700df (state: ACTIVE (5), host: mia-cg07-esx013.vmwcs.com, md: naa.5000c50067d8d9f7, ssd: naa.50025385a00a376a)
      RAID_1
        Component: 0c03ed52-2aa3-32b6-36a8-0011010700df (state: ACTIVE (5), host: mia-cg07-esx015.vmwcs.com, md: naa.5000c5006900c843, ssd: naa.50025385a00c508e)
        Component: 0c03ed52-7457-31b6-20ba-0011010700df (state: ACTIVE (5), host: mia-cg07-esx017.vmwcs.com, md: naa.5000c500690143d7, ssd: naa.50025385a00c5080)
  Disk backing: [vsanDatastore] 0c03ed52-e50b-b174-4eea-0011010700df/test-vm-default-policy.vmdk
    DOM Object: 1203ed52-5649-8be2-c1ec-0011010700df (owner: mia-cg07-esx013.vmwcs.com, policy: hostFailuresToTolerate = 1, proportionalCapacity = 100)
      Witness: 1203ed52-424b-3e11-89a7-0011010700df (state: ACTIVE (5), host: mia-cg07-esx016.vmwcs.com, md: naa.5000c5006901415b, ssd: naa.50025385a00c5090)
      RAID_1
        Component: 1203ed52-df00-3d11-dbd1-0011010700df (state: ACTIVE (5), host: mia-cg07-esx012.vmwcs.com, md: naa.5000c500690142df, ssd: naa.50025385a00c5084)
        Component: 1203ed52-1e00-3b11-8d8e-0011010700df (state: ACTIVE (5), host: mia-cg07-esx013.vmwcs.com, md: naa.5000c50067d8d9f7, ssd: naa.50025385a00a376a)
```

In the preceding listing, two of the VMs' objects are displayed; the VM Home namespace directory and the VM disk/VMDK. Both of these storage objects have replicas in a RAID-1 configuration, indicating that they are adhering to a number of failures to tolerate policy setting. Because there are only two components in each object, we can assume that the number of failures to tolerate policy value is set to 1 in the policy of this VM. We can verify that conclusion by checking the DOM object line of each object, which explicitly displays the policy settings, and indeed we can see host failures to tolerate = 1 in both cases. Again, although this descriptor specifies host failures to tolerate, it also covers other components such as disk and network. One other interesting point is that the VMDK in this case has a proportionalCapacity of 100, meaning that it is thickly provisioned on the VSAN datastore and not thinly provisioned, which is the default.

Of course, possibly the most useful part of this output is that it details where the components are stored. You can see host, magnetic disk ID, and the ID of the SSD fronting the magnetic disk in the disk group. And, finally, you can see whether the components are healthy. In this case, all components appear in the Active state, which is normal.

Finally, we also have information displayed about the witness components. These should not need explanation at this stage of the book, but suffice it to say that they play a major role when failures occur, and count as a vote to allow storage objects reach a quorum and continue to remain accessible when a failure occurs in the cluster.

Now that we have examined objects related to a VM, sometimes it is also good to know what objects/components are actually on a physical disk. This is where disk_object_ info comes in. With this command, you can display the contents of a physical disk that has been claimed by VSAN and have RVC display the components that are on this disk. This command is run against the cluster, but an additional argument is required whereby the disk identifier must be provided. This is easy to get, and the previous vm_object_ info command can provide this information, as can ESXCLI or the vSphere UI. If we use the NAA ID of the magnetic disks from the previous command, we can display all the objects and components on that disk drive.

Again, this is another command that provides a lot of useful information. In this example, we have switched to a different VSAN cluster to show some variety to the outputs. The following output has been truncated for readability; in this case various "DOM objects" have been left out:

```
/localhost/ie-datacenter-01/computers> ls
0 ie-vsan-cluster-01 (cluster): cpu 109 GHz, memory 331 GB
/localhost/ie-datacenter-01/computers> vsan.disk_object_info 0 naa.600508b1001c36662525d1d217c882f87
2014-03-14 11:37:57 +0000: Fetching VSAN disk info from hosts (may take a moment) ...
2014-03-14 11:38:00 +0000: Done fetching VSAN disk infos
Physical disk naa.600508b1001c3662525d1d217c882f87 (525a5dee-1f35-b3b5-cac9-c55d047ea601):
   DOM Object: 16782053-64de-7b11-a685-001517a69c72 (owner: 10.27.51.2, policy: hostFailuresToTolerate = 1, proportionalCapacity =
100)
      Context: Part of VM ie-vdpa-01: Disk: [vsanDatastore] 2e742053-2895-3151-e630-001517a69c72/ie-vdpa-01_2.vmdk
      Witness: 17782053-0097-fb35-a525-001517a69c72 (state: ACTIVE (5), host: 10.27.51.2, md: naa.600508b1001cdb46f505bf98eef9e9b4,
ssd: eui.c68e151fed8a4fcf0024712c7cc444fe)
      Witness: 17782053-9c0b-fa35-cf2a-001517a69c72 (state: ACTIVE (5), host: 10.27.51.2, md:
**naa.600508b1001c3662525d1d217c882f87**, ssd: eui.c68e151fed8a4fcf0024712c7cc444fe)
      Witness: 17782053-2abf-fa35-44b9-001517a69c72 (state: ACTIVE (5), host: 10.27.51.4, md: naa.600508b1001c8119ca0ab3a6fe0d2b19,
ssd: eui.a15eb52c6f4043b5002471c7886acfaa)
      RAID_1
         RAID_0
            Component: 17782053-b020-f935-eb15-001517a69c72 (state: ACTIVE (5), host: 10.27.51.3, md:
naa.600508b1001c784579103bf9baf41797, ssd: eui.d1ef5a5bbe864e27002471febdec3592)
            Component: 17782053-744b-f835-a4ca-001517a69c72 (state: ACTIVE (5), host: 10.27.51.3, md:
naa.600508b1001c034feb6ff0871db13c4b, ssd: eui.d1ef5a5bbe864e27002471febdec3592)
         RAID_0
            Component: 17782053-2a68-f735-e951-001517a69c72 (state: ACTIVE (5), host: 10.27.51.4, md:
naa.600508b1001c1380cc97bc5345465552, ssd: eui.a15eb52c6f4043b5002471c7886acfaa)
            Component: 17782053-b807-f635-1568-001517a69c72 (state: ACTIVE (5), host: 10.27.51.2, md:
naa.600508b1001cdb46f505bf98eef9e9b4, ssd: eui.c68e151fed8a4fcf0024712c7cc444fe)
```

What is nice about this output is that it shows you the object and the context. In other words, you can tell which VM storage object the particular component is a part of. Not only that, it shows all the other components that make up the storage object, and where those other components are located in the VSAN cluster. It also highlights the disk ID that we provided as an argument to the command by including some ** characters at the beginning and the end of the identifier.

What can be deduced from this output is that the disk that we are interested in contains quite a number of components. Some of the components are part of a VM disk/VMDK, whereas other components are used to make up namespace directories of VMs, and others may be part of the VM's swap. This output is extremely useful for troubleshooting once again because it allows you to see the status of components on disks. Once again, in this output, everything appears to be in a good, normal Active state.

This brings us to the final object_info command. This now uses an actual VSAN object identifier to display the status of a storage object. So, rather than looking at all objects belonging to a VM, or all components storage on a magnetic disk, we can now look in detail at a single storage object in the cluster, be it a namespace directory or a VM disk. This is very useful for tracing the status of a particular object, especially if log files are displaying messages related to an object ID and you are not sure which VM or which magnetic disk has the object in question. In the following example, we chose a VM disk's ID, and ran the command as follows, with the arguments of cluster and then object ID:

```
/localhost/ie-datacenter-01/computers> vsan.object_info 0 d4502253-e81d-00b8-6351-0010185def78
DOM Object: d4502253-e81d-00b8-6351-0010185def78 (owner: 10.27.51.3, policy: hostFailuresToTolerate = 1, proportionalCapacity = [0, 100])
  Witness: d5502253-10e6-321a-656d-0010185def78 (state: ACTIVE (5), host: 10.27.51.1, md: naa.600508b1001c530aff02e0c5c7971e1d, ssd:
eui.48f8681115d6416c00247172ce4df168)
  RAID_1
    Component: d5502253-3461-321a-d275-0010185def78 (state: ACTIVE (5), host: 10.27.51.3, md: naa.600508b1001c034feb6ff0871db13c4b, ssd:
eui.d1ef5a5bbe864e27002471febdec3592)
    Component: d5502253-b00b-311a-ff45-0010185def78 (state: ACTIVE (5), host: 10.27.51.2, md: naa.600508b1001c3662525d1d217c882f87, ssd:
eui.c68e151fed8a4fcf0024712c7cc444fe)
  Extended attributes:
    Address space: 43285303296B (40.31 GB)
    Object class: vdisk
    Object path: /vmfs/volumes/vsan:524ed5e9ee77b654-b7895b53dcad7c5e/c2cd2153-24a4-45a5-b0a1-001517a69c72/hbrdisk.RDID-7b82ee6b-b12e-4364-b72c-
c0ba2a4101d0.12.61153313595688.vmdk
```

This now gives us a nice detailed view of the makeup of the object. We can see that there is a RAID-1 configuration with two components, indicating that this has a policy setting that has number of failures to tolerate set to 1. All of this can be verified by the DOM Object line of the output, which indeed includes hostFailuresToTolerate = 1. We can also see that the object class is vdisk, a VM disk (VMDK). Once again, the command displays useful information about the location of each of the components, and all components are in an Active good state.

Using the various object_info commands, an administrator should be able to trace where each of the various storage objects belonging to a VM reside in the cluster and verify that they are in good working order. If issues arise that require an administrator to find components and troubleshoot, these commands are invaluable.

cmmds_find

The `cmmds_find` command can be extremely useful, especially if an ESXi host posts an error message with the ID of a particular VSAN object and you need to figure out what that said object actually relates to. The `vsan.cmmds_find` (cmmds for Clustering Monitoring, Membership, and Directory Services) can be used to display information about a particular object in the VSAN cluster.

-t DISK_USAGE

This first option is useful as it displays disk usage information in the cluster. The most important output is the Health column; this will immediately tell you whether any disks are in an unhealthy state.

```
/localhost/vsphere5.5-u1> vsan.cmmds_find ~/computers/vsphere5.5-u1/ -t DISK_USAGE

+---+------------+------------------------------------------+------------+----------+------------------------------------+
| # | Type       | UUID                                     | Owner      | Health   | Content                            |
+---+------------+------------------------------------------+------------+----------+------------------------------------+
| 1 | DISK_USAGE | 52777432-f127-f001-d081-800a04cafb0e     | 10.27.51.4 | Healthy  | {"capacityReserved"=>18874368,     |
|   |            |                                          |            |          | "iopsReserved"=>0,                 |
|   |            |                                          |            |          | "throughPutReserved"=>0,           |
|   |            |                                          |            |          | "l2CacheReserved"=>0,              |
|   |            |                                          |            |          | "l1CacheReserved"=>0}              |
| 2 | DISK_USAGE | 5214b1a5-b6b1-3a3a-f8b6-ee4ecc7a8d0e     | 10.27.51.4 | Healthy  | {"capacityReserved"=>0,            |
|   |            |                                          |            |          | "iopsReserved"=>0,                 |
|   |            |                                          |            |          | "throughPutReserved"=>0,           |
|   |            |                                          |            |          | "l2CacheReserved"=>0,              |
|   |            |                                          |            |          | "l1CacheReserved"=>0}              |
| 3 | DISK_USAGE | 5269ded0-91a2-4986-4d5e-e946d252730f     | 10.27.51.3 | Healthy  | {"capacityReserved"=>14680064,     |
|   |            |                                          |            |          | "iopsReserved"=>0,                 |
|   |            |                                          |            |          | "throughPutReserved"=>0,           |
|   |            |                                          |            |          | "l2CacheReserved"=>0,              |
|   |            |                                          |            |          | "l1CacheReserved"=>0}              |
| 4 | DISK_USAGE | 52f226e9-7664-34a1-b6be-3f27c4d2671e     | 10.27.51.3 | Healthy  | {"capacityReserved"=>7509901312,   |
|   |            |                                          |            |          | "iopsReserved"=>0,                 |
|   |            |                                          |            |          | "throughPutReserved"=>0,           |
|   |            |                                          |            |          | "l2CacheReserved"=>0,              |
|   |            |                                          |            |          | "l1CacheReserved"=>0}              |
| 5 | DISK_USAGE | 5251dfbe-2106-16ca-e6eb-c8389a7eebdd     | 10.27.51.3 | Healthy  | {"capacityReserved"=>0,            |
|   |            |                                          |            |          | "iopsReserved"=>0,                 |
|   |            |                                          |            |          | "throughPutReserved"=>0,           |
|   |            |                                          |            |          | "l2CacheReserved"=>0,              |
|   |            |                                          |            |          | "l1CacheReserved"=>0}              |
| 6 | DISK_USAGE | 52de5de0-ff71-02fa-b671-558abd3280e1     | 10.27.51.4 | Healthy  | {"capacityReserved"=>25165824,     |
|   |            |                                          |            |          | "iopsReserved"=>0,                 |
|   |            |                                          |            |          | "throughPutReserved"=>0,           |
|   |            |                                          |            |          | "l2CacheReserved"=>0,              |
|   |            |                                          |            |          | "l1CacheReserved"=>0}              |
+---+------------+------------------------------------------+------------+----------+------------------------------------+
```

-t DISK

The -t `DISK` option is rather useful as it displays details about all the disks in the cluster. There are also some interesting attributes displayed in the Content column, including capacity, and whether the disk is an SSD (`isSsd`).

-u UUID

The -u `UUID` option enables an administrator to look at the particular component in even more detail.

From the preceding output, a number of additional Types are available. These are HEALTH_STATUS and DISK_STATUS. Any of these can be passed to the `vsan.cmmds_find` command with the -t option.

We have barely scratched the surface of what this command is capable of. The more observant of you will have noticed that this command is very similar to the `cmmds-tool` available in the ESXCLI. That is quite correct, and many of the options used with `cmmds-tool find` can also be used here.

fix_renamed_vms

There is not much to add to the description of the `fix_renamed_vms` command. As it states, vCenter Server can rename some VMs if the VSAN datastore access become unavailable for whatever reason. This leaves the VMs with a long pathname as the name of the VM, and these are used in the vSphere web client as the name of the VM—not very user-friendly. This command renames those VMs from the long pathname to the shorter more human-readable form.

obj_status_report

`obj_status_report` is a nice command to verify that all objects and components in the cluster are in a good, healthy state and that no objects or components have been orphaned (in other words, no longer associated with a VM).

The `obj_status_report` command once again runs against the cluster. The output is split into two sections; the first displayed non-orphaned objects, and the second displays orphaned objects. It also verifies that any component found is in a healthy state (that is, has an Active state that we observed in the previous outputs):

```
/mia-cg07-vc01/mia-cg07-dc01/computers> vsan.obj_status_report 0
2014-02-08 12:52:25 +0000: Querying all VMs on VSAN ...
2014-02-08 12:52:25 +0000: Querying all objects in the system ...
2014-02-08 12:52:26 +0000: Querying all disks in the system ...
```

```
2014-02-08 12:52:26 +0000: Querying all components in the system ...
2014-02-08 12:52:27 +0000: Got all the info, computing table ...

Histogram of component health for non-orphaned objects

+-------------------------------------+-----------------------------+
| Num Healthy Comps / Total Num Comps | Num objects with such status |
+-------------------------------------+-----------------------------+
| 7/7                                 | 1                           |
| 3/3                                 | 7                           |
| 5/5                                 | 2                           |
+-------------------------------------+-----------------------------+
Total non-orphans: 10

Histogram of component health for possibly orphaned objects

+-------------------------------------+-----------------------------+
| Num Healthy Comps / Total Num Comps | Num objects with such status |
+-------------------------------------+-----------------------------+
+-------------------------------------+-----------------------------+
Total orphans: 0
```

What you are looking for in the output of this command is any non-orphaned objects that are not in a healthy state, as well as any orphaned objects. Both of these would require further troubleshooting to determine why they are not healthy, and in the case of orphaned objects, how they can be cleaned up.

check_state

check_state is a great command for getting the big picture of your VSAN environment. It carries out a number of fundamental tasks. It checks to make sure all VSAN objects are accessible, it checks to make sure that all VMs are healthy and accessible, and it also checks that any VMs deployed on the VSAN cluster are in sync from both an ESXi host perspective and vCenter Server perspective. Any anomalies are reported when the command is run:

```
/mia-cg07-vc01/mia-cg07-dc01/computers> vsan.check_state 0
2014-02-08 13:00:19 +0000: Step 1: Check for inaccessible VSAN objects
Detected 0 objects to not be inaccessible

2014-02-08 13:00:20 +0000: Step 2: Check for invalid/inaccessible VMs
2014-02-08 13:00:20 +0000: Step 3: Check for VMs for which VC/hostd/vmx are
out of sync
Did not find VMs for which VC/hostd/vmx are out of sync
```

I strongly recommend running this command at regular intervals, perhaps as part of a maintenance cycle. This will ensure that any anomalies are caught early.

This command also has a very useful option for reconnecting orphaned VMs: **--refresh-state**. It runs as follows:

```
/mia-cg07-vc01/mia-cg07-dc01/computers> vsan.check_state --refresh-state 0
2014-04-30 21:19:18 +0000: Step 1: Check for inaccessible VSAN objects
2014-04-30 21:19:18 +0000: Step 1b: Check for inaccessible VSAN objects,
again2014-04-30 21:19:19 +0000: Step 2: Check for invalid/inaccessible VMs

Detected VM 'ie-vdpa-01' as being 'orphaned', reloading ...
reloadVirtualMachineFromPath ie-vdpa-01: success

2014-04-30 21:19:23 +0000: Step 2b: Check for invalid/inaccessible VMs
again
2014-04-30 21:19:23 +0000: Step 3: Check for VMs for which VC/hostd/vmx are
out of sync

Did not find VMs for which VC/hostd/vmx are out of sync
```

hosts_stats, disk_stats, and vm_perf_stats

Now we come to some statistics and metrics commands. Like the `object_info` command previously, there are stats commands for hosts, disks and VMs. Let's begin with the `host_stats` command. This is a very useful command. Not only does it show the current magnetic disk configuration (referred to as HDDs or hard disk drives) in the output, but it also shows you what might happen if a single host in the cluster failed. In this example, we navigated to the cluster object in the inventory and ran the `vsan.hosts_stats` command from there, selecting the full cluster as an argument:

```
/mia-cg07-vc01/mia-cg07-dc01/computers> ls
0 cg07-cluster01 (cluster): cpu 126 GHz, memory 697 GB
/mia-cg07-vc01/mia-cg07-dc01/computers> vsan.hosts_stats 0
Current utilization of hosts:
```

Host	NumHDDs	Capacity Total	Used	Reserved
mia-cg07-esx015.vmwcs.com	1	1117.75 GB	2 %	2 %
mia-cg07-esx017.vmwcs.com	1	1117.75 GB	2 %	2 %
mia-cg07-esx011.vmwcs.com	1	1117.75 GB	0 %	0 %
mia-cg07-esx014.vmwcs.com	1	1117.75 GB	0 %	0 %
mia-cg07-esx018.vmwcs.com	1	1117.75 GB	0 %	0 %

```
| mia-cg07-esx016.vmwcs.com | 1        | 1117.75 GB | 0 %  | 0 %      |
| mia-cg07-esx012.vmwcs.com | 1        | 1117.75 GB | 4 %  | 4 %      |
| mia-cg07-esx013.vmwcs.com | 1        | 1117.75 GB | 4 %  | 4 %      |
+---------------------------+--------+------------+------+----------+
```

```
Simulating 1 host failures:
The command shows current VSAN disk usage, but also simulates how
disk usage would evolve under a host failure. Concretely the simulation
assumes that all objects would be brought back to full policy
compliance by bringing up new mirrors of existing data.
The command makes some simplifying assumptions about disk space
balance in the cluster. It is mostly intended to do a rough estimate
if a host failure would drive the cluster to being close to full.
```

```
+------------------------------------------------+-------------------------+
| Host with most data on it:                     |mia-cg07-esx013.vmwcs.com |
| Data to be newly mirrored:                     |40.76 GB                 |
| Capacity before failure:                       |8815.06 GB free, 1% used |
| Capacity after failure, before re-mirroring:   |7738.08 GB free, 1% used |
| Capacity after failure, after re-mirroring:    |7697.31 GB free, 2% used |
+------------------------------------------------+-------------------------+
```

The idea behind the simulation of a host failure is, as it says in the command output, to see whether any disk drive would reach close to capacity if VM storage objects were rebuilt to meet policy requirements in the event of a failure. This is a very useful command to determine whether VSAN could continue to meet the availability requirements of your VMs during a failure. This is a very useful command for capacity planning because if a host failure meant that policy compliance could not be achieved, another failure in the cluster could mean that your VMs become unavailable. This failure could be a host, disk, or even the network.

In the preceding output, there are eight hosts in the cluster, but each is only contributing a single magnetic disk. However, the cluster is very underutilized, so a host failure has little or no impact on the amount of disk space that my VM storage objects consume. We are nowhere close to filling up the magnetic disks on this cluster.

Now we come to the vsan.disks_stats command. Basically, this command can tell you how well your cluster is balanced from a components per magnetic disk basis. It also displays useful information about the amount of disk space that is available and consumed. Other useful information pertains to performance, such as read/write operations and latencies. However, performance will be covered in more detail in the following sections.

Let's look at some outputs, first from a cluster-wide view. The following output has been truncated for readability, with the output of five hosts removed.

```
/mia-cg07-vc01/mia-cg07-dc01/computers> vsan.disks_stats 0
+---------------------+--------------------------+--------+------+------------+-------+----------+-------+----------+
|                     |                          |        | Num  | Capacity   |       |          |       | Device   |
| DisplayName         | Host                     | isSSD  | Comp | Total      | Used  | Reserved | Used  | Latencies|
+---------------------+--------------------------+--------+------+------------+-------+----------+-------+----------+
| naa.50025385a00c5085| mia-cg07-esx011.vmwcs.com| SSD    | 0    | 83.47 GB   | 0 %   | 0 %      | 0r/0w | 0d/0q/0k |
| naa.5000c5006900c7cf| mia-cg07-esx011.vmwcs.com| MD     | 5    | 1117.75 GB | 0 %   | 0 %      | 0r/0w | 0d/0q/0k |
+---------------------+--------------------------+--------+------+------------+-------+----------+-------+----------+
| naa.50025385a00c5084| mia-cg07-esx012.vmwcs.com| SSD    | 0    | 83.47 GB   | 0 %   | 0 %      | 0r/0w | 0d/0q/0k |
| naa.5000c500690142df| mia-cg07-esx012.vmwcs.com| MD     | 4    | 1117.75 GB | 4 %   | 4 %      | 0r/0w | 0d/0q/0k |
+---------------------+--------------------------+--------+------+------------+-------+----------+-------+----------+
| naa.50025385a00a376a| mia-cg07-esx013.vmwcs.com| SSD    | 0    | 83.47 GB   | 0 %   | 0 %      | 0r/0w | 0d/0q/0k |
| naa.5000c50067d8d9f7| mia-cg07-esx013.vmwcs.com| MD     | 4    | 1117.75 GB | 4 %   | 4 %      | 0r/0w | 0d/0q/0k |
+---------------------+--------------------------+--------+------+------------+-------+----------+-------+----------+
```

As you can see, there is a somewhat uniform distribution of components across all hosts and all disks in this cluster. VSAN's own initial placement algorithms take control of this. Once again, we have each host listed, and each magnetic disk and SSD from those hosts, along with component count, capacity, and various performance counters. We may also run this command from a host perspective (by traversing to the host object) rather than a cluster perspective, but it doesn't really show any additional data.

This is an extremely useful command for verifying that you have a balanced cluster. This is why VMware is making a best practice recommendation to have identically configured ESXi hosts in the VSAN cluster. This will optimally balance the components across ESXi hosts and across magnetic disks. If you proceed with building a VSAN cluster with a selection of different ESXi hosts, it may lead to an unbalanced cluster, and certain ESXi hosts in VSAN working harder than other hosts, possibly leading to performance issues.

The final stats command is vsan.vm_perf_stats. This command, when run with a VM as an argument, provides input/output operations per second (IOPS), throughput, and latency information on a per-VM basis. This can prove extremely useful for investigating performance issues on individual VMs. The command gathers two sets of performance information, separated by a time gap of 20 seconds. This allows the display to average out the performance over that sample period. However, VSAN provides a much nicer way of examining performance information through the VSAN Observer tool, which we will look at in detail very shortly.

resync.dashboard

`resync.dashboard` is an extremely useful command to check how well or quickly storage objects in VSAN are resynchronizing. This could be occurring for any number of reasons, including a host failure with components being rebuilt elsewhere in the cluster or indeed a change in the policy setting that requires a new object to be re-created and synchronized against the old object. Remember that changes to a VM storage policy may occur on-the-fly. What happens is that a new replica with the new layout is created and is synchronized against the original preexisting components. When this completes, the original components are discarded. And this all takes place while the VM continues to run.

The `vsan.resync_dashboard` command is run against the cluster object in RVC, and it displays all objects that are resynchronizing as well as the number of bytes that are still left to synchronize. Here is an example taken from a cluster when we placed a host into maintenance mode and requested that full data migration take place. This means that VSAN needs to migrate all the components and objects from the ESXi host entering maintenance mode to other ESXi hosts in the cluster. Here we see one object to sync with 0.18GB bytes to sync left:

```
2014-02-10 12:02:47 +0000: Querying all VMs on VSAN ...
2014-02-10 12:02:47 +0000: Querying all objects in the system ...
2014-02-10 12:02:48 +0000: Got all the info, computing table ...
+---------------------------------------------+-----------------+---------------+
| VM/Object                                   | Syncing objects | Bytes to sync |
+---------------------------------------------+-----------------+---------------+
| vm-ftt-of-1-sw-of-2                         | 1               |               |
|    [vsanDatastore] vm-ftt-of-1-sw-of-2.vmx  |                 | 0.18 GB       |
+---------------------------------------------+-----------------+---------------+
| Total                                       | 1               | 0.18 GB       |
+---------------------------------------------+-----------------+---------------+
```

enter_maintenance_mode

You can use the `enter_maintenance_mode` command to place the ESXi hosts participating in VSAN into maintenance mode. Refer to Chapter 7, "Management and Maintenance," for further information about what maintenance mode options are available.

lldpnetmap

lldpnetmap is an extremely useful RVC command for troubleshooting network issues. The Link Layer Discovery Protocol (LLDP) is a vendor-neutral link-layer protocol used by network devices to advertise their capabilities. For those of you familiar with Cisco Discovery Protocol (CDP), this is a vendor-neutral equivalent. When this command is run against a VSAN cluster, it will display LLDP info for all the hosts in the cluster if such information exists.

apply_license_to_cluster

apply_license_to_cluster is another straightforward RVC command that can be used to license the VSAN cluster if you did not want to do this task via the vSphere Web Client. It takes an option of --license-key.

check_limits

Along with vsan.check_state, we recommend running the check_limits command at regular intervals when you are running a large number of VMs on your VSAN cluster. Way back in the requirements chapter, a number of VSAN limits were discussed. One of these limits was the number of components that could exist on an ESXi host participating in a VSAN cluster. The number in this initial release of VSAN is 3000. In the output from the vsan.check_limits, the number of existing components as well as the limit is displayed. Another VSAN limit is the number of socket connections per host that can be carried by the Reliable Datagram Protocol (RDT), VSAN's communication bus. This information is also displayed, along with the number of sockets currently in use. We have truncated some of the output of the command for readability.

```
/mia-cg07-vc01/mia-cg07-dc01/computers> vsan.check_limits 0
2014-02-08 13:10:41 +0000: Gathering stats from all hosts ...
2014-02-08 13:10:43 +0000: Gathering disks info ...
2014-02-08 13:10:43 +0000: Fetching VSAN disk info from <hosts> (may take a moment)

+-----------------------------+---------------------+--------------------------+
| Host                        | RDT                 | Disks                    ||
+-----------------------------+---------------------+--------------------------+
| mia-cg07-esx011.vmwcs.com   | Assocs: 13/20000    | Components: 6/3000        |
|                             | Sockets: 15/10000   | naa.5000c5006900c7cf: 0% |
|                             | Clients: 0          | naa.50025385a00c5085: 0% |
|                             | Owners: 2           |                          |
```

```
| mia-cg07-esx012.vmwcs.com | Assocs: 5/20000   | Components: 4/3000        |
|                           | Sockets: 7/10000  | naa.50025385a00c5084: 0% |
|                           | Clients: 0        | naa.5000c500690142df: 3% |
|                           | Owners: 0         |                          |
| mia-cg07-esx013.vmwcs.com | Assocs: 16/20000  | Components: 5/3000        |
|                           | Sockets: 14/10000 | naa.5000c50067d8d9f7: 3% |
|                           | Clients: 0        | naa.50025385a00a376a: 0% |
|                           | Owners: 2         |                          |
+---------------------------+-------------------+--------------------------+
```

reapply_vsan_vmknic_config

The reapply_vsan_vmknic_config command reconfigures the VSAN network on a particular VMkernel network interface card (NIC) on an ESXi host. This command could prove useful if changes are needed on the physical network layer and you need the VSAN network to recognize these changes. The following output demonstrates what you will see when running this command:

```
/localhost/ie-datacenter-01/computers/ie-vsan-cluster-01/hosts>
vsan.reapply_vsan_vmknic_config
Host: 10.27.51.2
   Reapplying config of vmk2:
     AgentGroupMulticastAddress: 224.2.3.4
     AgentGroupMulticastPort: 23451
     IPProtocol: IPv4
     InterfaceUUID: 80381f53-bc26-2968-3cf2-001517a69c72
     MasterGroupMulticastAddress: 224.1.2.3
     MasterGroupMulticastPort: 12345
     MulticastTTL: 5
   Unbinding VSAN from vmknic vmk2 ...
   Rebinding VSAN to vmknic vmk2 ...
```

recover_spbm

Take a scenario where you have lost your vCenter Server that manages your VSAN cluster. After deploying a new vCenter Server, the one remaining task is to rebuild your VM storage policies. But how do you find out what the policy settings were? This is where the recover_spbm command can really help.

First, it displays which VMs are running on VSAN without any policies. By that, we mean running with policies that are not defined in vCenter. The VMs continue to honor their original policy settings where possible, even if the vCenter Server is no longer available. Once VMs running with policies that are no longer in vCenter Server are discovered by the `recover_spbm` command, you are given options on how to recover them:

```
/localhost/ie-datacenter-01/computers/ie-vsan-cluster-01/hosts>
vsan.recover_spbm 0
2014-03-14 12:23:02 +0000: Fetching Host info
2014-03-14 12:23:02 +0000: Fetching Datastore info
2014-03-14 12:23:02 +0000: Fetching VM properties
2014-03-14 12:23:02 +0000: Fetching policies used on VSAN from CMMDS
2014-03-14 12:23:03 +0000: Fetching SPBM profiles
2014-03-14 12:23:03 +0000: Fetching VM <-> SPBM profile association
2014-03-14 12:23:03 +0000: Computing which VMs do not have a SPBM Profile
...
2014-03-14 12:23:03 +0000: Fetching additional info about some VMs
2014-03-14 12:23:03 +0000: Got all info, computing after 0.76 sec
2014-03-14 12:23:03 +0000: Done computing


Found 0 missing SPBM Profiles.
Found 0 entities not associated with their SPBM Profiles.
```

In the preceding output, there are no VMs running with undefined policies. vCenter Server has a full list of policies used by all VMs. There are a number of additional options available, such as looking at the missing policies in more details, re-creating the missing policies, and automatically associating the missing policies with VMs. This is a very useful RVC command when there is a vCenter Server failure, or indeed when migrating VSAN to a new vCenter Server.

SPBM Commands

Another very useful set of commands that are available in RVC are the SPBM (storage policy-based management) commands. As you might imagine, these are very useful commands for working on storage policies.

The output that follows displays a list of the commands available, and most of them should be pretty obvious.

```
> help spbm
Commands:
profile_delete: Delete a VM Storage Profile
profile_apply: Apply a VM Storage Profile. Pushed profile content to
Storage system
```

```
profile_create: Create a VM Storage Profile
device_change_storage_profile: Change storage profile of a virtual disk
check_compliance: Check compliance
namespace_change_storage_profile: Change storage profile of VM namespace
vm_change_storage_profile: Change storage profile of VM namespace and its
disks
device_add_disk: Add a hard drive to a virtual machine

To see commands in a namespace: help namespace_name
To see detailed help for a command: help namespace_name.command_name
```

In VSAN, a number of RVC commands to examine the SPBM settings are also available. At this point, you will know that to deploy a VM on VSAN, you create a VM storage policy for the VM, which may stipulate the number of mirror copies of the VM disk (number of failures to tolerate) or indeed a stripe width for the VMDK. SPBM is the underlying technology that controls this aspect of VSAN. In this post, we can look at some of these SPBM extensions in RVC.

Let's first take a look at the SPBM extensions. There are eight in total in RVC. The names are pretty self-explanatory:

```
spbm.check_compliance
spbm.profile_apply
spbm.device_add_disk
spbm.profile_create
spbm.device_change_storage_profile
spbm.profile_delete
spbm.namespace_change_storage_profile
spbm.vm_change_storage_profile
```

If you navigate to a VM in RVC, you can then use these commands against the individual VMs and devices. Let's look at some examples. First I want to check the compliance of a particular VM, named win1:

```
/localhost/CH-Datacenter/vms> ls
0 Discovered virtual machine/
1 VMware vCenter Operations Manager: cpu 0.00/-0.00/normal, mem 0.00/-0.00/
normal
2 win1: poweredOn
3 win2: poweredOn
4 win3: poweredOn
5 win4: poweredOn
6 win5: poweredOn
7 win6: poweredOn
```

```
8 vSphere Data Protection 5.5: poweredOn

/localhost/CH-Datacenter/vms> spbm.check_compliance 2
+-----------------+---------+------------+
| VM/Virtual Disk | Profile | Compliance |
+-----------------+---------+------------+
| win1            | FT=1    | compliant  |
|    Hard disk 1  | FT=1    | compliant  |
+-----------------+---------+------------+
Number of 'compliant' entities: 2
```

The next step is to apply a new profile. The profiles can be found in ~/storage/vmprofiles. In this example, we have two profiles available:

```
/localhost/CH-Datacenter> ls storage/vmprofiles/
0 FT=1
1 FT=1,SW=2
```

We will now change the profile on one of our VMs from FT=1 (number of failures to tolerate =1) to FT=1, SW=2 (number of failures to tolerate = 1 and number of disk objects to stripe = 2) using the command spbm.vm_change_storage_profile as follows:

```
/localhost/CH-Datacenter/vms> ls
0 Discovered virtual machine/
1 VCops-VM: cpu 0.00/-0.00/normal, mem 0.00/-0.00/normal
2 win1: poweredOn
3 win2: poweredOn
4 win3: poweredOn
5 win4: poweredOn
6 win5: poweredOn
7 win6: poweredOn
8 VDP-VM: poweredOn
/localhost/CH-Datacenter/vms> spbm.vm_change_storage_profile 2 -p ~/
storage/vmprofiles/FT=1,SW=2/
ReconfigVM win1: success
```

Of course, the reconfiguration will take a little time. By issuing the command spbm. check_compliance, it can be observed that hard disk 1 belonging to the VM that uses the storage policy that was just modified is now noncompliant:

```
/localhost/CH-Datacenter/vms> spbm.check_compliance 2
+-----------------+-----------+-------------+
| VM/Virtual Disk | Profile   | Compliance  |
+-----------------+-----------+-------------+
```

```
| win1               | FT=1,SW=2 | compliant    |
|    Hard disk 1     | FT=1,SW=2 | nonCompliant |
+------------------+-----------+--------------+
Number of 'compliant' entities: 1
Number of 'nonCompliant' entities: 1
```

And, of course, we can use the very useful vsan.resync_dashboard command to see how much data is still synching while the reconfiguration is taking place (the output has been truncated and the VM ID has been removed.)

```
/localhost/CH-Datacenter/computers> ls
0 CH-Cluster (cluster): cpu 86 GHz, memory 45 GB
/localhost/CH-Datacenter/computers> vsan.resync_dashboard 0
2013-12-12 16:56:58 +0000: Querying all VMs on VSAN ...
2013-12-12 16:56:58 +0000: Querying all objects in the system from 10.20.177.18 ...
2013-12-12 16:56:59 +0000: Got all the info, computing table ...
+-------------------------------------------+------------------+---------------+
| VM/Object                                 | Syncing objects  | Bytes to sync |
+-------------------------------------------+------------------+---------------+
| win1                                      | 1                |               |
|[vsanDatastore] <vmid>/win1-000001.vmdk |                  | 48.00 GB      |
+-------------------------------------------+------------------+---------------+
| Total                                     | 1                | 48.00 GB      |
+-------------------------------------------+------------------+---------------+
```

You can repeatedly run this command, and when the Bytes To Sync is 0, everything is synchronized. Some very useful commands, I'm sure you will agree.

One final note: If you want to use one of the SPBM commands that requires a "device" as an argument, you must use the disk devices as found in ~/vms/device/.

PowerCLI for VSAN

We know that many of our customers are interested in automating many tasks in the vCloud Suite. VSAN is no different. To get you automation as quickly as possible, a set of VSAN PowerCLI cmdlets has been released as a fling from VMware R&D.

Once the module has been downloaded from the VMware fling site (flings.vmware.com) and correctly installed, a set of VSAN cmdlets is now available for working on VSAN.

The new VSAN-specific cmdlets are as follows:

- Get-VsanDisk

- Get-VsanDiskGroup

- New-VsanDisk

- New-VsanDiskGroup

- Remove-VsanDisk

- Remove-VsanDiskGroup

- New-Cluster

- Set-Cluster

- New-VMHostNetworkAdapter

- Set-VMHostNetworkAdapter

Table 10-1 demonstrates how you might use these cmdlets.

Table 10-1   PowerCLI Cmdlets for VSAN

Task	Cmdlet
Retrieve disk mpx.vmhba2:C0:T1:L0 from a specific host	`Get-VsanDisk -VMHost MyVMHost` `-CanonicalName "mpx.vmhba2:C0:T1:L0"`
Retrieve a VSAN disk group that has a disk with canonical name mpx.vmhba2:C0:T2:L1	`Get-VsanDiskGroup -VMHost MyVMHost` `-CanonicalName "mpx.vmhba2:C0:T2:L1"`

Get disk group info and then add a disk to it	`$dg = Get-VsanDiskGroup -VMHost MyVMHost`
	`-CanonicalName "mpx.vmhba2:C0:T2:L1"`
	`$d = New-VsanDisk -VsanDiskGroup $dg`
	`-CanonicalName "mpx.vmhba3:C0:T2:L0"`

Create a new VSAN disk group that contains a magnetic disk and an SSD	`New-VsanDiskGroup -VMHost MyVMHost`
	`-SolidStateCanonicalName`
	`"mpx.vmhba2:C0:T1:L0"`
	`-HardDiskCanonicalName`
	`"mpx.vmhba3:C0:T1:L0"`

Remove disk mpx.vmhba3:C0:T2:L0 from a VSAN disk group	`$dg = Get-VsanDiskGroup -VMHost MyVMHost`
	`-CanonicalName "mpx.vmhba2:C0:T2:L1"`
	`Get-VsanDisk -VsanDiskGroup $dg`
	`-CanonicalName "mpx.vmhba3:C0:T2:L0" |`
	`Remove-VsanDisk`

Remove a disk group from a host	`$dg = Get-VsanDiskGroup -VMHost MyVMHost`
	`-CanonicalName "mpx.vmhba2:C0:T2:L1"`
	`Remove-VsanDiskGroup -VsanDiskGroup $dg`

VSAN and SPBM APIs

Many administrators who are interested in automation might be interested in the application programmable interfaces (APIs) that VMware has made public both for VSAN and for SPBM. VSAN- and SPBM-specific APIs are available as part of the vSphere 5.5 API. This allows you to programmatically access many VSAN operations and enable many tasks to be automated should you want to do so. Although this might not be useful to everybody, we decided to include it for completeness; however, we urge administrators who are interested in developing automation through the API to get further details from the API specification.

Just like with RVC, you should be aware of two main categories of operations when working with VSAN:

- VSAN-specific operations
- VM storage policy operations

Let's look at some examples.

Enable/Disable VSAN (Automatic Claiming)

Use `ReconfigureComputeResource_Task()` and set `spec->vsanConfig->enabled` to either true or false and `spec->vsanConfig->defaultConfig->autoClaimStorage` to true.

Manual Disk Claiming

Each ESXi host provides a vsanSystem manager at `configManager->vsanSystem` that provides the following methods for disk management:

- `AddDisks_Task()`
- `InitializeDisks_Task()`
- `QueryDisksForVsan()`
- `QueryHostStatus()`
- `RemoveDisk_Task()`
- `RemoveDiskMapping_Task()`
- `UpdateVsan_Task()`

Change the VM Storage Policy

The following command may be used to change the VM storage policy for a VM Home and virtual disk:

Use the `ReconfigVM_Task()` and set **spec->vmProfile** to the VM storage policy ID.

It may also be used to change the VM storage policy for VM virtual disk only:

Use the `ReconfigVM_Task()` and set `spec->deviceChange->device` to the specific virtual disk to be reconfigured and set `spec->deviceChange->vmProfile` to the VM storage policy ID.

Enter Maintenance Mode

Use the `EnterMaintenanceMode_Task()` and set `spec->maintenanceSpec->vsanMode->objectAction` to the specific data accessibility mode.

Create and Delete Directories on a VSAN Datastore

Use the `DatastoreNamespaceManager` that provides the following two methods:

- `CreateDirectory()`
- `DeleteDirectory()`

CMMDS

CMMDS is an internal VSAN manager for accessing low-level CMMDS (Clustering Monitoring, Membership, and Directory Services), object, and disk management APIs.

Each ESXi host provides a vsanInternalSystem manager at `configManager->vsanInternalSystem`, which provides the following methods for working with the lower-level system of VSAN:

- `QueryCmmds()`
- `QueryObjectsOnPhysicalVsanDisk()`
- `QueryPhysicalVsanDisks()`
- `QueryVsanObjects()`

SPBM

For VM storage policies, VSAN leverages the SPBM framework that allows administrators to create policies that define specific storage capabilities such as performance and reliability that can then be applied to a VM. The SPBM API is exposed as a separate API endpoint in vCenter Server and will be required if you want to create additional VM storage policies leveraging VSAN storage capabilities. Table 10-2 outlines some SPBM API calls.

Table 10-2   SPBM API calls

Task	SPBM API Call
Query list of available VM storage profiles defined	`PbmQueryProfile()`
Create VM storage policy	`PbmCreate()`
Delete VM storage policy	`PbmDelete()`
Check VM storage policy compliance	`PbmCheckCompliance()`
Given a VM Home or virtual disk, provide associated VM storage profile	`PbmQueryAssociatedEntity()`
Given a VM storage profile, provide the associated VM Home or virtual disk	`PbmQueryAssociatedProfiles()`

Troubleshooting VSAN on the ESXi

So far, we have looked at a lot of tools that are cluster centric, such as the RVC tool. Although we did discuss some ESXCLI commands available to administrators on an ESXi host, you also need to know where to look to find errors messages and log files. This small section highlights which log files to monitor, as well as some other utilities you might need to use when troubleshooting VSAN.

Log Files

You can find the VSAN log files in the ESXi host locations outlined in Table 10-3.

Table 10-3   VSAN Log File Locations

Log File Description	Log File Locations
CLOM (cluster-level Object Manager logs)	`/var/log/clomd.log`
OSFS (presents VSAN object storage as a file system)	`/var/log/osfsd.log`
vCenter/ESXi communications	`/var/log/hostd.log`
	`/var/log/vpxa.log`

VSAN vendor provider	`/var/log/vsan/vpd.log`
ESXi log	`/var/log/vmkernel.log`
	`/var/log/vobd.log`
	`/var/log/vmkwarning.log`

You may also find references to the major software components of VSAN, such as LSOM, RDT, DOM, and PLOG. GSS recommends searching the VMkernel log files for entries containing these keywords when troubleshooting VSAN issues. If you are unfamiliar with these software components, revisit Chapter 5. It provides detailed information about the role played by each of the components.

VSAN Traces

We briefly touched on the trace utility back in the ESXCLI section of this chapter. VSAN uses a compressed binary trace format for logging multiple messages per I/O. The traces go into /var/log/vsantraces/. These traces are not human readable and must be extracted before they can be viewed. To decode the VSAN traces into human-readable "log messages," you can run the following commands on the ESXi host:

```
# cd /var/log/vsantraces/
# zcat <file>.gz | /usr/lib/vmware/vsan/bin/vsanTraceReader.py > <file>.txt
```

When this command is run, *<file>*.txt will contain a human-readable form of the trace.

VSAN VMkernel Modules and Drivers

ESXi 5.5 comes preshipped with the components required to build a VSAN cluster. No additional VIBs or software components need to be added to the host to successfully create a VSAN cluster and build a scaled-out VSAN datastore.

When VSAN is successfully configured, you will observe new VMkernel modules loaded for the purposes of implementing VSAN. The VMkernel module names are vsan, rdt, plog, and lsomcommon.

When a VM does a write operation, the write goes to SSD, and then VSAN regularly flushes (or evicts) the SSD contents to magnetic disks. The plog module implements the VSAN elevator algorithm. It looks at the physical layout of the magnetic disk and decides when to flush SSD contents to it.

The vsan module can be thought of as the module for both the LSOM and DOM components. As these modules are heavily intertwined, the lsomcommon contains shared code for these components.

The rdt module is the Reliable Datagram Transport module responsible for cross-cluster VSAN communication.

Performance Monitoring

One of the most important aspects of managing storage is to be able to monitor and troubleshoot performance issues. VSAN is no different. In this section, we share with you various tools that are at a vSphere administrator's disposal for monitoring and troubleshooting VSAN performance-related issues.

ESXTOP Performance Counters for VSAN

In the initial release of VSAN, there are no VSAN datastore–specific performance counters in `esxtop`. However, it can still be a very useful tool when you want to examine VM activity, VMDK performance, host status, memory usage, and of course, disk activity on an ESXi host basis. Esxtop is quite easy to use; at a shell prompt on an ESXi host, simply type **esxtop**. Figure 10-1 shows some sample `esxtop` output.

```
 1:33:20pm up 49 days 15:04, 514 worlds, 0 VMs, 0 vCPUs; CPU load average: 0.01, 0.01, 0.02
PCPU USED(%): 1.3 3.9 1.3 0.5 1.5 0.3 0.5 0.1 4.1 0.4 0.3 0.1 0.4 0.5 0.2 0.4 AVG: 1.0
PCPU UTIL(%): 2.9 4.2 3.2 1.4 2.8 0.7 1.3 0.5 4.4 0.8 0.5 0.9 1.0 0.6 1.1 AVG: 1.7
CORE UTIL(%): 6.6     3.6     3.2     1.5     4.9     0.9     1.4     1.3     AVG: 2.9        .

      ID       GID NAME              NWLD   %USED    %RUN   %SYS   %WAIT %VMWAIT    %RDY   %IDLE  %OVRLP   %CSTP  %MLMTD  %SWPWT
21789709  21789709 esxtop.10111864      1    3.82    3.66   0.00   95.41       -    0.00    0.00    0.00    0.00    0.00    0.00
    2019      2019 hostd.100001493     26    3.79    3.63   0.00 2572.30       -    0.03    0.00    0.00    0.00    0.00    0.00
       2         2 system             121    2.39    3.46   0.00 11985.29      -    0.60    0.00    0.09    0.00    0.00    0.00
    2465      2465 sh.1000015170        1    0.48    0.49   0.00   98.58       -    0.00    0.00    0.00    0.00    0.00    0.00
16577438  16577438 cmmdsd.10085114      2    0.36    0.14   0.26  198.00       -    0.00    0.00    0.03    0.00    0.00    0.00
       8         8 helper             166    0.30    0.30   0.00 16447.55      -    0.03    0.00    0.00    0.00    0.00    0.00
    1324      1324 vmkiscsid.10000      2    0.13    0.03   0.11  198.13       -    0.01    0.00    0.00    0.00    0.00    0.00
    3161      3161 vpxa.1000015525     11    0.07    0.11   0.00 1089.66       -    0.01    0.00    0.02    0.00    0.00    0.00
    2097      2097 rhttpproxy.1000      8    0.06    0.08   0.00  792.46       -    0.05    0.00    0.01    0.00    0.00    0.00
    1686      1686 vmware-usbarbit      2    0.04    0.04   0.00  198.11       -    0.00    0.00    0.00    0.00    0.00    0.00
16577352  16577352 clomd.100051145      1    0.03    0.03   0.00   99.03       -    0.00    0.00    0.00    0.00    0.00    0.00
21789616  21789616 sshd.1011186413      1    0.03    0.03   0.00   99.03       -    0.00    0.00    0.00    0.00    0.00    0.00
    1216      1216 net-lacp.100001      3    0.02    0.03   0.00  297.20       -    0.02    0.00    0.00    0.00    0.00    0.00
      10        10 ft                   5    0.02    0.02   0.00  495.39       -    0.00    0.00    0.00    0.00    0.00    0.00
       9         9 drivers             13    0.01    0.02   0.00 1288.04       -    0.01    0.00    0.00    0.00    0.00    0.00
    3537      3537 openwsmand.1000      3    0.01    0.02   0.00  297.19       -    0.01    0.00    0.00    0.00    0.00    0.00
    1867      1867 logchannellogge      1    0.01    0.01   0.00   99.06       -    0.00    0.00    0.00    0.00    0.00    0.00
     891       891 vmsyslogd.10000      4    0.01    0.01   0.00  396.34       -    0.00    0.00    0.00    0.00    0.00    0.00
    4185      4185 sfcb-ProviderMa     10    0.01    0.01   0.00  990.67       -    0.00    0.00    0.00    0.00    0.00    0.00
    2815      2815 dcbd.1000015353      1    0.01    0.01   0.00   99.06       -    0.00    0.00    0.00    0.00    0.00    0.00
    1540      1540 chardevlogger.1      1    0.00    0.01   0.00   99.07       -    0.00    0.00    0.00    0.00    0.00    0.00
11277855  11277855 osfsd.100579090      1    0.00    0.01   0.00   99.06       -    0.00    0.00    0.00    0.00    0.00    0.00
    1915      1915 sensord.1000014      1    0.00    0.00   0.00   99.07       -    0.00    0.00    0.00    0.00    0.00    0.00
    4556      4556 sfcb-ProviderMa      9    0.00    0.01   0.00  891.61       -    0.00    0.00    0.00    0.00    0.00    0.00
11277140  11277140 swapobjd.100579      1    0.00    0.00   0.00   99.06       -    0.00    0.00    0.00    0.00    0.00    0.00
     952       952 vobd.1000014253     18    0.00    0.00   0.00 1783.55       -    0.00    0.00    0.00    0.00    0.00    0.00
```

Figure 10-1   `esxtop` output

Help can be accessed by typing in the character h while `esxtop` is running. The following display options are available:

- c: CPU

- i: Interrupt

- m: Memory

- n: Network

- d: Disk adapter

- u: Disk device

- v: Disk VM

- p: Power management

However, we do have a tool that provides VSAN-centric performance statistics, namely the VSAN Observer tool. We will examine this shortly.

vSphere Web Client Performance Counters for VSAN

Similar to esxtop, the vSphere Client does not have any specific performance counters for VSAN datastore, either. If you navigate to the VSAN cluster object in the vCenter Server inventory, select the **Monitoring** tab, and then select **Performance** view, there is an option to change the chart options. You will notice that once again nothing specific for the VSAN datastore is available.

However, the performance views available in the vSphere Client for both the VMs and the VMDKs work perfectly, even when the VM is deployed on the VSAN datastore. Figure 10-2 shows performance information, in this case highlighting read latency and write latency of VMDKs.

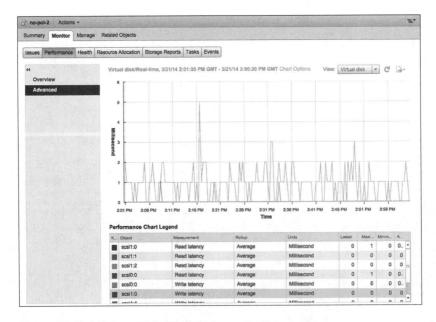

Figure 10-2   vSphere Web Client Performance view

As mentioned in the esxtop section, the VSAN Observer tool is what we can use to display information about VSAN performance. We shall look at this tool next.

VSAN Observer

The vSphere Web Client in vSphere 5.5 U1 ships with a number of built-in VSAN management functions. For example, you will find VSAN datastore as well as VM-level performance statistics in the vSphere Web Client. If you require in-depth VSAN performance, however, down to the physical disk layers, understanding the cache hit rates, reasons for observed latencies, and so on, the vSphere Web Client will not deliver this level of detail in vSphere 5.5 U1. That is where the VSAN Observer comes in.

VSAN Observer comes with the vSphere vCenter Server in version 5.5 U1. The VSAN Observer is part of the Ruby vSphere Console (RVC), an interactive command-line shell for vSphere management, and RVC is part of both the Windows vCenter Server and VCVA (appliance version of vCenter) in vSphere 5.5 U1.

Let's talk a bit about requirements and how to deploy the VSAN Observer before delving into what it can do for you.

VSAN Observer Requirements

VSAN Observer is a performance tool that has been specifically written to display VSAN performance information. It requires a modern web browser and a working Internet connection (because certain open source software components need to be downloaded for it to work). It also requires vCenter 5.5 U1 Server, either the Linux appliance version (VCVA) or the Windows version. Ruby vSphere Console and RVC are preinstalled in vCenter Server 5.5 U1.

You have two deployment options:

- You can use RVC inside your production vCenter Server that is managing your VSAN clusters.

- You can deploy an additional vCenter Server, just to get RVC and the VSAN Observer tool.

In a lab environment, the former is likely more convenient. Administrators need to be aware that the VSAN Observer opens up an unencrypted and unhardened HTTP server. Doing this on your production vCenter Server may very well be against your security policies, which is why VMware created the standalone option. In such a case, deploying an additional server to run RVC may be a better option for you.

Running the `vsan.observer` command with the name of your cluster as an argument will launch VSAN Observer. This command will gather statistics from vCenter Server and VSAN every *x* seconds. The default interval value defaults to 60 seconds for statistics collection, but you may specify a smaller or larger interval via the `--interval` parameter. It will currently collect information for a 2-hour period.

Typically, you want to run the command with the `-run-webserver` option, which opens an unencrypted HTTP web server on port 8010. You can change the port number with the `--port` option. Because we have already looked at the steps to launch RVC on a Windows version of vCenter Server in the previous version, let's now look at the steps required to get RVC up and running (and thus launch the VSAN Observer) on the vCenter Server Linux appliance (VCVA):

1. Open an SSH session to your vCenter Server Appliance:

   ssh root@<name or ip of your VCVA>

2. Open RVC using your root account and the vCenter name, in my case:

   rvc root@localhost

3. Now do a `cd` in to your vCenter object (you can do an `ls` to see what the names are of your objects on any level), and if you press the <tab> key it will be completed with your datacenter object:

   cd localhost/<Name-of-your-datacenter> /

4. Now do a `cd` again. The first object is computers and the second is your cluster. In my case that looks like the following:

   cd computers/<Name-of-your-VSAN-cluster>/

5. Now you can start the VSAN observer using the following command:

   vsan.observer . --run-webserver --force

6. Now you can see the observer querying stats every 60 seconds, and as mentioned you can stop this by pressing **Ctrl+C**. The collection will stop automatically after a period of 2 hours.

After completing these preparation steps, you can now examine the in-depth VSAN performance data. Begin by opening a web browser and pointing it at http://<*rvc-vc-ip*>:<*observer-port*>. The <*rvc-vc-ip*> is the IP address of the host running RVC, not the IP address of the vCenter Server that you are monitoring (although they could be the same). The port defaults to 8010, but you may have changed it via the `--port` option. We recommend using Google Chrome, but any modern browser should work. Internet Explorer

8 is not considered a modern browser, but may still work to some extent. Older versions of IE will definitely give you problems.

Figure 10-3 shows what the VSAN Observer landing page looks like.

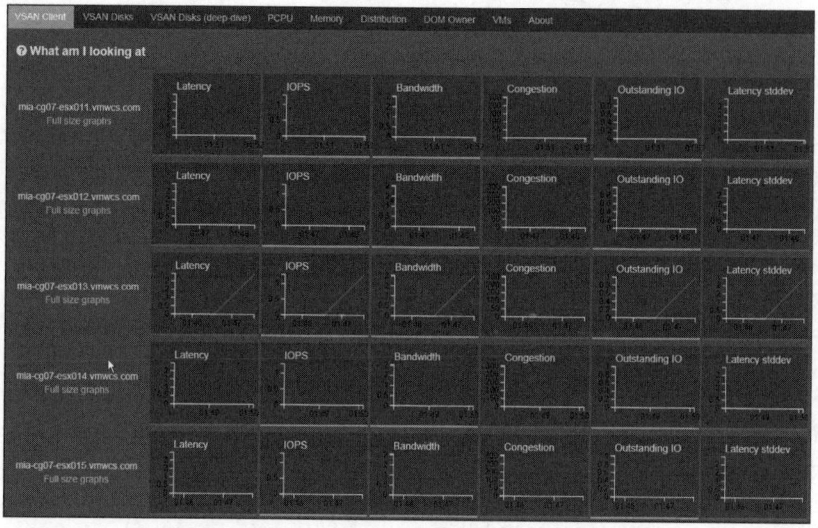

Figure 10-3   VSAN Observer: VSAN Client view

You can also ask the command to generate a stats bundle, a single smaller archive file that contains the same information the web browser would show you, which you can then save, email to colleagues, or email to VMware support. The command option is as follows:

```
vsan.observer <cluster> -generate-html-bundle /tmp
```

This will dump the stats bundle to the /tmp folder on the vCenter Server.

The command will run until you tell it to stop via **Ctrl+C**. Note that it will keep the entire history of your observer session in memory until you press **Ctrl+C**, meaning if you run it for many hours it will use multiple gigabytes of RAM. This is another reason why you may prefer to run the VSAN Observer on a dedicated vCenter Server.

Examining VSAN Observer Performance Data

When you first open up VSAN Observer, the primary indicator of an issue that is abnormal is that there will be a red underline for the graph in question that is outside normal operating boundaries. Graphs in VSAN Observer typically show green for normal state, or gray if there is no information or not enough information yet available. Red is your indicator to start investigating, and is displayed when 20 percent of the samples taken during the sampling period are outside the configured threshold.

The VSAN Observer UI is organized by subsystem. You should start with the VSAN Client view, which gives you an overview over what level of service the VMs are getting from VSAN. Every host in a VSAN cluster (and hence every "VSAN Client") is consuming storage distributed across all other hosts in the cluster, so seeing a performance issue on the VSAN Client on host A may in fact be due to overloaded disks on host B.

The "VSAN disks" view allows you to look at VSAN from that perspective, checking how nodes that contribute storage to the VSAN datastore are doing in terms of servicing I/O from their local disks. You can then further drill down into a deep-dive of the VSAN disks layer on a per-host basis, seeing how VSAN splits I/O among SSDs and HDDs.

Figure 10-4 shows the VSAN disks view. As you can see, there is a lot of information displayed here. This view shows everything from latency, IOPS, bandwidth, congestion, outstanding I/O, and a standard deviation on latency, which is how much latency has deviated from the average. Once again, you are looking for charts with are underlined in red; these highlight a metric that is outside the norm. That is where investigation into disk-related issues should begin. For latency, the threshold level is set to 30 milliseconds. Bandwidth is measured in kilobytes per second (KB/sec). Congestion is a measurement of 1 to 255; 1 means there is no congestion, 255 means it is fully congested. The threshold value for congestion is set to 75.

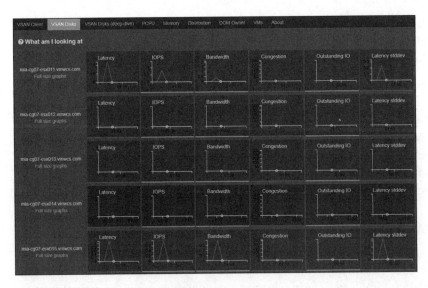

Figure 10-4   VSAN Observer: VSAN disks

VSAN shares compute resources with the rest of ESXi; that is, VSAN is consuming a slice of the same CPU and memory resources that the VMs running on a given host are also consuming. VSAN has been designed to consume no more than 10 percent of CPU resources. You can inspect the VSAN PCPU (physical CPU) and memory consumption in dedicated tabs in the observer, which may also be useful in detecting performance bottlenecks due to CPU or memory limits.

Figure 10-5 shows the memory consumption of not just the VSAN components, but also other consumers of memory of the various ESXi hosts participating in the VSAN cluster.

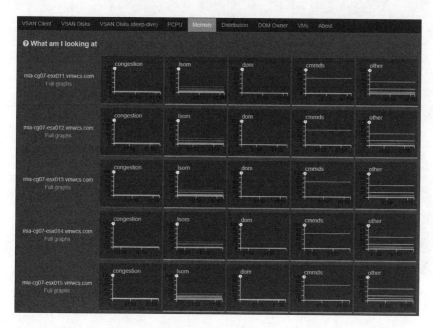

Figure 10-5   VSAN Observer: Memory

Because VSAN is a type of storage that is managed in a very VM-centric way (per-virtual disk using VM storage policies), you can also look at performance on a per-VM or even per-virtual disk level in the VSAN Observer. Start in the VMs tab and select the VM that you want to get more detail on.

Figure 10-6 shows the VM Home space from one VM. For each component that makes up the object, information such as latency, IOPS, read cache (RC) hit rate, and cache evictions are all displayed. This is excellent information for determining whether any issues exist with any of the components that make up the storage object of a particular VM that may be exhibiting performance issues. Evictions are a reference to the fact that entries in the cache are being flushed out of cache to magnetic disks. High values here could suggest that there could be contention for cache resources, possibly implying that flash has not been sized correctly. Read cache hit rate is also an interesting graph, because anything below 100 percent implies that we have had a read cache miss and have had to go to magnetic disk to retrieve a data block, which will increase latency.

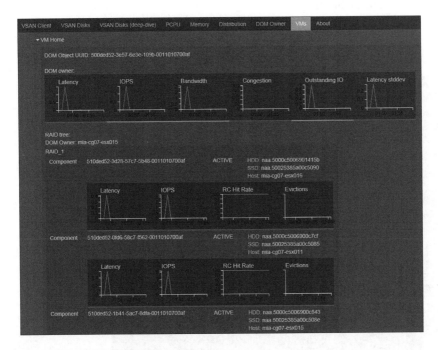

Figure 10-6   VSAN Observer: VMs view

Last but not least, there are tabs for auxiliary information (on cluster balance, distribution of objects, significant cluster events, and so on). Every time you switch tabs, the graphs update automatically and reflect the latest information gathered by RVC in the background.

Most tabs contain information about how to read the information presented in the graphs. However, a lot of them require familiarity with storage performance. Having said that, the more you use the VSAN Observer tool, and the more familiar you get with how your environment should be running in steady state, the more useful this tool will become when you need to troubleshoot issues that occur outside the norm.

As you can imagine, we have only scratched the surface of what you can do with VSAN Observer.

Sample VSAN Observer Use Case

As a way of demonstrating the usefulness of VSAN Observer, we reached out to Simon Todd, one of the VMware Support Technical Leads for VSAN, and asked him about how he has used VSAN Observer to troubleshoot a performance issue on VSAN. Simon kindly shared the following scenario, including symptoms and root cause.

The problem statement from the case that Simon shared was this: "During I/O testing, VMs performed slow, and some VMs reported as inaccessible." Troubleshooting began by looking at the log files, after which issues were quickly identified. First, DOM reported TimeTooLong for an operation, as shown in Figure 10-7.

```
2013-12-05T17:21:38.356392 [26141117] [cpu27] [22a870d2 OWNER write]
DOMTraceOpTookTooLong:2645: {'op': 0x4136c85f78c0, 'obj': 0x412eca2b4c40,
'objUuid': '58cc9852-d985-9aae-8bd9-0006f62b11ec', 'time msec': 103129}
```

Figure 10-7   DOMTraceOpTookTooLong

The investigation team also noticed that LSOM was reporting a very high congestion figure of 255, as shown in Figure 10-8.

```
2013-12-05T17:21:35.586223 [27666780] [cpu3] [3184]
LSOMTraceRcLSOMVAAllocFailure:1055: {'status': 'VMK_NO_MEMORY'}
2013-12-05T17:21:35.586224 [27666781] [cpu3] [3184] LSOMTraceRcScanError:
3332: {'rclPacked': 0x0, 'objectSlot': 14000, 'rclIndex': 0, 'rdt': 0x0,
'inFlight': 0x0}
2013-12-05T17:21:35.586224 [27666782] [cpu3] [3184]
LSOMTraceRcDomCompletion:1461: {'status': 'VMK_NO_MEMORY', 'time':
'00:00:00.000003', 'heapCongestion': 0, 'vaCongestion': 0, 'iopsCongestion':
0, 'congestion': 255}
```

Figure 10-8   Congestion at 255

It was now time to turn to VSAN Observer to see whether it could help with locating the root cause of the problems witnessed in the log files. Immediately, when VSAN Observer was launched and the VSAN Client view was opened, it was clear that there were significant latency problems, as shown in Figure 10-9. There were also congestion issues reported, as per the congestion errors found in the logs.

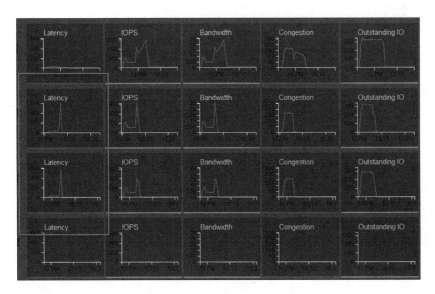

Figure 10-9   Latency issues

The abnormal issues are reported with the red underscores, so this is brought to an administrator's immediate attention. By clicking any of the graphs, it will be enlarged with additional detail. In this case, one of the latency graphs was expanded, and further detail is given about the latency values. As shown in Figure 10-10, the read latency value reported in the graph was extraordinarily high, in the region of 60,000 milliseconds, or 60 seconds.

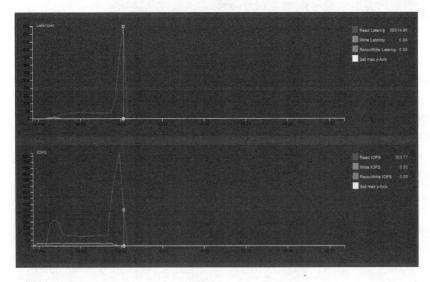

Figure 10-10   Latency and IOPS detail

One thing that stood out was the fact that the IOPS figure was relatively low, but the latency value was high. Why is this? Further investigation was needed. As we have said, there are some other interesting VSAN Observer views to look at. The next interesting view is the VMs. What was observed on this view is that there were a lot of cache evictions occurring for one of the VM's components. Looking at other VMs revealed similar behavior. So, it looks like the root cause of our latency and congestion issues are due to the flash device struggling to deal with the workload. It seems that it has to regularly evict blocks from the cache to make room for new data blocks, as shown in Figure 10-11 by the orange peak in the Evictions graph.

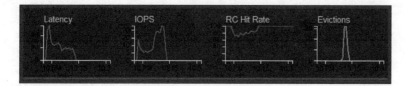

Figure 10-11   Evictions

This led to the support team asking this customer about the type of flash device that was being used in this environment. It turned out that the flash device used in this particular configuration was a Class A flash device, only capable of 2,500 IOPS maximum. The flash devices in each of the hosts were being maxed out by the workload that the customer was trying to deploy on this VSAN cluster resulting in this unwanted behavior. Unfortunately for the customer, it was impossible for VMware support to fix this issue, as this was an unsupported flash device (VMware does not support any Class A flash devices).

Hopefully, this use case showed some of the usefulness of VSAN Observer and how it can be used to identify bottlenecks, but also demonstrated what kind of impact the selection of a flash device can have on performance of your infrastructure. You should familiarize yourself with what is the norm for your environment so that anomalies are readily observed, although the red underscore when values are above the threshold also helps. This use case should also drive home the importance of correctly sizing your VSAN environment; so once again, you should review Chapter 9, "Designing a VSAN Cluster," for guidance on how to correctly size your VSAN cluster and avoid issues like the one discussed here from occurring in your environment.

Summary

As you can clearly see, an extensive suite of tools is available for troubleshooting and monitoring a VSAN deployment. We heard from a lot of VMware customers that they no longer wished for their storage to be a "black box" where visibility into performance was next to impossible. With this extensive suite of CLI and UI tools, customers can drill down into the lowest levels of VSAN behavior.

Index

vmware PRESS

Essential Virtual SAN
Administrator's Guide to
VMware VSAN

Cormac Hogan
Duncan Epping

Safari
Books Online

FREE
Online Edition

Your purchase of *Essential Virtual SAN* includes access to a free online edition for 45 days through the **Safari Books Online** subscription service. Nearly every VMware Press book is available online through **Safari Books Online**, along with thousands of books and videos from publishers such as Addison-Wesley Professional, Cisco Press, Exam Cram, IBM Press, O'Reilly Media, Prentice Hall, Que, and Sams.

Safari Books Online is a digital library providing searchable, on-demand access to thousands of technology, digital media, and professional development books and videos from leading publishers. With one monthly or yearly subscription price, you get unlimited access to learning tools and information on topics including mobile app and software development, tips and tricks on using your favorite gadgets, networking, project management, graphic design, and much more.

Activate your FREE Online Edition at
informit.com/safarifree

STEP 1:   Enter the coupon code: YOTOJFH.

STEP 2:   New Safari users, complete the brief registration form.
Safari subscribers, just log in.

If you have difficulty registering on Safari or accessing the online edition,
please e-mail customer-service@safaribooksonline.com